God's Ordinary People:

No Ordinary Heritage

God's Ordinary People:
No Ordinary Heritage

Jessica L. Rousselow   *Alan H. Winquist*

Taylor University Press
Upland, Indiana

Library of Congress Catalog Card Number: 96-61465
ISBN: 0-9621187-4-5

Cover design by Angela Angelovska and Donald R. Wilson.

Front cover includes three photographs located in the Taylor University Archives. They are: The Student Volunteer Band, 1909 on the left; The Women's Military Training Corps, 1917 on the right; and the Cosmopolitan Club, 1920s in the center. The African ivory vase is from the Wengatz Collection, Taylor University Archives and the photograph album is from Ruth Warring Rousselow's family.

Dedication:

This volume is dedicated to all of "God's Ordinary People" in each of our lives who enabled us to appreciate the extraordinary nature of our Christian heritage.

The authors

GOD'S ORDINARY PEOPLE: NO ORDINARY HERITAGE

NO ORDINARY HERITAGE

God's Ordinary People:

No Ordinary Heritage

PREFACE AND ACKNOWLEDGEMENTS

The authors see two main streams flowing through Taylor University's history. First, from its inception as Fort Wayne Female College in 1846, there has been a commitment to equal educational opportunities for both genders and for all economic classes. In the nineteenth century, classical studies formed the core of the curriculum. In the twentieth century, the liberal arts commitment has remained central. The second stream is the focus on Christian service nationally and internationally. During the nineteenth and early part of the twentieth century, most of the Christian service was sponsored by the Methodist Episcopal Church, currently identified as The United Methodist Church. The international thrust centers on the life of Bishop William Taylor for whom the school was renamed in 1890. It is the thesis of this volume that the meshing of these two points has made Taylor University unique in Christian higher education.

The six chapters in this book are arranged around these streams. Chapter One, "In the Beginning... Were the Women," focuses on the Fort Wayne years from 1846 to 1890. This was the period when the egalitarian approach to education was established as well as the commitment to classical studies as the heart of a college education. Basic questions asked by this chapter are: what was happening to women in America between 1846 and 1890, and in light of this what was occurring at Fort Wayne Female College and later Fort Wayne College? Did the College reflect, lead or resist societal trends? Was the College a place where women were granted a voice? What sort of educational experience was given the women students in the nineteenth century?

The period around 1890 was a watershed time. Fort Wayne College was struggling as an institution. As enrollment was plummeting and a financial crisis was looming, the school came under the control of the National Association of Local Preachers (NALP), a group within the Methodist Episcopal Church dedicated to reclaiming the Holiness tradition of John Wesley. For the members of the NALP, Bishop William Taylor, internationally renowned evangelist and preacher, was their hero. Chapter

GOD'S ORDINARY PEOPLE:

Two, "The World Was His Parish" is a summary of Bishop Taylor's achievements, but more particularly how they impacted Taylor University. The Christian service stream had emerged. A special emphasis in this chapter is the unique relationship that developed between the African continent and Taylor University. William Taylor was named the Missionary Bishop of Africa at the General Conference of the Methodist Episcopal Church of 1884. In this chapter Bishop Taylor's missionary methods is critically evaluated.

Chapter Three - "Servant Leaders: Women Students and Women Faculty Role Models" - returns to the first stream, equal educational opportunities for both genders, by studying the institution in its new setting in Upland 1893 to the 1950s. The first section emphasizes women students' experience on campus during the first half of the twentieth century by examining leadership training opportunities provided them. The second section of the chapter focuses on the experience of women faculty members. Special attention is given to women who provided significant leadership in key areas of the College.

Chapters Four, Five and Six return to the Christian service emphasis. "To the Corners of the Earth..." features Taylor alumni who have entered overseas missionary service carrying forth Bishop Taylor's legacy. Chapter Four presents a sampling of Taylor University Missionary couples working in the service of the Methodist Episcopal Church. A special emphasis is on the unique relationship with Africa. Chapter Five focuses on women missionaries world wide. It has been stated in the College publications such as *The Echo* and *The Gem* that an impressive ten percent of all Taylor graduates before 1949 worked on a mission field. "From the Corners of the Earth...", the title of the last chapter, describes the international students who have come to Taylor, and who nearly all until 1960 entered full time Christian work.

This project has several aims. First, we are indebted to William Ringenberg's detailed survey of the overall history of the University. Our aim, however, is to highlight a number of God's ordinary people and neglected voices—women, missionaries, and international alumni—in Taylor's history. Another aim is to demonstrate Methodism's significant role at Taylor which lasted into the 1950s. We wish to convey a sense of pride in Taylor's heritage and the accomplishments of her alumni. The book is written first and foremost for the Taylor community, but perhaps others by reading it will become interested in learning about this University's unique heritage.

We could not possibly include everyone in this study. Those included are based not only on achievement, but also on availability of historic documentation. We have included an appendix where brief biographical sketches of other significant Methodist missionaries prior to 1945 are included. We see this study as merely a beginning. There will be a need to probe into other topics such as a study of Taylor missionary alumni after the Methodist era. Also, a study should be conducted on the sons and daughters of missionaries who have attended Taylor and have made a significant impact on their world. The nature of this project is an unfolding one where additions and corrections will be necessary.

The idea for this project came during a dinner conversation two years ago when the authors began to brainstorm about ways in which they might contribute to Taylor University's forthcoming sesquicentennial celebration. This has been a challenging research project, frequently with little documentation. In many ways it has been like putting together a giant jig saw puzzle with different size pieces. The Wright Administration Building's disastrous fire in 1960 destroyed much valuable resource material. Nevertheless, we have found many of the missing pieces at the General Commission on History and Archives of The United Methodist Church, Madison, New Jersey; Commission on Archives and History, The United Methodist Church California-Nevada Conference, Berkeley, California; Holt-Atherton Special Collections, University of the Pacific Libraries, Stockton, California; Fort Wayne Allen County Public Library; Allen County Historical Society Archives; and our own Taylor University Archives. We have also conducted extensive interviews with Taylor alumni and friends, former faculty members, and Bishop Taylor's descendants.

It would be impossible to acknowledge everyone. Special thanks go to David Dickey, Bonnie Houser, Lois Weed, and Yolanda Taylor of the Taylor University Library and Archives; to Dale Patterson, Mark Shenise,

God's Ordinary People:

Dr. Kenneth E. Rowe, Jocelyn Rubinetti and staff of the General Commission on History and Archives, The United Methodist Church, Madison, New Jersey; Jean Schoenthaler, Director of the Drew University Library and Archivist; Dr. Stephen E. Yale, Director of the Methodist Archives, Graduate Theological Union, Berkeley, California; and Ms. Daryl Morrison, Head of the Holt-Atherton Department of Special Collections, University of the Pacific Libraries, Stockton, California. We have conducted numerous interviews and are particularly indebted to Edmund Chambers, Walnut Creek, California; Diana C. Johnson, Redwood City, California; Mr. and Mrs. Edward Koskinen, Soledad, California; Mr. and Mrs. Stanley Koskinen, Salinas, California; Rev. Darrel Thomas, Stockton, California; Rev. Paul Sweet, San Francisco; Rev. Donald Fado, Sacramento, California; Dr. Clarice Lowe and Edwin Lowe, Houston, Texas; Bishop and Mrs. Ralph Dodge, Dowling Park, Florida; John Monroe Vayhinger, Woodland Park, Colorado; Dr. K. Paul Kasambira, Peoria, Illinois; Thomas R. Logsdon, New York; and a number of people closely connected with Taylor University living in Indiana including Iris Abbey, Dr. Hazel Carruth, Alice Cleveland, Betty Freese, Alice Holcombe, Dr. Elmer Nussbaum, Jennie Lee, Bonnie and Don Odle, Dr. William Ringenberg, Ruth Brose Rogers, and Frances Willert.

We are very grateful for the fine photographic assistance from Taylor University's Jim Garringer, Jerry Hodson, and Craig Hider, and from George Goodwin, Morristown, New Jersey. We are very appreciative of the Taylor University Press staff of Dan Jordan, Roger Judd, and Barbara Hotmire, and help from Jackie Armstrong and Sandy Johnson. We are particularly indebted to Angela D. Angelovska and Donald R. Wilson for their skilled assistance in layout and design. We also wish to thank Taylor University for awarding us financial assistance and for the University's willingness to publish this manuscript. We are grateful for the encouragement from President Jay Kesler, Dr. Daryl Yost, Dr. Dwight Jessup, Gene Rupp, Dr. Charles "Chip" Jaggers, Chuck Newman, and Nelson Rediger.

CATALOGUE AND REGISTER

OF THE

FORT WAYNE FEMALE COLLEGE

AND

FORT WAYNE COLLEGIATE INSTITUTE,

FOR THE

Year ending April 25, 1855.

FORT WAYNE, IA.

Cincinnati:

PRINTED AT THE METHODIST BOOK CONCERN.

R. P. THOMPSON, PRINTER.

1855.

Chapter One

IN THE BEGINNING...WERE THE WOMEN

*T*he world of 1846, the year of Fort Wayne Female College's founding, was very different from that of 1996. The late 1840s marked the greatest expansion of the United States westward since the Louisiana Purchase of 1803. A treaty signed between the United States and Great Britain finally solved the Oregon Territory controversy, placing the present states of Washington and Oregon in United States territory. The Mexican-American War began in that year, ending three years later with the United States acquiring the Southwest including the present states of Texas and California. On January 24, 1848, gold was discovered on the south fork of the American River in northern California, and the gold rush was on. The following year Bishop William Taylor and family began the long voyage from the East Coast via Cape Horn to San Francisco, the beginning of his worldwide fame as evangelist and preacher. Brigham Young led the Mormons from Nauvoo City, Illinois to the Great Salt Lake, Utah, arriving in the promised land of the West the following year. Iowa became a state in 1846 followed two years later by Wisconsin. Leading the nation during this great expansion was President James Knox Polk.

The 1840s was the decade for the beginning of two great migrations across the Atlantic — the Irish escaping from the horrors of the potato famine, and the Swedes attempting to leave behind poverty and religious restrictions. In 1846 the town of Nantucket, the world's largest whaling port, and a center for the women's suffrage movement, went up in flames. The 1840s and 1850s was the era of the great clipper ships. The Smithsonian Institution was established in 1846, and John Deere's iron plow was invented. Elias Howe's invention of the sewing machine, also in that year, had an enormous impact on the life of women. Two years later the first American women's rights convention met in Seneca Falls, New York.

Internationally, Liberia was proclaimed Africa's first independent nation in 1847. Europe was about to explode into violent revolutions the following year. The industrial workers (proletariat) were rising up against their employers, the bourgeoisie, and Karl Marx wrote the *Communist Manifesto*. One year earlier, in 1847, Britain's Factory Act had restricted the working day for women and children between thirteen and eighteen to ten hours a day!

Culturally, three women writers—George Sand, Charlotte and Emily Bronte—were writing in Europe, as were Fyodor Dostoevsky, Hans Christian Andersen, Herman Melville, and Henry Wadsworth Longfellow. Mendelssohn composed his oratorio "Elijah" in 1846. The following year Thomas Alva Edison was born in Ohio and Alexander Graham Bell in Scotland, and the first successful appendectomy was performed.

Even though there had been attempts to create a system of public education free to all citizens since the Revolutionary War, no such system had yet been put in place in 1846. Indiana had provided for public education in the State Constitution, but no funding had been made available for this purpose. Instead, the State Legislature had placed the responsibility for education on the cities and towns. The census of 1840 had ranked Indiana sixteenth on the national scale of literacy, the lowest rate among the Northern States with only one in seven persons being able to read and write. There were several colleges in existence in the state including: Hanover (1827); Indiana University (1838); Indiana Asbury (1839); and Notre Dame (1842). However, none of these institutions was open to women. The world was truly standing on the threshold of a new age!

By the year 1846, Fort Wayne, Indiana had already undergone significant expansion. It was located in a very propitious setting, where three rivers came together making transportation relatively convenient. This in turn contributed to the growth of commerce which led to the accumulation of wealth by at least some of the city's inhabitants. It was perhaps natural that they should turn their thoughts to education and culture.

In the 1840s, the Methodists were somewhat behind other denominations in the building of educational institutions. Speaking during the anniversary celebration of the Methodist Episcopal Sabbath School on Jan 27, 1845, Joseph K. Edgerton, a leading Fort Wayne citizen, lamented:

> It is a matter of regret, however, that, while the influence of the Methodist Church is so great, and its position so highly favorable, it has disappointed public expectation, and failed of its duty, and subjected itself to observation and reproach, by not using as strenuous and effectual efforts as it might use in the cause of education. Though it has done much, it is still, in this respect, behind other denominations which are its inferiors in numbers and strength.[1]

Indiana Asbury, renamed DePauw University in 1884, had been founded by the Indiana Methodist Episcopal Conference in 1839 as an all male institution. The Indiana Methodists had split in 1844 creating the North and South Conferences. Indiana Asbury was located in the South Conference, and the North Conference desired a college of its own. It would seem reasonable to assume that the educated and cultured wealthy citizens of Fort Wayne such as the Rockhills, the Hamiltons and the Rudisils coveted the same kind of educational opportunities for their daughters as those available to their sons. It is also possible that some of these Fort Wayne residents were loathe to send their daughters away to the well established eastern female seminaries. Perhaps even Oberlin College near Cleveland where women were welcome seemed a bit remote. Whatever their motivations, which at this distance in time can only be a matter of conjecture, a group of Fort Wayne's leading citizens along with the North Indiana Conference of the Methodist Episcopal Church undertook to create a female college in Fort Wayne in 1846. If the *Fort Wayne Sentinel* was representative of the sentiment in the community, it appears that this move was viewed as extremely positive. The Conference action was reported in the December 12, 1846 edition:

> We are glad to see this commendable attempt by the Methodist Episcopal Church of this beloved state to elevate the standard of female education. It is high time that it should be done. Justice to woman demands it; justice to a succeeding generation demands it.[2]

A TRUE COLLEGE

The public record leaves little room to doubt that the intentions of the founders of Fort Wayne Female College were to create a true college, not a female seminary or preparatory school, even though the latter was the more customary form of institution in which young women of the first half of the nineteenth century were

4

educated. Perhaps the founders made the choice to create a college because Fort Wayne already had two female seminaries—one, under the direction of the Misses M. L. Wallace and H. M. Raymond, had opened in November 1844.[3] The second, under the direction of Mrs. L. A. Sykes, had begun operating in October, 1845.[4] *The Sentinel,* reporting on the granting of the charter for the Fort Wayne Female College by the State of Indiana in its 1847 edition, 26 June stressed that the Board of Trustees was vested with the power to confer "the highest literary degrees and honors usual in female colleges upon such young ladies as may satisfactorily complete the prescribed course of study."[5]

The college catalogue for 1853-54 makes clear what these degrees were. "Young Ladies having completed the English Course of Study, and sustained therein satisfactory examinations, will receive an English diploma, an M.E.L. or Mistress of English Literature. Those who, in addition to the English Course, shall have completed the Course in the Languages, will receive a Classical Diploma, a L.B.A. (Lady Baccalaureate)."[6] During the early decades most of the young women received the M.E.L. degree.

By 1850, the faculty was considering opening a male department, but only "in such a manner and under such regulations, as shall not interfere with the rights and privileges of the Female Department of the college."[7] It was not until 1853 that a separate school, the Fort Wayne Collegiate Institute, was organized for young men, and in 1855 the two schools were united under the name Fort Wayne College.[8] It is important to note that even though the institution became coeducational, the commitment to educating women was not diminished. This commitment to gender equality was reaffirmed in the 1858 catalogue: "Both males and females can pursue a regular course of study and graduate with the degrees and honors usually conferred by other Colleges." President Reuben D. Robinson asserted that this was the best policy since "young gentlemen and young ladies ... mutually encourage each other to practice good manners, to be prompt and correct in recitations, and to be pious."[9] In fact the integration of males into the formerly female college seemed to proceed more smoothly than the integration of females into Indiana Asbury where the young men barred the entrance to the chapel in an effort to keep the five young women from entering, and the student newspaper published articles referring to their presence as "a sad oppression, grievous to endure."[10]

Fort Wayne Female College compares favorably to both Indiana Asbury and Oberlin Institute in terms of the degrees offered and earned by women. Between 1850 and 1860 forty-one women received classical degrees from Fort Wayne Female College and its successor Fort Wayne College. During a similar time period, (1836-1845) thirteen women received full classical degrees from Oberlin Institute.[11] The great majority of women who were accepted to study at Oberlin were concentrated in the "Young Ladies Course" which was not as rigorous as the college course since it omitted classical Latin, Greek and history; all were included in the curriculum of Fort Wayne Female College.[12] The curriculum for women at Oberlin was less rigorous than the male curriculum because it was felt that the feminine mind was not "strong enough to conquer the difficulties of Latin and Greek."[13]

THE WOMEN CAME

In addition to those women who received degrees, more than

300 attended Fort Wayne Female College for some period of time during the decade of the 1850s. The enrollment register printed in the 1853 catalogue shows a total of 131 young women excluding those in the Primary Department; the 1856 register lists a total of 141 women students; and the 1858 register contains the names of seventy-seven females.

The first available alumni record dates from the year 1871 and covers the graduating classes of the 1850s and 1860s. All but five of the women were married. Most lived in Indiana, Michigan, Illinois and Ohio, although one had moved East to Washington D.C. and one traveled West to Nebraska. Several were married to ministers, two were the wives of doctors and one wed a politician. There was no information given about the lives of the five single women. It is possible that they lived with their parents or other family members. It is equally possible that they earned their own living in one of the several occupations open to women of the first half of the nineteenth century including dressmaker, milliner, barber, artist, music teacher, and mistress of a select school.[14]

It should be noted that in the early part of the nineteenth century the purpose of education was to provide intellectual experiences designed to equip the mind for successful living not to prepare people for particular vocations. The purpose of Fort Wayne Female College was to "develop the intellectual powers, to train the mind to habits of close thought and reasoning, and to educate the heart in the purest principles of Christian morality."[15]

It has been observed that from its founding, the young women who attended Fort Wayne Female College studied the same curriculum as the young men in Fort Wayne Collegiate Institute. When male students were first integrated into the institution, female students outnumbered them. However, this state of affairs soon changed and the number of males and females equalized throughout the remainder of the decade. Beginning with the 1870s, enrollment patterns shifted dramatically with more males than females matriculating in most departments. The only exception to this pattern was the area of music and painting, "the ornamentals," which continued to enroll almost one hundred percent women. When the Normal School was introduced in 1875-76, nearly twice as many women as men were attracted to this new program. Throughout the decade of the 1880s, males maintained the enrollment edge in all four classes, especially the freshman academic class and the commercial and business courses while women continued to dominate music and art. After 1875, the student register did not indicate which students were

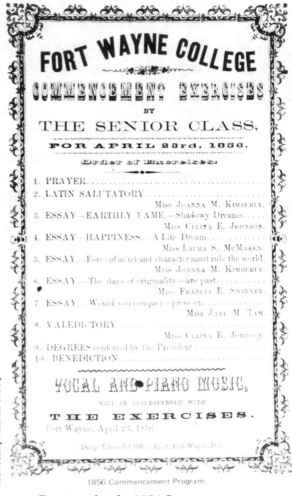

Allen County Historical Society

1856 Commencement Program.

Program for the 1856 Commencement

taking the normal course; therefore, it is impossible to trace any shifts between genders in this area. Between 1879 and 1889 sixty-seven males and forty-four females graduated from Fort Wayne College.[16] Considering the number of students both male and female who attended the college for at least a single term during this decade, the number of graduates remained almost infinitesimal, possibly because the high cost of education prevented many students from remaining in school until a degree program was completed.

THE WOMEN ACHIEVED

One of the ways which the faculty, parents and board members used to determine their success in achieving their educational goals was to conduct public oral examinations for all students at the end of each term. The first such public examination was conducted in December 1847, and several members of the Board attended the event and reported their perceptions to the next meeting of the trustees. After praising the deportment of the students, the committee gave a detailed summary of the various subjects in which the young women were examined, lauding the performance of the students in all areas. Their comments about composition are particularly interesting because the young ladies read their own essays in this public forum—a practice which was not followed in most educational institutions at this time including Oberlin Institute where men read the women's speeches and essays which they had written. [17] The committee pronounced themselves "greatly delighted with the examination" and felt that the "parents and trustees" had "cause to congratulate themselves" on the quality of education their daughters were receiving in the fledgling college.[18]

The Fort Wayne newspaper reported on the term examinations

and commencement exercises for 1850 as effusively as the trustees had reported two years earlier. The writer was particularly impressed by the promptness and thoroughness with which answers to the various questions and problems were presented. This "demonstrated that the mind had been well disciplined, and trained to the habit of close and independent thought." The writer was further impressed by the sense of self confidence in their knowledge and skills which the young women presented. [19]

A woman who had been a student in the College in 1856 remembered the occasion of her public examination seventy years later and shared her memories with a reporter from the *Indianapolis Sunday Star*. Mrs. A. J. Marvin recalled how some of the students

Mrs. A. J. Marvin, Student of Fort Wayne Female College in 1856.

had accidentally discovered a human skeleton on the grounds of the college. "The bones had been collected by one of the professors who had drilled the class very thoroughly on the name and use of each bone. At the public examinations he placed all the bones in a large box and required each member of the class to draw one—and having done so, to name it, and discuss it in an intelligent manner." She concluded her account by saying that they all did very well in this exercise "bringing great glory upon themselves." [20]

This self confidence and independence of thought which the college sought to instill in its female students was not always fully appreciated by the adults in power. One situation which very nearly ended disastrously occurred in 1852.

10

Miss Eliza Cooper gave a valedictory address in which she made some remarks that the Acting President, A. C. Heustis, deemed "highly disrespectful and insulting" to himself. He, therefore, stopped her examinations and made an official complaint to the Board in which he said he was "unable to confer on her the honors to which she had been elected." The Board called Miss Cooper to defend herself against these charges which she did by saying that the offending language "was in jest." The Board called several witnesses before arriving at the conclusion that the President was "in part justified" in his complaint. The President of the Board was instructed to admonish Miss Cooper privately "of the impropriety of her course in this case," and President Heustis was "requested to proceed with the examination and graduation of Miss Cooper to the degree to which she had been elected by the Board."

As a further result of this situation, the Board passed two resolutions. The first stated that public statements about college personalities of an "unkind character should not be tolerated." The second one called for "compositions, papers, declamations and orations" to be examined and approved by the President or a member of the faculty before they could be read or spoken in public.[21]

WOMEN WORKED AND CREATED

In addition to classroom drills, recitations, essays and compositions—all devices used to train the intellect— two literary societies were formed in Fort Wayne Female College, the Excelsiors and the Philosophians. The literary societies were student run organizations and constituted a venue in which the women's voices were honored. The societies elected officers and conducted weekly meetings which were given over to literary and musical exercises, and they had a library of their own collection. After the college became coeducational, these two societies were joined to form the El Dorados, an all female society; and a new organization, the Thalonians, was created for the male students. Classes were suspended during the Civil War and when the College reopened in 1869 this pattern of gender segregation in the literary societies was continued temporarily. However, in 1875 the El Dorados and the Thalonians joined together in the Union Literary Society. This arrangement did not last very long. Before the end of the decade, the Union Society had split into two groups each having male and female members. They were named the Thalonians and the Philaletheans. These societies met every Friday evening, and the exercises consisted of "debating, reading essays, reciting choice selections, and music." [22]

THIRD QUARTERLY

GRAND CONCERT.

Fort Wayne College Institute of Music

Allen County Historical Society

Fort Wayne College Concert Program.

The 1898 *Gem* contained short historical sketches of both the Thalonians and the Philaletheans. According to the Thalonian historian:

> For several years the influence of the gentle sex was unknown in the literary hall, but at last the beneficial results of this influence were recognized and equal rights and privileges were given to ladies and gentlemen. Many of the leading women of Fort Wayne and vicinity were Thalonians in their college days.

The Philalethean historian summed up the purpose of that society as being "to secure mental development and culture along literary lines; to give its members training in public reading and speaking; and to cultivate a taste for the lofty, the beautiful, the true." The list of Fort Wayne College members who had achieved some prominence since graduation contained two women, Mrs. Rheua Nickey Stemen, whose husband George was a Fort Wayne physician, and Cora M. Gordon, who became a journalist in Tacoma, Washington.

The graduation exercises which were conducted December 13, 1873 reflected the equality of education enjoyed by the female students of Fort Wayne College. That evening three young women read original essays. One of these essays, "My Fortune is in My Own Hand", must surely have articulated the kind of competence which its author, Miss Hallie C. McCarn, was apparently taking with her as she graduated. An amazing rhetorical exercise occurred at this commencement when a debate was presented on the question "Is fashion more oppressive than taxation?" Miss E. L. Harper took the affirmative and Mr. R. S. Reed the negative. "Good arguments were advanced on both sides." In order to fully appreciate the significance of this debate, one must recognize that in 1873 it was still not considered respectable or appropriate in many places for a woman to occupy a public platform and debate against a male opponent. [23]

God's Ordinary People:

The 1880s, when the Fort Wayne College was under the leadership of W. F. Yocum, began with great promise. The number of students kept increasing. A large addition was built to the College building, and the future looked very bright. The graduation exercises held during commencement week of 1885 inaugurated the new Chapel which comfortably seated 1000 people. *The Fort Wayne College Index*, edited by Mrs. W. F. Yocum, provided a comprehensive recapitulation of the festivities. Two young women graduates were singled out for particular commendation for the quality of their speeches. They were Nora Alleman and Melissa McConnahey. Miss Alleman delivered two speeches during the week long celebration. The first was the valedictory address at the Thalonian reunion which was praised as "one of the best exercises of the afternoon" due to its "pointedness and beauty of thought." Her second effort was an oration delivered at the commencement exercise itself and was said to have "electrified the audience" of a thousand by her "earnest delivery" and "perfect enunciation." However, the star performance was delivered by Miss Melissa McConnahey who "stepped boldly to the front, and without manuscript or notes delivered an impassioned plea for the freedom of women in the ranks of professional and industrial labor." Her address was entitled "What Can a Woman Do?" and she cited many examples of women's achievements. It was the opinion of the reporter that Miss McConnahey afforded a good example of the equality of intellect in the sexes. [24]

The commencement of 1885 was especially important because it was the first reunion of all students who had attended the College. The speaker chosen to address the alumni, friends and students was a woman, Mrs. Maude M. Shoemaker Dilla, graduate of the class of 1882. The title of her address was "The Lessons of Student Life", and it presented an eloquent argument for the value of a liberal, classical education in all of life's various arenas. [25]

CURRICULAR GOALS

American colleges were not originally organized as they are today. The concept of academic departments and divisions evolved

Taylor University: The First 125 Years.

Women Students Fort Wayne College

over a long period of time. Initially, the individual courses provided the basic building blocks for the curriculum. In Fort Wayne Female College and its successor, Fort Wayne College, courses were offered over three terms during each academic year. For example, in the 1850s, students enrolled in the Collegiate Course were expected to study three subjects each term. Freshman studied Virgil, *Cyropaedia* (Xenophon's longest work in which he sets forth an ideal system of kingly government) and algebra in the first term; Sallust (a Roman historian and politician), Herodotus, and a continuation of algebra in the second term; Cicero's *Orations*, Xenophon (Greek historian and essayist), Isocrates (Athenian philosopher and rhetorician) and rhetoric in the third term. The sophomore and junior years were patterned in somewhat the same way. Each term included two courses in classical language and literature and a third course taken from one of the following areas: mathematics, history and political science, or natural science. The senior year maintained the same three term, three course pattern, but focused on mental, moral and natural philosophy, logic, rhetoric and theology. If one desired to study a modern language, some courses in German would be substituted for some of the classical language courses. [26]

In the 1880s, the Fort Wayne College changed its curricular goals dramatically. They ceased offering the full four year collegiate curriculum and concentrated on what they called the "Academic Course" which was recommended to those who desired "a good education" but who could not "afford the time or money to take a complete classical college course." The courses studied were basic in that they focused on the primary aspects of a curricular field, i.e. arithmetic instead of algebra, McGuffey's *Reader* instead of English literature. In addition, a "college preparatory course" was offered in order to prepare students to enter a college such as DePauw University at the sophomore level. The first two years of this program were actually the same as the "Academic" but the last three years added many more Latin, English literature, advanced mathematics and science courses. The justification given for this departure from the mandate of the college as chartered was that educational needs of ordinary citizens were shifting. The country was growing and the economy was expanding. There were many opportunities in the world of commerce which had not previously been available and trained employees were needed. Therefore, the institution opted to provide "a first rate course of *secondary instruction* and an ample preparation for the business pursuits" of the country. Thus courses were added to the curriculum in such areas as business letter writing and bookkeeping.[27] The full collegiate course was reintroduced during the academic year 1889-90, the last year in which the college operated as Fort Wayne College.

With the change in name from Fort Wayne College to Taylor University came changes in curricular structure. The most obvious was the incorporation of the Medical College allowing for the division into two "departments"—the Literary and the Medical. The 1890-91 catalogue announced that the new University offered seven courses of study including: The Normal Course, The Scientific Course, The Classical Course, The Music Course, The Business Course, The Medical Course, and The Art Course.[28] This would seem to be quite an ambitious undertaking given the fact that the entire faculty of the Literary Department consisted of seven people, one of whom, C. B. Stemen, was also Acting President, Agent, and Professor of Surgery in the Medical Department. Such a feat was only possible because the actual subjects studied overlapped all the curricula except the medical course, where there was generally a different set of faculty members.

God's Ordinary People:

Women's Choir on the steps of Fort Wayne College

SHIFTING MORES AND CONSCIOUSNESS

The culture of Fort Wayne College as it had developed over the first forty-four years was significantly altered when the school became Taylor University and began to identify more with the National Association of Local Preachers and the Holiness Movement than with the General Conference of the Methodist Episcopal Church.[29] During the 1850s the only specific allusion to the religious nature of the College appeared in the "Standing Rules" which admonished that "each student will be expected to attend Church in the forenoon on the Sabbath, at such place of worship as her parents or guardian may desire." The young women were also forbidden to "walk on the streets or commons for pleasure, collect in each other's rooms for idle conversation or amusement" or engage in any other activity usually forbidden in a Christian home on the Sabbath.[30]

These rules regarding the observance of the Sabbath remained largely unchanged in the 1870s. The official statement of the College in regard to religious faith remained disconnected from any particular denominational doctrinal statement, although the official sponsorship of the Methodist Episcopal Church was always acknowledged. Instead of focusing on theology, the catalogue stressed the fact that Fort Wayne College sought to "cultivate social virtues" and to "strictly enforce moral decorum."[31] The catalogue issued at the end of the decade which covered the years 1877-1879 contained a section entitled "Religious Exercises." The first one was morning prayers which were held daily and attendance was required. Secondly, there was a voluntary daily prayer meeting, and thirdly students were "required to attend some orthodox church on Sunday forenoon." The church could be Catholic or Protestant according to the desire of the parents or the students.[32]

God's Ordinary People:

By the mid 1880s the extended list of rules had been abandoned. In its place there was a statement about the nature of living together in a college community where the goal was to "awaken the conscience of the students to a strict regard for the rights of others, and to a sense of their duty to themselves, to society, and to God." The catalogue acknowledged that most of the students at Fort Wayne College were "young men and women of maturity" and, therefore, were not in need of many regulations. There were only four items on the "Things Required" list, one of which was "attendance at Church at least on Sunday morning." The list of "Things Prohibited" did not appear. [33]

The last catalogue issued under the name of Fort Wayne College included a rather lengthy statement about the moral and religious instruction carried out in the College. It acknowledged the affiliation with the Methodist Episcopal Church, specified that attendance was required at the daily chapel exercises which used the Methodist liturgy, stated that attendance at the church of one's choice was expected at least on the Sabbath morning, and characterized the College as "not objectionably denominational" but "distinctively Christian." The paragraph concluded by discussing the fact that there was a student run prayer meeting which had been going on for some years, and acknowledged that many students had "been quickened into new life" and faith and some students "had been converted" to faith as a result of these meetings. [34]

When Thaddeus Reade assumed the presidency in 1891, the religious tone of the catalogue underwent a transformation. Reade wrote an introductory essay to the catalogue covering the year 1891-92. He declared that the aim of Taylor University was to "build up a Great University on the basis of evangelical

Christianity." He characterized the school as "in no sense secular" and as "religious and Christian through and through." The announced intention was to "lead all our students to a saving knowledge of Christ." [35] The following year Reade declared, "Never in the whole history of the Institution was the moral and religious tone higher." [36] The 1895 catalogue informed the reader that "during the year two special meetings were held in the school to promote a revival of religion among the students and as a result nearly all of our students were brought to Christ." [37] In addition to this rather marked shift in religious language, the statement of rules changed somewhat. The list of "Things Required" grew from four to six. The two new ones required young men and women in their association with one another to "exercise the utmost prudence," and also required "attendance at the Sunday afternoon lecture." The "Things Prohibited" list included drinking intoxicating liquors, using tobacco, playing cards, using profane or obscene language, defacing University property, and noisy, disorderly or unseemly conduct of any description." [38]

The move from Fort Wayne to Upland in 1893 signaled extensive changes in the curricular structure as well as in the religious ethos of the institution. The Medical School was left behind, and the seven courses of study which had been announced in 1890 were reduced to four: the Classical Course leading to the B.A. degree, the Philosophical Course leading to the Ph.B., the Scientific Course leading to the B.S., and the Normal Course which led to a diploma certifying the graduate to teach in the public schools. Almost everyone on the faculty of eleven was scheduled to teach multiple subjects. Presumably, classes continued to enroll students from all four different courses.

A few years later, another organizational change occurred. The 1897-98 catalogue stated:

> It is our intention to develop several distinct though not separate schools which, taken together shall constitute the University. Looking to this end we announce the following: Upland Normal College, Wright College of Liberal Arts, and Reade Theological Seminary; and as preparatory to the College of Liberal Arts, Taylor Academy.[39]

The result of this organizational change was merely to realign the separate courses. The subjects taught remained much the same as they had been since the birth of the institution in 1846 including the same Greek, Latin and English authors. Students still attended topical lectures and participated in Socratic recitation periods and wrote copious essays in conjunction with the language and literature courses as well as those in history, geography, and other social sciences. With the addition of some modern equipment, laboratory experiences were added to the scientific lectures and recitations. [40]

The Normal School curriculum was a pre-professional program designed to train teachers for the public schools. The curriculum focused on the subject areas which were studied in the common schools of the day including arithmetic, penmanship, reading and elocution, grammar, geography, history, physiology, spelling and defining. It was a three year diploma program of study and included courses in the history and philosophy of pedagogy. One professor, Lillian F. St. John, was responsible for teaching all of the Normal courses. [41]

The Reade Theological Seminary offered two degree tracks, the English Theological Course and the Latin Theological Course. The former paralleled the Scientific Course in the College of Liberal Arts and the latter was similar to the Classical Course. The only additional subject area was homiletics. [42] It is interesting to note that no particular faculty member was assigned to teach homiletics although it was required in both theological tracks for at least three terms.

EARLY WOMEN FACULTY

One of the most significant ways in which women have impacted the history of Taylor University is through their contributions as faculty members. The first faculty of Fort Wayne Female College consisted of the President, A. C. Heustis and his wife and three young women, Abigail Keis, Elizabeth Irving and Jane Irving. All of the surviving catalogues from the nineteenth century list one or more women faculty members. They taught a variety of courses in nearly all areas of the curriculum. Most held one degree, either an M.E.L. or an A.B. Those who taught music and art appear to have been trained musicians and artists but did not possess college degrees until the 1890s when the bachelor of music became common. Those who taught in the primary department normally were not credited with possessing full degrees. Presumably, they had graduated from some female seminary or preparatory school in order to be qualified to teach at the primary level.

It is difficult to make exact comparisons between the qualifications of male and female faculty during the first part of the century. Most of the male professors held seminary degrees, frequently an A.M. The highest degree held by any woman faculty member at this time was the Ph.B. It must be remembered that any institution which granted the Ph.B. or the A.B. could also grant the A.M. if a student applied to study a particular subject area with

23

a professor for an additional year beyond the bachelor's degree. By the 1890s there were some women who had earned the A.M. Two examples were F. Ella Lingo who taught fine arts and French beginning in 1894 and Mabelle C. Reade who joined the faculty in 1899. Her subject area was Greek, and she was granted a leave of absence the following year to study for the Ph.D. Unfortunately, she did not return to Taylor.

The Gem

Mabelle C. Reade, Professor of Greek.

One curricular area in which women faculty made a significant impact was English and classical and modern languages. Fort Wayne College catalogues dating from the 1850s did not identify English as a specific course. Rather, the elements of English grammar were taught in the Preparatory Department in conjunction with the elements of Latin grammar.[43] However, when we reach the 1870s we find a faculty position designated "Professor of Latin and English" and the position was filled by Jennie M. Fitch, A.B.[44] By the year 1875-76, a faculty position held by Lucy E. Robinson in English literature appeared in the catalogue.[45] By the end of the decade English literature and elocution were combined and Emma L. Knowles, M.E.L. was the professor. She was assisted by Belle K. Buckland who also held the M.E.L. degree. This decade also marked the introduction of a modern language—German. In 1871, Adelia A. Hitchcock, A.B., was Professor of Greek and German, and Lizzie C. Kable was the listed professor for German and English in 1876.[46] It will be noted that while women occasionally taught classical languages, these subjects were more often taught by males holding A.M. degrees from a seminary. This was also a period of time in which both male and female professors were not necessarily identified with a single course or in some cases even with a single subject area. For example, the 1881 catalogue informed the reader that Lizzie C. Kable was now teaching mathematics and English rather than German.[47] The following year there were considerable changes in the "Board of Instruction." For the first time, there were no women teaching English, Latin, Greek or German. In fact, one male professor was teaching the first three subjects and another was teaching German.[48] By the middle of the decade a woman was again teaching English literature, rhetoric and elocution, though Latin, Greek and German remained the domain of a male professor who possessed an A.M. French had been added as a modern language and was to be taught by Adele Roth.[49] The decade ended in financial and curricular crisis. The last catalogue issued by Fort Wayne College in 1889-90 indicated that the position of professor of English, elocution and German, along with several other curricular areas, remained vacant at the time of publication.[50]

NINETEENTH CENTURY PEDAGOGICAL METHODS

The Fort Wayne College catalogues did not begin describing course content and methodology until the 1880s. The first such description stressed that "correct use of language" was the main focus of the English course. However, "spelling and the analysis of English sentences" were also important parts of the study of English and would not be neglected. "Standard English authors" provided the basis for the literature classes.[51] The following year, the literature studied in the English courses was specified more exactly. "Fifteen masterpieces representative of the different periods of the development of English Literature" would be selected for study. Students were required to write original critical essays about the various masterpieces and to read these essays to the class during one two-hour long recitation period. Peer critics were then employed to "make a fair criticism of the essayist and his work." A general discussion followed in which all students were expected to participate. [52]

The methods used to teach modern languages were surprisingly modern. The primary objective was "to develop facility in conversation." In order to achieve this goal German was spoken in class. Reading German authors and writing compositions in German was also a part of the course. The grammar textbook was used as an aid for the advanced student especially in the writing of essays. [53]

Latin and Greek were "taught according to the methods of the best American Colleges." Great attention was given to grammar and translation. Here the goal was to render literal meaning while preserving the smooth flow of English sentences. [54]

During 1891-92, Grace Husted, B. Sc., joined the faculty and, was given the assignment of teaching German, rhetoric and Bible history. [55] The following year her assignment was changed to include English history. [56] English literature did not reappear until 1894-95 when it along with Latin was assigned to Husted. An additional faculty member, Mabel Seeds B.L., also was assigned to teach Latin. French was reintroduced during 1895-96 with the coming of Ella Lingo, A.M. [57]

Fort Wayne Female College truly broke new ground in the realm of educational opportunity in Indiana. While it was not the first women's college in the country, it was among the first, and it was the first in the state, a fact which deserves to be celebrated. In addition, the college laid a firm foundation of classical liberal arts education available to all without discrimination. At the same time, the basis for flexibility and responsiveness to societal needs was built into the curriculum. This foundation has withstood the tests of time and remains important in the Taylor of 1996.

God's Ordinary People:

PATRON'S DAY SONG.

IN MEMORY OF BISHOP TAYLOR.

Howard G. Hastings, '05.   Ethel W. Elder, '05.

1. The name of Bish-op Tay-lor spreads Far as the o-cean wave;
2. To-day the Bish-op's work goes on; Good deeds can nev-er die.
3. Long live our school for God and right, And wor-thy of her name!
4. A-loft may Tay-lor's ban-ner wave, And loud her prais-es swell.

Both land and sea he trav-eled o'er, Seek-ing the lost to save.
And while we cher-ish here his name, He dwells with God on high.
May we still keep the stand-ard high, The prin-ci-ples the same.
And all up-hold old Tay-lor U, Wher-ev-er we may dwell.

CHORUS.

For Tay-lor U. we'll bold-ly stand, Ex-tolled her name shall be;

Her fame shall spread from shore to shore, Wide as the boundless sea.

Taylor University Archives

Bishop Taylor song written and composed by Taylor University students.

28

Chapter Two

BISHOP WILLIAM TAYLOR: THE WORLD WAS HIS PARISH

*I*n 1890, three years before relocating to Upland, Fort Wayne College was renamed Taylor University in honor of famed Methodist evangelist and missionary organizer, William Taylor (1821-1902). President Jay Kesler has commented that "we [today at Taylor University] have neglected him at our own expense. Bishop Taylor is a far greater figure than we realize. He inculcates what Taylor University is all about better than any other person... The Taylor University we have today - the spirit of the students - is about as parallel to him and his spirit as it can get."[1] Kesler noted that the National Association of Lay Preachers (NALP) which was in charge of Fort Wayne College in the late 1890s was made up of men who like Taylor frequently were self-educated through "a rigorous reading program" outside formal schooling. The NALP represented independence as distinct from a hierarchical emphasis, and a return to the Holiness tradition which emphasized a second work of grace as exemplified by John Wesley in his 1838 Aldersgate experience. Furthermore William Taylor "represented evangelical Christian faith at a time when frontier religion was beginning to be brought into disrepute and people were seeking respectability." Educated people particularly in the East were seeking to return to their European roots; in contrast Taylor reflected a simpler frontier Christianity.[2]

29

THE EARLY YEARS

Taylor was born on May 2, 1821 in Rockbridge County, in the western part of Virginia, the first of eleven children to Stuart Taylor and Martha Hickman Taylor. Bishop Taylor in *Story of My Life* recounted a number of details about his family background. The Hickmans had originated in Delaware but his mother's grandfather had migrated west, bought land and slaves, and raised his family in the Presbyterian faith. William Taylor's paternal grandfather, James Taylor, was one of five brothers who emigrated from Armagh, Ireland, to Virginia between 1755 and 1765. They acquired land and slaves in Rockbridge County. James married a daughter of Captain Audley Paul of Scottish-Irish background.

> The Pauls were religiously opposed to slavery, and so indoctrinated the rising generation of the Taylors into antislavery sentiment that as fast as they came into possession of slaves by inheritance they set them free. My father [Stuart Taylor] emancipated the last of the race of them, being one of the younger of the fourteen children of James and Ann (Paul) Taylor.[3]

Former Taylor University President John Paul noted that in the 1850s Stuart Taylor with one thousand dollars obtained from his son, William, paid for his former slaves' passage to Liberia.[4]

Taylor recalled that soon after his parent's marriage, the family joined the Presbyterian Church. But one day his father passed Lambert's Church where a minister named Joseph Spriggs was preaching. His father became curious because of the large congregation which had assembled, but was somewhat wary of the Methodists because they were "a sect everywhere spoken against" in that part of Virginia.[5] Nevertheless Stuart Taylor went in and became "struck" by the sermon. Two weeks later in August 1832 a Methodist camp meeting was held at Cold Sulphur Springs about ten miles from the Taylor home. Stuart Taylor quietly took his son, William, to the meeting, using the excuse that he had to drive a herd of cattle in that direction. For three days they listened to the preaching and then finally Stuart Taylor responded to the call. On their return home, Stuart Taylor said to his son:

> William, I am converted. Yes, William, I am converted to God; converted among the Methodists. God bless the Methodists! I hated and dreaded them, but God has wonderfully saved me at a Methodist camp meeting.[6]

After his conversion, Stuart Taylor obtained a preacher's license, and for forty years was an evangelist traveling from one revival meeting to the next. John Paul noted that perhaps from the experience of his father, William Taylor developed the idea of self supporting missions.[7]

William Taylor also had a deep religious experience in August 1841 at a camp meeting at Panther Gap, some ten miles from his home. Following this conversion, he was first appointed as a junior preacher on the Franklin Circuit (Virginia). He was admitted on trial to the Baltimore Conference in 1843, and two years later was granted full membership. On September 21, 1845, Taylor married Isabelle Anne Kimberlin who had been born in Virginia in 1825.[8] In 1848, having been noticed by Bishop Beverly Waugh, Taylor was appointed the preacher of a rather prestigious church in north Baltimore.

MINISTRY IN CALIFORNIA

Later that same year, Bishop Waugh interviewed Taylor as a candidate for the proposed Methodist work that was being envi-

William Taylor as a young man.

sioned for California. One month later the Bishop decided on Isaac Owen and Henry Benson, professor of Greek at Indiana Asbury University (today DePauw) to be the two pioneer Methodist preachers to California. But Benson declined the invitation, and Waugh then turned to Taylor. On April 19, 1849, Taylor, his wife Anne, and one child, Morgan Stuart, born in 1847, departed from Baltimore on board the ship "Andalusia," a voyage bound for San Francisco around Cape Horn. Taylor was the ship's chaplain, but he had trouble relating to the crew and passengers on board. For example, initially William and Anne Taylor took a dim view of the dancing which took place every evening. A few days out of Valparaiso, a severe storm caused damage to the ship. The crew and male passengers began to do repair work on Sunday, August 5, before the worship service, much to Taylor's annoyance. Ann Booth, one of the passengers, noted:

> Poor man [Taylor], his simplicity amuses while it sometimes is annoying-no doubt he is perfectly sincere, and would

himself practice what he preaches to others but his fastidiousness never was more out of place than on the present occasion when common sense suggests the necessity of yielding to the emergency of the case.[9]

However, Taylor eventually realized he needed to be more adaptable and towards the end of the voyage was no longer as judgmental in his sermons. Ann Booth commented:

He refrains from using that denunciating style that used to characterize his sermons, and instead thereof, he employs persuasive arguments, which are much more effectual. The passengers appear to appreciate the motive which has induced this change, and testify their approbation by giving their general attendance.[10]

While on the long arduous sea voyage, a daughter, Oceana, was born on January 22, 1849 off Cape Horn, but she died in San Francisco in August 1850. The Taylors had a total of eight children, but only four sons survived into adulthood. The following is a list of the Taylor children and their descendants:

Morgan Stuart Taylor - born 1847 in Washington DC; died
    1919 in Alameda, California buried in Mountain View
    Cemetery, Oakland; he was an attorney.
  children - Ethel Anne Taylor Chambers (1886-1979) - she died in
    Guanajuato, Mexico.
    Ethel married George Eric Chambers and had two
    children, Edmund Stuart Chambers (1917-) and
    Barbara Jean Chambers (1919 -).
    Edmund Stuart's daughter is Diana C. Johnson .
    Barbara Jean married Edward Koskinen—
    they have a daughter (Janice) and son (Stanley).
    Lulu Irene Taylor Post (1889-1989) - buried in MountainView
    Cemetery, Oakland.
Oceana Wilson Taylor - born in 1849; died in 1850 (buried in Yerba
    Buena Cemetery, San Francisco).
William Taylor Jr. - born 1851 in California; died 1853 in
    San Francisco (buried in Yerba Buena Cemetery, San

Anne Taylor and two sons, Edward K. (left) and Ross (right)

Francisco).

Charles Reid Taylor - born 1853 in California; died 1865 on the East
     Coast.

Osman Baker Taylor - born 1854 in California; died from small pox in
     1856 in Brooklyn, New York (buried in Greenwood Cemetery,
     Brooklyn).

Ross Taylor - born 1857 in Rockbridge County, Virginia; died 1919 in
     Ohio. His children: Stewart L., William Ross, Rossada Taylor
     Hittinger, Dorothy Taylor Hayes. Ross worked with his father
     in his Africa missions.

Edward Kimberlin Taylor - born 1860 in Elmira, New York, died 1930
     in California (buried in Mountain View Cemetery, Oakland)
     Edward Kimberlin became a prominent lawyer in Alameda,
     California; twice elected mayor, and also State Senator.
     He had two daughters, Miriam (1890-1905) who died in a
     horse accident and Eunice (1896- died in infancy).

Henry Reed Taylor - born 1867 in South Africa; died 1917 (buried in
     Mountain View Cemetery, Oakland). Henry Reed became a
     journalist - was city editor of the *Alameda Encinal*; he had one
     daughter - Marjorie Taylor Proudfoot (1892-1982) of
     Alameda, California — buried at Mountain View Cemetery.[11]

Taylor preached for seven years in California, a large part of
his ministry to the "Forty-niners." Standing on a whiskey barrel
in Portsmouth Square, San Francisco, Taylor spoke to thousands.
An historic plaque of the Methodist Historical Society which was
formerly on the Square and now in the possession of the Temple
United Methodist Church, San Francisco, noted that:

> Here on December 3, 1849 William Taylor preached to miners
> who crowded this park the first of 600 sermons on this city's
> streets and docks Later he preached on six continents but was
> commonly known as "California" Taylor

He was recognized for his powerful preaching skills, commanding
personality, and extraordinary energy and vitality. In 1881, he noted
he was six feet tall and weighed 207 pounds.

God's Ordinary People:

John Paul identified five ministries in which Taylor was engaged between 1849 and 1856. He was pastor of the first Methodist Episcopal Church of San Francisco; founder of other Methodist congregations in San Jose, Santa Clara, and Santa Cruz; famed street preacher (his preaching took him to brothels and saloons); hospital missionary; and minister to sailors through his Seamen's Bethel which was a boarding house. The latter unfortunately burned, and Taylor and his colleagues were left with a large debt. Part of the debt, however, was paid off when Taylor wrote two books, *Seven Years Street Preaching in San Francisco* (1857), and *California Life Illustrated* (1858). However, it was never fully paid. In 1856, Taylor was granted a leave of absence from his California work.

In California, Taylor aided the poor, ministered to the sick, defended Native Americans, and preached in Chinese labor camps. Along with Edward Bannister and Isaac Owen, two Methodist preachers, Taylor founded California Wesleyan College, located first in San Jose, then moved to Stockton and renamed College of the Pacific (its present name is University of the Pacific). Taylor may have been one of the first to recognize the importance of California apart from its gold. He made the following observations:

> Indeed it [California] is altogether a very attractive country...
> There is a charm in its climate, its scenery, bays, rivers, valleys,
> mountains, and ocean; its varieties of production, mineral and
> vegetable, and its game...[12]

It can be said Taylor was one of the founding fathers of San Francisco, and there are several landmarks in the Bay Area related to this fact. The San Francisco Public Library contains two mural paintings commemorating America's nineteenth century westward expansion. They were painted by Frank Vincent DuMond for the 1915 Panama-Pacific International Exposition. "Pioneers Leaving the East" is in the second floor Humanities Room, and "Pioneers Arriving in the West" in the Circulating Room. The former depicts a group of pioneers leaving New England for the West with a wagonful of household goods. Included in the mural is a jurist, a school-mistress, a child, and a preacher whom the artist has depicted as William Taylor, though some of his facial features are, according to a librarian, resembling those of the artist's mother. In The Church of the Good Shepherd Methodist in Richmond, California is a memorial window entitled "The Twelve Apostles of California." William Taylor is included with such important historic figures as early Roman Catholic missionary Junipero Serra, explorer Jedediah Strong Smith, naturalist John Muir, cowboy and entertainer Will Rogers, and poet Edwin Markham.

The African News, Taylor University Library

Anne Taylor

California became the home for Anne Taylor and the children while William Taylor preached around the world. While in Australia in the 1860s, Taylor sent eucalyptus tree seeds to Anne Taylor who planted them; it is believed this tree was first introduced into California by the Taylors. William Taylor spent the last two and a half years of his life in Palo Alto, and was buried in Mountain View Cemetery, Oakland along with his wife and other members of the family who died later. This 200 acre cemetery with its rolling terrain was designed in the early 1860s by Frederick Law Olmsted, known for his Central Park work in New York City. The most impressive part of the cemetery is "Millionaires' Row" with large marble and granite monuments for such luminaries as railroad tycoon Charles Crocker, "Chocolate King" Domingo Ghirardelli, and two former California governors. Nearby, commanding an impressive view of the cities of Oakland and San Francisco, is the nearly six foot monument to the Taylors. The United Methodist Church has designated it an historic site. Taylor is identified as Bishop of Africa (he was given that title by the Methodist General Conference in 1884) with the biblical inscription "The People who sat in darkness saw great light."

In downtown San Francisco, at 100 McAllister (at the corner of McAllister and Leavenworth) is the 28-story neo-Gothic style building formerly known as the William Taylor Hotel built by the Methodist Church and dedicated in 1929. This 500 room hotel was at that time the tallest building in San Francisco and reputed to be the highest hotel west of Chicago. On the street level was the Great Hall, a Gothic-style church accommodating 1500 worshipers, designed by architect Lewis P. Hobart whose masterpiece was San Francisco's Grace Cathedral. Unfortunately, the Depression forced the Methodists to sell the building, and in 1936 it reopened as the swank Empire Hotel. During World War II it was sold to the federal government and the Great Hall was subdivided and plastered over to become a military induction center. The building was vacated in

1976, but shortly thereafter it was purchased by its present owner, the Hastings College of the Law and converted into a student residence hall. The former Great Hall has been "rediscovered" and is now used by the George Coates Performance Works. Unfortunately there are no historic plaques on the building noting that it was originally the William Taylor Hotel.[13]

WORLD EVANGELIST - SUMMARY OF TAYLOR'S OVERSEAS MINISTRY

In the period from 1856 until he was designated Missionary Bishop of Africa by the General Conference of the Methodist Episcopal Church in 1884, Taylor traveled and preached in all six populated continents, and ultimately journeyed an astounding 250,000 miles. As an evangelist, up to that time in history, he may have had no equals save St. Paul and John Wesley. Taylor's life is well documented because with help from editors he wrote eighteen books including *Christian Adventures in South Africa* (1867); *Pauline Methods of Missionary Work (1879); Ten Years of Self-Supporting Missions in India* (1882); *Story of My Life (*1896); and *The Flaming Torch in Darkest Africa* (1898), the latter containing an introduction by famed explorer Henry Morton Stanley.[14] Taylor wrote the manuscripts during the long voyages across the world's oceans. It is claimed tens of thousands of copies were sold, thereby providing income for his family and his self-supporting missions. *The African News* was a periodical focusing on Taylor's mission enterprises. It was published from 1889 to 1894. It was then known as *Illustrated Africa* (1894-1896), and as *Illustrated Christian World (1896-1898)*.

In October 1856 the Taylor family left California by ship, sailing via Panama for the East Coast. From 1856 to 1861, Taylor was a

Bishop Taylor's Magazine.

BISHOP WM. TAYLOR,

EDITOR AND PROPRIETOR.   RESIDENT IN AFRICA.

Information from and About Africa.

Missionary News

— OF —

Africa AND Other Mission Fields

T. B. WELCH, M.D.,
Associate Editor, Vineland, New Jersey.

VOL. I. 1889.

PUBLISHED BY

T. B. WELCH & SON, VINELAND, NEW JERSEY.

successful preacher in the East and Midwest, as well as in parts of
Canada. Unfortunately, he was not successful in obtaining funds
to pay off the San Francisco debt. Taylor noted in his book *The
Model Preacher* that he visited Fort Wayne College in 1859.

> A few weeks since, I spent a night at Fort Wayne College.
> Brother Robinson [R.D. Robinson, Taylor University president
> between 1855 and 1877]..., his good lady [Mary K. Mahurin
> Robinson] and myself having returned from church, were
> conversing in the parlor, when a messenger came in and
> handed the President a telegraph dispatch.[15]

The message related that Mary Robinson's father had died in
Lafayette, Indiana. At that time few would have thought in a third
of a century this school would be named in William Taylor's honor.
Taylor visited the University again during the 1895-6 academic
year in Upland.

While in Canada, Taylor heard stories about Australia and felt
called to that continent. In 1862, he sailed for Australia by way of
England. After spending seven months in England and Ireland, he
visited Paris, France; Palestine; Asia Minor; Syria; and Egypt, then
on to Ceylon, and finally Australia and New Zealand where he
preached for three years, adding thousands to the Methodist
churches. His family joined him towards the end of his stay. They
were to return together to California but then Taylor became
interested in preaching opportunities to Europeans in India.
Unfortunately, his son, Morgan Stuart, fell ill and doctors advised
South Africa would have a much more conducive climate than India
in order for him to regain full health. In 1866 and 1867, for seven
months Taylor preached in South Africa, his first visit to the African
continent. This was a turning point in Taylor's preaching career
because it was the first time he spoke to people not of European

background. England and Scotland were visited in 1867 where Taylor met William and Catherine Booth, founders of the Salvation Army. His family returned to California, and Taylor went on to Barbados and British Guiana in 1868. From 1869 to 1875, Taylor was back in Australia as well as Ceylon and India. It was in India where Taylor developed the "self-supporting" missionary strategy which he termed the "Pauline System." The Indian experience was disappointing for him because he was not fully effective in communicating with the indigenous people.

In 1875, Taylor returned to England, this time helping Dwight L. Moody in his London evangelistic campaign. During the seven year period between 1877 and 1884, the focus was on South America and the West Indies. Taylor made three trips to South America, the first being in 1877-8 where he organized a system of self-supporting schools in Chile and Peru. During 1880 he was on the east coast of South America, and from 1882 to 1884 again on the west coast.

The final phase of Taylor's missionary odyssey was Africa. Taylor was a lay delegate from the South India Conference at the 1884 Philadelphia meeting of The General Conference of the Methodist Episcopal Church. At the conference there was noticeable tension between the "outsiders" and the New York "insiders."[16] Another problem that had to be faced was the floundering church in Liberia. Methodism had been introduced into this West African nation earlier in the nineteenth century resulting at first in a strong church. But by the 1880s it was beset by a number of problems. Thus it was decided to elect a Missionary Bishop to address the problems of the Liberian Church. There was an effort to elect a black bishop, but then William Taylor was nominated.

> ...His candidacy drew support from a number of parties. Those opposed to electing a black bishop, those in favor of Taylor's Self-Supporting Missions and the Holiness forces had a candidate [Taylor] who united their conflicting interests.[17]

He was elected on the first ballot as Missionary Bishop of Africa. Paradoxically, Taylor was interested in leadership for blacks, especially Africans, and yet his election was a defeat for a person of color. He saw his election as a vote of confidence in his "Pauline Method" of missions. But the Missionary Bishop's position was considered different from "regular" bishops, and this was clearly shown in the salary issue. It was decided that his salary would not come out of the Episcopal Salary Fund, but rather the treasury of the Missionary Society. Subsequently, Taylor refused to accept this arrangement but fortunately had a financial backer in New York who paid for his support.[18]

Between 1884 and 1896, Taylor made seven trips to Africa. His primary task was to straighten out the problems of the Liberian Church. But Taylor was not satisfied merely focusing on Liberia. He dreamed of developing a chain of self-supporting mission stations across the continent, from Angola and the Congo in the west to Mozambique and the Indian Ocean in the east. He went about attracting volunteers for service in Africa. The first group of missionaries to Angola arrived in Luanda on March 20, 1885. These men and women were willing to trust God and the indigenous people for their support. But Africa was a very difficult place to sustain self-supporting missionaries, and some either died or returned to the United States, their spirit and health broken. Nevertheless, many persevered, particularly in Angola, developing a healthy Methodist

Church. Bishop Taylor's great physical strength began to weaken. In Brussels, Belgium, he fell ill, and in 1896 the General Conference retired him. Taylor made one final trip to Africa. In 1896-7 for fifteen months Bishop Taylor preached and traveled in South Africa which he had not visited since the successful meetings thirty years earlier. In 1899 he made his last trip to the eastern United States and then retired to Palo Alto where he died in 1902.[19]

THE AFRICA YEARS: PART ONE - SOUTH AFRICA

It was accidental in many ways that Bishop Taylor came to South Africa in 1866. His son, Morgan Stuart, was ill and the doctors thought it advisable the family should go to South Africa rather than India. The Taylors arrived at Table Bay in Cape Town from Australia at the end of March 1866. In the history of South African Methodism, the year 1866 was the beginning of a period of extraordinary growth. "The first African campaign, of only a few months, was to be attended with magic results that surpassed and surprised Taylor's faith."[20] But it did not start out successfully. Taylor began his revival services among whites at the Wesleyan Church on Burg Street, Cape Town.[21] The crowds were not large, and Taylor was disappointed. He then moved on to Port Elizabeth and Uitenhage, continuing to preach to the whites but again the crowds were sparse. However, in Grahamstown, eastern Cape Province, "the clouds broke, and resulted in a rising tide of mighty spiritual power and blessing."[22] After a couple of weeks, Taylor went on to King William's Town where the crowds were disappointing again. But in that city in the eastern Cape, Taylor was introduced to Charles Pamla, a 32 year old Zulu who had been converted and who had received theological instruction at the Native

44

Theological Institution in Annshaw. He was a good student and developed into a fine preacher "of commanding presence, of great natural gifts, fluent in speech, able to preach in five different languages."[23] In King William's Town, Taylor preached to whites, and Pamla more successfully to blacks. Taylor was very impressed with Pamla. He decided that at the revival at the Annshaw mission station which began on June 14, 1866 he would preach to blacks with Pamla translating. The meeting was a complete success. The altar call following the sermon attracted more than one hundred. Taylor was astonished. "I believe Charles gave every idea and shade of thought as naturally and as definitely as if they had originated in his own brain."[24] Taylor commented:

Charles Pamla, South African evangelist, preacher

> ... he uttered every sentence from his heart, just as I did myself, so that by the union of two heads and two hearts, the Holy Spirit's power, we worked a double heart battery, which seemed to give the preaching through an interpreter much greater power than singly and directly without an interpreter.[25]

Whenever Pamla was present, Taylor's sermons were successful. Taylor in turn was identified by the Africans as "Iskunisivutayo" ("Burning Fire Stick or Torch"). His last book, published in 1898, was called *The Flaming Torch in Darkest Africa*. In Durban two months after the successful meetings at the Annshaw mission station, Taylor and Pamla bade farewell to each other. Pamla recalled Taylor took his hand and cried. Taylor said:

> He [Pamla] has a philosophic cast of mind, can grasp the most abstruse principles readily, forgets nothing worth remembering, and after interpreting my sermons twice per day for nearly two months, it became a work of supererogation for me to preach through him, for he could do it as well, or better, without me. I had prayed that God would allow me to remain, at least a few years, to lead a victorious host of native evangelists into the interior of Africa; but I now saw that God would answer my prayer indirectly, by giving my mantle to my Elisha [Pamla], and take me away, if not to heaven, to some other part of His vast dominions, where He may have greater use for me.[26]

This was the first time Taylor had spoken to groups who were not primarily white. He clearly became fascinated by Africa, and some eighteen years later he would return as Missionary Bishop of Africa.

Taylor was paternalistic in the sense that he believed black evangelists needed his guidance and leadership. Yet having Pamla assist him was quite different from what was happening in the Wesleyan Church. Generally Wesleyan missionaries until 1866 were hesitant to allow Africans to become evangelists and to have any significant responsibilities. Thus 1866 was a watershed year for South African Methodists. The following year a theological institute was established at Healdtown for black preachers, and in 1871 the first blacks including Pamla were ordained by the South African Wesleyan Church. Pamla became a noted evangelist in South Africa, and when he retired in 1913 it was observed he had converted over 25,000 Africans under his preaching. In June 1917 he died at the age of 83. Pamla had served the South African Methodist Church for nearly sixty years first as an unpaid evangelist and then as an ordained minister.[27]

Taylor was in South Africa at a time when there was considerable hardship in the Cape Colony from drought, disease, and war. Since Africans were overwhelmed by these crises, Taylor's preaching brought a sense of hope. Because their lives were being dramatically changed by Westernization, it has also been suggested that "only through conversion to the new faith was the gateway opened for one to share the benefits and advantages of that [new] society."[28] In no small part Taylor's preaching was a catalyst that transformed the Wesleyan Church into one of South Africa's largest

Commission on Archives and History, United Methodist Church, CA, NV Conference Berkeley, CA.

Willam Taylor in South Africa - 1866

denominations. It also catapulted Taylor into an international evangelist, and from that time on he frequently preached in areas of the world not inhabited for the most part by Caucasians. Clearly South Africa was the watershed event for Taylor's international ministry.

THE AFRICA YEARS: PART TWO - LIBERIA

Eighteen years after Taylor's successful evangelistic experience in South Africa, he again came to Africa. This time he returned as Missionary Bishop of Africa. The main purpose for selecting a

Missionary Bishop was to have oversight and to strengthen the work of the Methodist Episcopal Church in Liberia. The Liberian colony before its independence in 1847 was a narrow strip of coastline. Methodism had been introduced early in the colony's history and extended its work from Robertsport (Cape Mount) in the northwest to Harper (Cape Palmas), a distance of some three hundred miles.[29] Its work was primarily with the Americo-Liberians (the group descended from freed American slaves who began arriving in the 1820s) and not the indigenous population. For a variety of reasons its work was stagnant and its schools at Cape Palmas and Monrovia were in bad condition. Leadership was needed to revive the church, and at the 1880 General Conference the Liberians had asked for another Bishop, but no action was taken. Also at the 1880 General Conference the expansion of the church in Africa was actively discussed. Taylor bemoaned the fact that there was no Methodist work among the indigenous people of Liberia except the beginning of one in Kroo Town (Kru Town), Monrovia, headed by Mary Sharpe (some sources spell the name "Sharp").[30]   Taylor was also thinking in terms of expanding the work to other parts of Africa. But at this conference, Taylor recalled that the chairman of the Committee on Episcopacy stated:

> It is no use to elect a bishop for Liberia. Liberia is a very unfortunate approach to Africa, being hedged in by hostile and warlike nations, and cannot be made an acceptable gateway to the continent. If you could find some man like Livingstone, who would open up Africa, it would be wise to elect such a man...[31]

Four years later Taylor was chosen to be that person. Initially it was proposed that a black man be elected Missionary Bishop of Africa. But then someone suggested William Taylor. He was then elected overwhelmingly, and given two assignments — the oversight of Liberia and the expansion of the work to other parts of Africa.

Taylor wasted no time. His first task was to recruit a corps of missionaries fully committed to the concept of a self-supporting mission. He was reassured by the General Conference leadership that it would not interfere with his self-supporting mission approach. Before the end of 1884, Taylor had attracted some thirty men and women along with about a dozen children. His plan was to take some members of the group to Liberia to begin work among the indigenous population. Others would go to Luanda, Angola which he decided was to be the entry point into the interior of Africa.

By February 1886 Taylor was planning to expand Methodist work in Liberia to the Grebo people along the Cavalla River. Among the people in his party during the difficult journey to the Grebos was the famed black evangelist Amanda Smith.[32] Taylor's aim was to establish industrial missions based on coffee-raising at

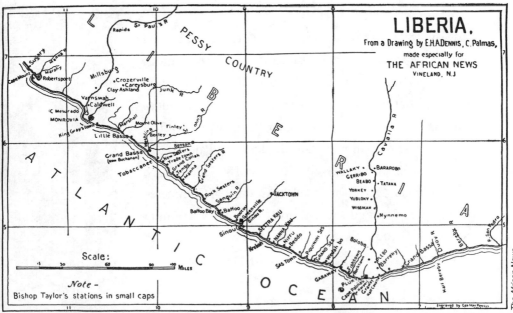

Methodist Missions in Liberia - 1880s

already existing trading posts along the Cavalla River. Bishop
Taylor also wished to expand the work among the coastal Kru (Kroo)
with whom he had a particular interest. A group of Kru had settled
near Monrovia and were being ministered to by Miss Mary Sharpe,
an independent Methodist missionary who had been laboring in
Liberia since 1879. Taylor led a group first to Garraway and later
Sas Town (Sasstown). One of the outstanding Taylor missionaries
who worked with the Kru for some nineteen years was Agnes
McAllister who arrived in Liberia in January 1889. She translated
a number of hymns into the Kru language and wrote a book, *The
Lone Woman in Africa*. McAllister described the violent clashes
among tribal groups in Liberia which was so significant in Samuel
Morris' early years. Bishop Taylor wrote the introduction to her
book, stating "Miss Agnes McAllister is a Christian
heroine. She has been in charge of Garraway Mission
Station on the Kroo [Kru] coast of West Africa for nearly
eight years, and has made a success of all departments of
our mission work."[33]

By 1895 there had been considerable expansion
among the indigenous population in Liberia. Ten stations
had been established in the Cape Palmas and Cavally
River district.[34] Over fifty missionaries had been sent to
Liberia by Taylor, a large number being women. The
Brooks mission station at Pluky in the Cape Palmas area
was under Elizabeth McNeil.[35] Born in 1865 in Fertility,
Pennsylvania, McNeil attended the College of Commerce
in Philadelphia and the Osborn Missionary Training
School in Brooklyn, New York. A few months after
joining the Methodist Church in 1887, she went to Liberia

The African News

under Bishop Taylor, serving there until 1892. She then returned to the United States for rest and change as she described it. While in America, she became a Deaconess by the Board of the Oregon Conference (her sister lived in Portland). In one year McNeil gave over one hundred talks on Africa and raised $1200 to build a new mission house. She then came back to Liberia in 1893 and during that year married Abraham L. Buchwalter who had been a missionary carpenter in Bishop Taylor's Liberian self-supporting mission

Mr. and Mrs. Stanley Koskinen

Bishop Taylor and possibly President D. H. Howard of Liberia photographed in 1884

Liberia Conference, Monrovia, 1888. Seated in center - Bishop William Taylor

General Commission on History and Archives, United Methodist Church, Madison, NJ

Bishops of the Methodist Episcopal Church - 1891

since 1890. They returned to the United States in 1895 due to Elizabeth Buchwalter's illness. But in 1897 they resumed their work in Africa, this time with the Inhambane East Central Africa Mission in southern Mozambique. Later they were connected with the Methodist work in Umtali (Mutare), Rhodesia. They retired in 1916 and returned to the United States, settling in southern California, where Mr. Buchwalter died in 1917. Mrs. Buchwalter continued to live in the Pasadena area until her death in 1942.

According to Bishop Taylor in *The Flaming Torch in Darkest Africa*, Elizabeth McNeil, while at the Brooks mission station before her marriage to Buchwalter:

> ...adopted a number of children, before they had become heathen, and they were soon witnesses to the saving grace of the Lord Jesus. Then with her little family of about twenty children she held open-air meetings under a breadfruit tree, and [the king and the chiefs] were soon attracted to them. Her method was to read and explain the Scriptures and then give their testimony before their heathen neighbors. They might have their doubts in regard to the statements of the foreign missionary, but the simple, straightforward story of the guileless little children carried conviction to their hearts. A great revival resulted, during which the king, several of his chiefs, and a number of his people were converted to God.[36]

One of the adopted children was Tia Bralah, a little Grebo girl who became known as Diana McNeil. She was born in Cape Palmas. According to her unpublished personal reflections written years later, Diana McNeil noted that "sometime before I was born [1889], 'Teacher' [Elizabeth McNeil] as all the mission children called the white missionary was instrumental in saving my mother's life." She explained that an older clan member was pursuing her mother with a weapon, and Diana's mother sought sanctuary in the mission school. Diana was then given by her mother to McNeil as

Elizabeth McNeil and
Tia Bralah (Diana McNeil)

Houston Chronicle, July 24, 1970

"a token of gratitude." Her mother wanted her to receive an education at the mission school.[37] Bishop Taylor:

wanted to bring a child from the mission to the United States as a sample of the kind of native people the churches here were serving in their missionary work. None of the missionaries were willing to let anyone of the children go so far away across the 'big big waters.' Disappointed, Bishop Taylor was about to give up the idea when 'Teacher' came forward to say she thought she knew one family, one of the recent converts who would be willing to let a little girl go. That happened to be my parents, my mother especially who still remembered her indebtedness to Teacher for saving her life and so I was brought to America the first time.[38]

Another reason why Elizabeth McNeil came back to America in 1893 was to escort the little three year old Liberian girl. Diana McNeil in her personal reflections could barely remember her early years in the United States but she did note that as she and McNeil traveled from East to West, sometimes accompanied by Bishop Taylor. "I became one of the attractions as I was brought forth on the platform after the speeches and taught to sing 'Jesus Loves Me This I Know'... I was quite a curiosity."[39] The purpose of this tour was to get people interested in the mission work in Liberia.

Diana McNeil recalled that during her stay in America she had forgotten any knowledge she may have had of her Grebo language. After one year, McNeil and Diana returned to Liberia, and Diana was enrolled in a mission school in Monrovia. Also during that

General Commission on History and Archives, United Methodist Church.

Bishop William Taylor and Tia Bralah (Diana McNeil) photographed in 1892.

year her sister, Minnie, had been admitted to the mission school. At this time, Elizabeth McNeil married A.L. Buchwalter. Diana McNeil returned with the Buchwalters to the United States and then to Mozambique. The Buchwalters were described as strict disciplinarians, Elizabeth being a small woman in stature, rather prim, reserved, but forceful.[40] At the age of eleven Diana was placed in a school in Lancaster, Pennsylvania, and then went with relatives of her foster parents to Monrovia, California where she graduated with high honors from the Monrovia high school. She then entered the University of Southern California in 1906 from which she graduated with honors in 1909. She took a Master of Arts degree in 1910, specializing in history. It has been said Diana McNeil was the first black to earn an undergraduate degree from that institution.[41] Later she attended the Chicago Missionary Training School, receiving the degree of Bachelor of Religious Education. Following graduation in 1912, she returned to Liberia as a member of the faculty of the College of West Africa, Monrovia. However, she came back to the United States in 1916 because of health problems. Diana McNeil accepted a faculty position at Philander Smith College, Little Rock, Arkansas, where she met and married Cato Pierson, teacher and minister. Their desire was to go to Africa as missionaries. But this never occurred because of Diana's pregnancy. Diana McNeil Pierson taught at Clark College, Atlanta, Georgia; at Rust College, Holly Springs, Mississippi; and at Wiley College in Marshall,

Taylor University Archives

Diana McNeil Pierson

Texas. In 1961 she retired from teaching, and lived with her husband in Dickinson, Texas where he was pastor of the Faith United Methodist Church. She died in 1971.

Diana McNeil Pierson's outstanding career in higher education for African-Americans was continued by her daughter, Dr. Clarice Lowe. She received her bachelor's degree in English from Wiley College, master's degree from Northwestern University in speech pathology and audiology, then went on for a Ph.D. at the University of Wisconsin where her doctoral dissertation was entitled "The Division of the Methodist Episcopal Church in 1844 An Example of Failure in Rhetorical Strategy." Dr. Lowe was Professor of English at Texas Southern University, Houston, and head of the Department of Communication. She taught at that institution from 1947 until her recent retirement.[42]

Elizabeth McNeil was also significant in the life of Samuel Morris. According to Jorge Masa in *The Angel in Ebony,* Morris became acquainted with McNeil who took a particular interest in Morris. She knew Rev. Stephen Merritt, secretary of Bishop Taylor's mission located in New York City. When Morris arrived in New York, he immediately sought out Merritt (see Chapter Six).

THE AFRICA YEARS: PART THREE - ANGOLA/CONGO REGION

The Methodist historian W.C. Barclay noted that "while the challenge of Liberia undoubtedly appealed to Taylor, with still more enthusiasm he approached the other half of his episcopal commission, the penetration of the continent with the Christian message."[43] Taylor became interested in Angola and the Congo region from the 1880 expedition of two German explorers, Paul Pogge and Hermann von Wissmann, as well as David Livingstone's earlier travels. Taylor decided to establish a series of mission stations starting in Luanda, then eastward into the interior, with the goal of establishing a string of stations across the continent to Portuguese East Africa (Mozambique). In 1885 a party of forty-four recruits including families with children were enlisted. The group was composed of "one or more thoroughly-trained financiers, two physicians-one male and one female- two or more experienced school-teachers, mechanics, farmers, trained evangelists..."[44] Several volunteers, however, withdrew before the actual work began. The group left New York City January 22, 1885 on a bitterly cold day.[45]

Before the group arrived, Taylor sent out Dr. William R. Summers and Charles W. Gordon to go to Luanda to pave the way. At last the first missionaries arrived in Luanda on March 20, 1885.

General Commission on History and Archives, United Methodist Church

The first group of Taylor's missionaries to Angola, photographed in Luanda - 1885.

Immediately they were faced with difficulties. During the wait in Luanda, all but one of the party became ill with "African fever", and one died. Taylor's son Ross, wife and four children under six years of age were part of the original group, but they decided to return home, a great disappointment to Bishop Taylor. Ross Taylor, however, continued to support his father's missionary efforts by editing *Illustrated Africa* (1894-96).

Taylor "chose six [of the original party] as an advance guard to select locations for mission stations in the interior of Angola."[46] From Luanda, the site of the first mission stations, the advance team traveled south from Luanda along the coast, and then eastward on the Cuanza River to Dondo, as far as the steamboat could navigate, where a mission station was established. Then they went on foot for over fifty miles to establish Nhange-a-Pepe. Some thirty-nine miles farther they climbed a higher elevation to reach Pedra Negras, then another sixty miles to Malange. Amos E. Withey was designated presiding elder of this district. Rather than proceed further inland, it was decided this would be the mission field. Dr. Summers, however, continued on to Luluabourg in the heart of the Congo Free State. Unfortunately he died there in 1888.

After the six Angolan mission stations were established, Taylor decided to go to Europe to meet the Portuguese and Belgian kings, and seek their support for his mission plans. They were receptive. In commenting about his meeting with Leopold II, king of Belgium, Taylor noted:

> He [Leopold] conducted me to a seat and sat down near me, and we talked forty minutes. His majesty is about six feet four in height, with symmetrical proportions, a grand, majestic-looking man, and very affable and kind. He said he had been long wishing to know how he could introduce

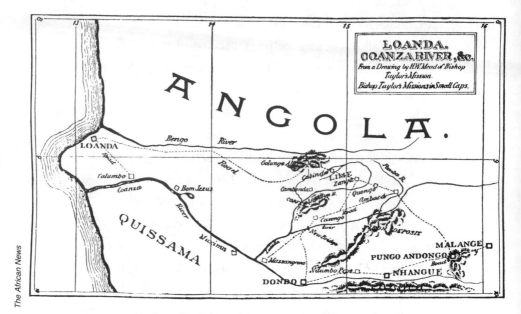

Bishop Taylor's missions in Angola - 1880s, 1890s

American industry and energy into Congo State, and proferred to render us every facility possible in planting missions in that country [Congo]; and we have ever felt the benefit of that interview in our effort to plant missions there.[47]

Taylor returned in 1886 with another group of recruits, this time traveling along the Congo River to its tributary, the Kasai.

Despite extraordinary problems at the beginning, notably sickness which cost the lives of a number of children, Taylor's self-supporting missions survived in Angola.[48] The spirit of the missionaries was remarkable, and they all learned Kimbundu. More mission stations were established. Amos Withey could report in 1895 that there were eight stations and substations, one of these being Quessua near Malange which became the most important Methodist center in Angola. "Our means of support are by trading, cattle-raising, mechanical industries, and farming. We have no salaries... We are hopeful, cheerful, trustful; rejoicing evermore, praying without ceasing, and in everything giving thanks."[49]

The stations along the Congo, however, were not successful despite Bishop Taylor's valiant efforts. Between 1887 and 1895, over fifty missionaries served in the Congo. A steamship named "Anne Taylor" in honor of the Bishop's wife was built to transport the missionaries. In 1896 there were six struggling stations on the Lower Congo but in his visit to the region in 1897, Bishop Joseph Hartzell, Taylor's successor, found only two missions still functioning. Most of the stations were abandoned either due to the death or departure of the missionaries. As a result the stations were disbanded and turned over to a Swedish group. It should be noted Bishop Taylor also established a mission in Natal and southern Mozambique.

Barclay summarized Bishop Taylor's missions and their successes and failures. Taylor was truly a "human dynamo" but also controversial. [50] In Liberia, he tried to tackle the educational problem with full force. Three closed seminaries were reopened. He appointed people who believed what he believed in. He also established new missions among the indigenous people. In the missions he wanted to include manual labor opportunities, and introduce large scale farms and orchards, and nursery schools for the instruction of children in Christianity. "Until Taylor's appearance, no white male missionary had been sent to Liberia in twenty-seven years. He personally brought to Liberia more than fifty men and women, mostly to take charge of his self-supporting work."[51] Taylor thought positively—there was always a solution.

God's Ordinary People:

As far as Angola and the Congo regions were concerned:

> ... [it] was entirely Taylor's field, initiated by him, directed by him, and independent of any controls, either by the Missionary Society or by the Liberia Conference with which it was organically related by District organization. What he accomplished, speaking practically, was a mere beginning, a string of missions stretched across the face of Angola and the Congo. They served to introduce Methodism; they made friends; they established good will; and they made a few converts. When they were removed from Taylor's control and were officially received by the Church's Missionary Society and organized into a Conference some were closed down...[52]

Herbert Withey preaching to Angolans.

Barclay noted that "one of the real values of the Taylor undertaking was in the spirit in which it was entered and in the faith which believed it could move mountains... The sense of conviction he communicated to his volunteers."[53] The extraordinary dedication of many of his missionaries can be documented. Ardella and Samuel Mead at the Malange station deeded all their worldly possessions to his mission. William Rasmussen from Denmark who worked at Vivi in the Congo, despite fever and poor health, returned over and over again to his post Then there was the dedication and commitment of the Withey family — Mr. and Mrs. Amos Withey and their son, Herbert, who became a close colleague of Mr. and Mrs. John Wengatz. H. Withey was a boy of twelve in the original group that went out in 1885. His daughter, Winifred, was a student at Taylor in the late 1930s; *The Gem* (1939) noted she was a senior and her married

Mrs. Winifred Withey Lucas, daughter of Herbert Withey.

name was Winifred Lucas. Herbert Withey was a linguist; he translated the New Testament into the Kimbundu language. He was also a photographer. The Methodist Archives in Madison, New Jersey has an extensive collection of his fine photographs, a wonderful pictorial source of Angola from the turn of the century into the 1930s. He also kept descriptive diaries over long periods of time. Withey had a high regard for Bishop Taylor.

> William Taylor was a man of apostolic spirit, a world wide evangelist, who had been wonderfully used of God... He had many friends and supporters who believed intensely in the

63

man and his methods. He was a man of consecration, faith, and daring, but withal characterized by strong common sense, ready to modify his plans as further light, experience, and providence might indicate.[54]

There were many early heroic missionaries in the service of Bishop Taylor's missions. Particularly brave and successful stories were two unmarried African-American women, Susan Collins and Martha

Susan Collins
Missionary in Angola

Drummer. Collins was born in Madison County, Illinois in 1851, the daughter of a former slave who gained his freedom when his master journeyed to Indiana and who subsequently served in the Union Army during the Civil War. Following a move to Iowa immediately after the war, Susan Collins and her father migrated to South Dakota to settle a land claim. She also opened a laundry business in Huron, South Dakota, then sold it, and entered a Bible training school in Chicago. In 1887 Collins was recruited by Taylor, and was first sent to the Congo,

Martha Drummer
Missionary in Angola

but then later to Angola. She served in Angola until 1900 without a furlough or salary. After a brief return to the United States, she returned to Angola under the auspices of the Women's Foreign Missionary Society (WFMS). Collins was alone at the Quessua station for four years, and later helped to found a girls' school at that station. Whenever missionaries became ill, it was always Miss Collins they called for who nursed them back to health. Collins returned to Fayette, Iowa after 33 years on the mission field where she died in 1940.[55]

Martha Drummer was born in southern Georgia in 1871, her father being a Methodist preacher. She was educated at Clark University in Atlanta. While at Clark she became interested in missions work in Africa. Upon graduating from Clark, Drummer enrolled at the Methodist Women's Training School for Deaconesses in Boston where she learned nursing. In 1906 she was sent by the WFMS of the Methodist Episcopal Church to Quessua, Angola. For twenty years Drummer worked in and around Quessua. She and Collins labored together under very difficult circumstances. Her nursing skill was in constant demand. In 1926, in poor health, Drummer retired to spend her last eleven years in Atlanta where she died in 1937. At a memorial service for Miss Drummer in Angola in 1938, it was noted that "we speak often of Mr. Withey as our Father; but Miss Drummer was our Mother, the one who led many of us to Christ and encouraged us through the years."[56]

DEVELOPMENT OF TAYLOR'S MISSIONS IN LIBERIA AND ANGOLA

Bishop Taylor was succeeded in 1896 by Bishop Joseph Hartzell who proceeded to consolidate the mission stations which Taylor had organized. In Liberia, Hartzell pushed for greater outreach among the Americo-Liberians, and concentrated on a smaller number of stations among the indigenous groups.[57] But Mary Sharpe was a relentless critic who had been working with the Kru people. She "condemned the Americo-Liberian church as morally and religiously degraded, utterly unfit to carry out the evangelization of the country."[58] She was not impressed by the administrative leadership of either Bishops Taylor or Hartzell. In her estimation, they came occasionally and left quickly. Regarding Taylor, Sharpe said, "The Bishop's influence here has no more than

Charter members of the Congo Mission Conference, 1897, Bishop Joseph Hartzell's (front center) first conference in Angola.
Herbert Withey - front right

feather's weight."[59]

In Angola, Hartzell also tried to organize the missions more efficiently. In 1897 he dropped two of the original five Angola mission stations founded by Taylor in 1885, retaining Luanda, Pungo Adongo, and Malange as well as Quiongua and Quessua. Hartzell began the idea of furloughs which had no place in Taylor's self-supporting plan. The missionaries were laboring under deplorable living conditions and Hartzell wanted to do something about that. He also discovered there had been few converts in Angola. During Hartzell's administration which ended in 1908, the Angola mission was extended with stations being set up under African leadership.[60] Although evangelization continued to be stressed under Hartzell, there was also interest in establishing

66

schools as, for example, the WFMS Girls' School at Quessua.

The Angola mission work was small in comparison to Methodist works in other parts of the world. In 1921 the Angola missionaries gathered in Conference session at Quessua and were organized as the Angola Mission Conference (previously it had been part of the West Central Africa Mission Conference). Only six missionaries answered "present"; there were also women workers including Susan Collins and Martha Drummer. The six included Herbert C. Withey and John C. Wengatz of the Taylor University class of 1910 (in 1937, another Taylor graduate, Ralph E. Dodge, entered the Conference). When the automobile was introduced, Wengatz in 1921 took a 250-mile trip into unoccupied mission territory south of the Cuanza River below the Quiongua-Quessua-Malange area. By 1926 the Mission had a new Songo-Bangalo District with Wengatz supervising a dozen African workers in eight churches with four schools.[61]

From time to time the Methodist work was restricted by Roman Catholic opposition, Portuguese colonial government regulations, harassment by minor public officials, and the drafting of African Methodists for forced labor. Contract labor was a serious issue, and John Wengatz spoke about its "evil appearance."[62] Wengatz saw the practice as sheer financial profiteering by the exploitation of drafted labor.

> The severe draft by the government on the young and the strong for plantation and road work that ought to be done by machinery, has an evil appearance and effect that is rapidly ruining the country. It is called contract labor but when the people are roped and tied up and led off under the lash and simply appointed to their task without any questions and scarcely any pay, for a period of six months, except their taxes, I fail to see the contract in it.[63]

God's Ordinary People:

In 1923, Mrs. Robert Shields, a leader in shaping the Mission's educational program, reported that some schools had to be shut down because the students were obliged to go pick cotton or work on the roads.[64]

Another issue which greatly involved the Methodists was the question over the use of vernacular languages. The Portuguese colonial authorities wanted the Africans to learn and speak Portuguese, thereby reducing the importance of the indigenous languages. This was challenged by Herbert Withey who was doing extensive translation work in the Kimbundu language. Withey saw the importance of the African language as a medium to communicate the Gospel. "It is the language which reaches their hearts, and we do not hesitate to predict that it will continue to be used, and hold its own, long after all the present day actors will have passed away."[65] A serious incident took place when the colonial government suspected that the Methodists had been feeding information to Edward A. Ross, an American sociologist, who published in *The Nation* (August 1925) an article entitled "Modern Slavery in Africa." The government subsequently harassed the Methodist missions at Quiongua, Malange, and Luanda, arresting African Christians.

In spite of all these difficulties the work continued to grow and many future leaders of an independent Angola were being educated. Today Methodism in Angola is divided into two parts, the United Methodist Church under the leadership of Bishop Emilio De Carvalho, and the Independent Methodist Church whose bishop is Zacarias Cardoso.[66] The United Methodist Church has approximately 35,000 members with 43 pastors; its headquarters is in Malange. The well organized Independent Church has some 140 pastors and 144 churches; some of the largest congregations of the Independent Methodist Church are in the Luanda area. Unfortunately the recent civil war in Angola has been destructive to Methodism. UNITA made Malange and its surrounding area a major target. The Malange church complex and headquarters building were damaged, and the mission station at Quessua, the largest Methodist mission in Africa and the heart of Angolan Methodism, was destroyed in 1992 and 1993.[67] Because of the strategic and symbolic value of Quessua, the Church is seriously considering the rebuilding of the mission. Many Angolan leaders have been raised in the Methodist Church including Agostinho Neto, former President of Angola (his father was a Methodist pastor). The grandfather of the current President, Jose Eduardo dos Santos, was a pastor of the Angolan Methodist Church. The governor of the Malange area, Dr. Flavio Fernandes, is a product of the mission school at Quessua. It has been observed that "it is estimated that at least 70% of the leadership in the government has received some of their education in mission schools and Quessua was one of the main centers of learning."[68]

CONFLICT BETWEEN BISHOP TAYLOR AND THE MISSION BOARD OF THE METHODIST EPISCOPAL CHURCH

Bishop Taylor, like any great leader, had admirers who were totally committed to his approach to missions as well as detractors. Herbert G. Withey noted that:

> I have great admiration for the character of Bishop Taylor, regarding him as one of the missionary heroes of all time. As a boy of 12 listening to him at a Camp Meeting in New England, soon after his election as Bishop I have always felt that I received my call as a missionary to Africa. It is a conviction that has stayed with me ever since and I have sought

to be not disobedient to the heavenly vision.

> Yes, I believe he was providentially directed to start a mission in Angola, with the idea of extending the line into the interior and perhaps eventually across the continent. The idea of going at once with a party of men women and children in to the far and savage interior without supporting stations from the coast was I would say overzealous and impracticable. But he was a man of strong common sense and while as he said he longed to grapple with impossibilities he had common sense, ready to modify his plans as seemed necessary as he went along.[69]

On the other hand, *The New York Times* headlined an editorial in 1885 "A Dangerous Crank." The article was in response to a dispatch from the American Consul in Sierra Leone to the U.S. State Department concerning Taylor's first group of 40 missionaries journeying to Angola

> This is the band led by an alleged Bishop and undoubted crank... He has with him many women and a large number of children, some of whom are mere infants. A madder project than that of marching these women and children into the heart of Africa was never conceived...

> Of the forty persons who are to be led into the wilderness by the 'crank' in question it is doubtful if a single one escapes the murderous savages through whom STANLEY fought his way on his journey down the Congo. If a remnant does survive to reach the proposed mission field it is very certain that not one of the women or children will be among them. These helpless people will die like sheep of the deadly coast fever, and the only consolation will be that they will escape the hardship and starvation which must be endured by those who survive.

> It was impracticable for our own Government to forbid these people to leave our shores, but it may be possible for the American Consuls in Africa to throw such obstacles in their way as will prevent them from attempting to carry out their

purpose. It would be quite proper to treat them as lunatics and to ship them home by the first vessel. That the leader is lunatic of a very dangerous kind is evident.[70]

In an article in *Methodist History*, church historian David Bundy noted several points of contention between Bishop Taylor and the Board of Missions of The Methodist Episcopal Church.[71] The first area of conflict concerned the question of mission autonomy. The Board viewed itself as administering all the missionary activities, while Taylor saw the Board as establishing Methodist churches around the world but without controlling their operations. Taylor disdained the idea that decisions for the missions could be made 10,000 miles away; this was "bondage" imposed by the home church.

The Board considered itself responsible for supplying funds for the missionary activities in order that they be used most effectively. In fact, the Board was jealous of retaining its funding power. Taylor disagreed. If God called workers, he stated, the money would be provided. He believed if missionaries received a salary from the United States, they would then live on an economic level different from the local ministers. This economic disparity would make it difficult for missionaries to function effectively with the indigenous people. Missionaries, believed Taylor, should conform to the culture of their new home. The Board, on the other hand, felt the task of evangelization was being neglected because Taylor's missionaries were spending too much time trying to support themselves economically. Taylor noted that if a missionary adapted well and had an effective ministry, there was no reason to have furloughs. In contrast, the Methodist Episcopal Board granted furloughs, though in the early years regular furloughs were not guaranteed, and the individual missionary had to apply. Taylor sought to raise money through direct appeals; the Board was not happy about this approach.

One can appreciate Taylor's argument that it is important for missionaries to live close to the people with whom they are serving. Taylor was not happy with the prospect of missionaries living together in "compounds" separated from the people. In short, Taylor was envisaging a strategy somewhat akin to the Peace Corps where volunteers live and work directly with the local people. On the other hand, one could question Taylor's assertion that the missionaries really would live that much better if they received financial aid from the United States. In fact, many missionaries supported directly by the Methodist Episcopal Church at least in the early years were continually experiencing financial difficulties.

The Board was worried that the emotional "call" was not enough to sustain most missionaries through difficult situations. The Board was also concerned that families not be subject to hardships and exposed to the possibility of untimely death. Taylor believed a missionary and his entire family "called of God" could function any place provided he/she learned the local language, and adapted to local foods and customs. Taylor ridiculed missionaries who insisted on North American style food, housing, and customs. He was saddened by deaths among his recruits, but he recalled his sorrow with the premature death of several of his own children. Death, in fact, was a glorious end to missionary service. He was very disappointed when his son Ross, wife, and four children, although among the first group to Angola, quickly returned to the United States when they realized the immense difficulties they would be facing. The Board, in contrast, was more concerned with the health of its missionaries. A recruit had to have "a clean bill of health" before going out as a Board missionary.

Taylor's "Pauline Method" was pragmatic, opportunistic, more spontaneous, and haphazard. He took advantage of all possible resources and openings for his missions. Therefore, he worked against the more organized approach of the Board. Whereas the Board worked together with other churches, Taylor's approach was to charge in without much planning and set up mission stations as quickly as possible.

How sound was Taylor's premise concerning self-support in Africa? An observer noted the food raised by the missionaries cost twice as much as that available in the open market. Furthermore since it was sometimes difficult to earn a living during six days, the necessities of earning a livelihood sometimes called for a compromise of Christian principles. Others described the destitute situation of the missionaries as being pitiable. Some claimed self-support wasted manpower, and that Taylor's missions were the most expensive in Africa. On the other hand, Taylor attracted missionaries "who were fearless, even more than that - rugged, robust, and with consuming drive."[72] Bishop Willis King of Liberia noted:

> It is not a mere coincidence that, in some ways, the most vigorous and loyal Methodists in Liberia, are those on the Kru Coast, where mission stations were first established by Bishop Taylor and his self-supporting missionaries. With little aid financially, and left for many years without missionary leadership, they have remained loyal to Methodist traditions, and have kept alive their Christian heritage under most difficult circumstances. They have vindicated the faith which Bishop Taylor had in the possibilities of men of all races and nationalities to enter into the Christian heritage.[73]

Professor Bundy also interprets Bishop Taylor's conflicts with the Board in sociological terms. As one proceeds through the nineteenth century, the Methodists were no longer considered "despised" by other groups. Especially in the industrial centers of the North and Midwest, Methodists were achieving social and political "respectability." Control of the Church was more and more coming in the hands of the urban upper middle and upper class Methodists, the nouveau riche, according to Bundy. This resulted in alienation between the two groups. Bundy sees Bishop Taylor representing the lower classes. When he returned to the United States after long periods of absence, Taylor observed that Methodism was changing and not necessarily for the good. What was happening in the American Church was also taking place within the Church in India - it was weakening because it was not forced to survive on its own. Taylor's greatest support was coming from many alienated people living in the rural North and Midwest where the Holiness Movement was having its strongest support. Bundy's arguments seem convincing though perhaps one should not ignore the fact that in many respects the Holiness Movement was clearly based on theological more than sociological reasons. The Holiness Movement leaders believed they were returning to John Wesley's emphasis on "entire sanctification" and "the second work of grace." In Taylor University's history, the Holiness Movement had become the most important influence by 1890 through the National Association of Local Preachers(NALP), and under the leadership of Thaddeus Reade. Reade certainly encouraged students from economically poorer backgrounds to attend Taylor, but there were still students coming from more affluent families attending the University. Nevertheless a division had been created between the alumni of Fort Wayne College prior to 1890, and the alumni of

Taylor University in the years to follow. In 1935 the Executive Secretary of the Alumni Association was Rev. Joshua Frank Cottingham, a former missionary in the Philippines. He was determined to invite alumni from the old Fort Wayne College for a grand 1935 commencement which might help to solidify the two constituencies.

BISHOP TAYLOR'S IMPACT ON TAYLOR UNIVERSITY

An extraordinarily large number of Taylor alumni have gone into mission work. This trend began in the 1890s when Fort Wayne College was renamed Taylor University. In the 1880s the NALP took over the leadership of the college, and their hero was clearly Bishop Taylor. In the 1890s President Thaddeus Reade desired the edification of the students' inner spirit more than improving their minds. Spreading the Gospel to every corner of the world was both Taylor and President Reade's goal.

Taylor has inspired scores of Taylor University students to explore the possibilities of mission service and be a part of the Great Commission of Matthew 28:18-20. At least before 1950 most were Methodists. Chapters Four and Five will discuss a number of earlier alumni including Oliver Moody, John and Susan Wengatz, Marshall and Lois Murphree, Ralph and Eunice Dodge, Leota Ratcliffe, Cora Fales, Floy Hurlbut, and others who heeded the call. The current Taylor World Outreach (TWO) program in which students spend several weeks on various Christian mission projects throughout the world is clearly in Bishop Taylor's dream of worldwide evangelism. The idea for TWO originated in the late 1970s with Christian education Professor Ruth Ann Breuninger when she conceived of the Lighthouse Program to the Bahamas.

God's Ordinary People:

This program has expanded. In January 1996, five teams were sent to the Bahamas, Ethiopia, India, Northern Ireland and Zimbabwe involving seventy-nine students.

Through the years, numerous articles in *The Echo* and yearbook (*The Gem* or *Ilium*) have focused on Bishop Taylor. An article in *The Echo* in April 1917 noted that:

> Methodism has produced some mighty men, but among her evangelists and missionaries she never produced a greater and more apostolic man than William Taylor... Bishop Taylor was not a college man, nor did he graduate from a theological seminary. His theology he beat out upon the anvil of experience. His homiletics he learned in the school house, the back woods, the camp meetings, in street preaching as well as in great churches... When William Taylor came around, people felt that a prophet of God had come in their midst. He was a man of the most potent personality. He had great visions, but he was eminently practical. He dreamed, but his dreams came true... William Taylor thought in continents. He was a kindly man, unselfish, unceasingly active, humble, and deeply spiritual. He knew God. He testified once that he had walked for over fifty years, without a break, with God. He blazed the way for the triumphs of Methodist missions throughout the world.[74]

This article reflected the strong admiration the Holiness wing of Methodism had for Bishop Taylor. It concluded by noting that for a number of years the University celebrated Taylor's birthday on May 2. Beginning in that year (1917) his birthday was celebrated with an oratorical contest on the life, character, and works of Bishop Taylor. A prize of $25.00 was awarded to the best orators, the prize to be divided into three parts. This oratorical tradition continued at Taylor throughout the 1920s and into the 1930s.

Taylor University celebrated Bishop Taylor's 105th birthday in 1926. The baccalaureate preacher for that year was Bishop W.F.

Oldham whom the *Taylor University Bulletin* (May 1926) identified as having been converted by Bishop Taylor. That issue also had an article appealing for people to purchase annuity bonds which "is a fine way to go into partnership with William Taylor and Thaddeus C. Reade [and others] who have lived and labored through Taylor to establish the breastworks of Zion and send out agents of blessing through the home land and to their regions beyond."[75] The William Taylor Foundation was originally established in 1933 to become the owner, operator, and policy maker of Taylor University. Today it has a new role as a major fund raiser for the University. "It assists in securing Taylor's future through new and innovative methods of developing resources."[76]

In 1928, President John Paul published his book *The Soul Digger or Life and Times of William Taylor*. Paul wrote the following poem commemorating Bishop Taylor's life and ministry:

THE GOSPEL FOR THE GLOBE

Around the Cape of Good Hope
    And over India's plains,
In bustling Australia
    And dear old England's lanes
Came California's prophet
    And old Virginia's son
        To publish grace
        And bless the race
Till myriads were won.

To fill his high commission
    He spoke as man to man;
A universal language

God's Ordinary People:

Was at his full command.
Each race called him their prophet-
The black, the brown, the white;
Their Hearts could hear
His message clear;
Through Taylor came their light.

All men to him were royal;
All should be sons of God;
There were no heathen children,
No chattels for the rod.
Sound reason had been planted
In every heathen mind,
And heaven's seal
Gave his appeal
Attest to all mankind.

The Southern Cross beamed on him
And friendly Pleiades;
He felt the charm of every land,
The romance of the seas;
He was at home in Northlands;
The tropic vales were dear,
And God was praised
And standards raised
In countries far and near.

That was a sacred morning
When William Taylor died,
As would a great, strong warrior,
His trumpet at his side.
Ten thousand maimed and sinful

Lined up on Eden's shore
To own his worth
Who while on earth
Had sent his wealth before.[77]

78

Another example of a literary effort in remembering Bishop Taylor's life was a theater piece entitled "Celebrating The Life of William Taylor; Circuit Rider, Evangelist, Missionary" written by Jessica Rousselow and performed by Taylor students in a 1986 chapel service.

The Gem of 1946 was dedicated to Bishop Taylor in commemoration of the centennial of the University. The dedicatory page read in part:

> Embodied in the record of his life are the spiritual experiences of the New Birth and the Sanctified Life. Likewise there are the achievments [sic] of a world evangel who saw, as did the founder of his Church, that the world was his parish. The name Taylor University, in honor of Bishop William Taylor, was given to the school not only because of the Spirit-filled life, the missionary zeal, but also because Bishop Taylor was the only man who had been elevated from the Laity- the ranks of the Local Preachers-to the high office of Bishop. Those traditional experiences of grace and those heroic endeavors in world evangelism which characterized Taylor have become the watchword of the institution which bears his name. In appreciation of the sacred trust which is ours to perpetuate we follow in his train.

In previous years, the school owned a couple of artifacts belonging to Bishop Taylor. A wooden cane was cut by him when he was in South America. It was sent to the University and was known as the mace which headed all academic processions.[78] The June 1927 *Taylor University Bulletin* noted that the Administration Building contained Bishop Taylor's baby cradle, and a painting of the Bishop was displayed over the chapel platform. These artifacts were destroyed in the Administration Building fire in 1960. In reviving interest in Taylor, the conference room on the second floor of the Helena Building was renamed the Bishop William

Taylor Conference Room in 1995. It contains a number of framed enlarged photographs of Bishop Taylor with an accompanying explanatory brochure.[79] For the University's sesquicentennial, Temple United Methodist Church of San Francisco loaned to the University a Bishop Taylor walking stick. It was used in academic convocations during the 1995-6 academic year and the 1996 graduation.[80]

During the 1996 homecoming, an official plaque was unveiled outside the Rediger Chapel/Auditorium. Present for the ceremony were several California descendants of Bishop Taylor. Also part of the homecoming celebrations was a presentation of Bishop Taylor's life and ministry by Reverend Don Fado of Sacramento, California.

There were probably two occasions when William Taylor visited Fort Wayne College (Taylor University). The first was when he visited Fort Wayne College in 1859.[81] William Ringenberg in *Taylor University The First 125 Years* noted the second visit was at the beginning of the 1895-6 school year. With respect to a possible visit in 1890, Ringenberg added that:

> The *Fort Wayne Sentinel* of October 8, 1890, reported that he was to come to the college during the following week, but subsequent editions of the paper did not mention that he actually came to Fort Wayne.[82]

CONCLUSION

Perhaps Bishop Taylor did more to expand the work of Methodism worldwide than any one in the nineteenth century. He took to heart John Wesley's "the world is my parish." His firm belief that God had taken William Taylor into a peculiar partnership "filled him with the intrepidity and assurance of an apostle."[83] He has been described as a restless man and a rugged individualist who identified himself against the "Eastern establishment", and with common sense which spared him from fanaticism. He was a good storyteller, and a man of wit. He had directness of speech, and his voice was of unusual melody, range, and power. Despite criticisms leveled at him for his maverick style of recruiting missionaries without "home support" and little preparation for the mission field, he always identified himself with the Wesleyan tradition. He may not always have been wise but thousands found Christ through his preaching. In his *Story of My Life* dedicated to "my Divine Sovereign," Taylor described his mission work as spreading out like the eucalyptus forests of California, a tree which he introduced into that state. Although some Californians are not happy with the spread of this imported tree, nevertheless it is a poignant analogy to Taylor's work. Truly he was a key man in the nineteenth century who transformed Christianity from a religion that appeared to remain only in the Western white dominated world to becoming a major worldwide faith. Bishop Taylor is surely one of the giants who in no small way was responsible for the rapid development and expansion of Christianity in Africa, Asia, and Latin America.

God's Ordinary People:

Taylor University 1927 Intercollegiate Negative Debate Team

Frances Bogue

Mary Elizabeth Beebe

Merrette Hessenauer

The Gem

82

Chapter Three

SERVANT LEADERS: WOMEN STUDENTS AND WOMEN FACULTY ROLE MODELS

ort Wayne Female College was founded for the purpose of providing a full collegiate education to young women. Fort Wayne College provided the same educational curriculum for women and men students. Taylor University reaffirmed the commitment to equal opportunity education for both genders. Although the balance between male and female students has at various times tipped in one direction or the other, there has never been a time since the mid 1850s when women students were absent from the campus. There is also no indication in the college catalogues that any curriculum was off limits to women.

THE LITERARY SOCIETIES

From the earliest days there was an extracurricular dimension to college life which was designed to contribute to the intellectual development and leadership potential of the students. The original organizations which operated beyond the curriculum but which, nevertheless, supported the educational objectives of the institution, were the literary societies. As noted in Chapter One, these two societies were both open to men and women. However, within the societies the opportunities for leadership were never equally distributed. Probably because the student body membership fluctuated from term to term throughout the year, the societies elected an entirely new slate of officers each term. By the time the institution moved to Upland, these officers included president, vice president, treasurer, recording secretary, corresponding secretary, censor, assistant censor, literary critic, music critic, three judges, sergeant at arms, and an editor or reporter.

Elections of officers were regularly reported in *The Echo* after 1913 and lists of officers appeared in *The Gem* from 1898. It was an extremely rare occasion when a woman was elected to the presidency of one of these organizations. Mabelle Reade had been president of the Thalonians in the 1890s and Annabelle Guy was president in 1913. Margaret James and Harriet Merrin had both been president of the Philaletheans in the early 1900s. Women almost never appeared as treasurers, but they frequently were assistant treasurers. It was rare for a woman to be elected reporter or editor in the first decade of the century. However, Olive Mae Draper edited the "Philo Standard" in 1915. Women reporters became more common in the 1920s and 1930s. There were two categories in which women clearly were the favorites: recording and corresponding secretaries. In fact, there were

The Gem

Annabel Guy. President of Thalonians.

virtually no males who served as secretaries in any of the extra curricular organizations. Women and men were both elected to the positions of critics, censors, and judges.

The Gem

Margaret James. President of Philaletheans.

The other arena in which leadership ability was developed was the presentation of weekly programs for the societies' membership and occasional programs for the entire campus community. These programs normally consisted of some combination of musical selections, readings or monologues, original essays, and debates. In the regular weekly meetings, members were given the opportunity to develop skills with a view toward being chosen to represent the group in the annual inter-society competition traditionally held during commencement week.

These program presenters were often listed in *The Echo* after 1913, and the winners of the competition were always featured in the paper's commencement issue. A survey of these reports did not reveal any clear pattern of gender bias. Nearly all programs included both male and female presenters. However, original essays and debates were more often presented by men, and readings were usually the province of women. Music was more evenly divided between men and women with women having a slight edge in representation. This could be explained because there tended to be more women then men studying music, especially during the first three decades of the century.

God's Ordinary People:

The November 2, 1914 issue of *The Echo* contained a report of a combined "Thalo-Philo Program." The event was declared "a marked success in every way." The program began with a "Faculty-Thalo-Philo mixed quartet," and continued with an oration by Mr. Norvelle. Miss Ross gave a reading which "kept the house in almost continuous laughter." Mrs. Vickery read an essay entitled "Conscience" which "contained very deep spiritual, philosophical and psychological truths." Miss Guy presented a reading which "held the audience practically spellbound from first to last." Two additional musical selections were provided by Misses Topp and Engle who sang a duet and Helen Raymond who executed a piano solo.

In the yearly competitions it was sometimes the case that a man would represent one society and a woman the other in a particular event. For example, in 1914 *The Echo* reported that the inter-society contest had five events. The categories included piano, vocal, original essay, reading, and original oration. Both the essay and the vocal solo categories pitted a male contestant against a female. In the essay contest the male contender won, and in the vocal solo the woman took the prize.[1] A very interesting event occurred at the 1916 commencement inter-society contests when Lulu Ruppert's rendition of "The Littlest Rebel" won over Barton Reese Pogue's presentation of "The Going of the White Swan."[2] In 1920 the first prize for the Preston Gold Prize Inter-society debate went to the Thalonian team composed of Alice Eskes and Frank Lee. They defeated a Philalethean team composed of two males. The issue debated was: Resolved, that the plan of adjustment boards recommended by the Second Industrial Conference at Washington for the settlement of disputes between capital and labor should be adopted.[3]

DEBATING CLUBS

The second type of organization to emerge in the College was the debating club. The first two clubs, the Eurekas founded in 1903 and the Eulogonians which began in 1906, were exclusively for males. The first debating club for women was the Willard Debating Society founded in 1903. This club existed through the academic year 1906-7. Then debate for women disappeared until 1913 when Professor Sadie Louise Miller helped a group of young women organize the Soangetahas. The name was a Miami Indian

The Willard Debating Society.

word which meant "strong-hearted maidens." The goals of the organization were to train the members to think logically and quickly and to appear before a public audience with ease and self control.[4] The organization was seen as evincing the fact that "our school is awake to the spirit of the times." The women of Taylor were aware that woman's sphere was no longer simply within the narrow circle of domestic duties, and there was an increasing need for women to become involved in church and state. One way to prepare for these enlarged responsibilities was to practice the art and techniques of platform debate.

The Soangetahas met weekly for the purpose of learning how

87

to debate. They followed the pattern of the male clubs engaging in two types of practice debates, extemporaneous and formal. The first type generally selected questions which were related to campus life, but the formal debates dealt with larger issues of national policy or religious controversy. They also spent some sessions in parliamentary drill where the goal was to learn how to participate in a formal public meeting using correct procedures.

From its inception through the mid 1930s the Soangetahas maintained seriousness of purpose which was relieved by the general fun of the extempore debates. The Club enjoyed a steadily rising membership and its activities were regularly reported in the pages of *The Echo*. At the beginning of each term, the Soangetahas would engage in rush activities. This was an all out effort to attract new members. The club was divided into the Blues and the Golds, and the two groups had a contest to determine which of them could get the most new women to sign up for membership in the organization. The first meeting after "rush" was usually a purely social event in which the losers had to fete the winners in some way. Normally,

The Gem

Soangetaha Debating Club.

this meant a picnic or a full scale dinner followed by a humorous program. For example, in the fall of 1915 the featured event at this post-rush dinner was an extempore debate on the resolution that "the potato masher is a more effective household tool than the rolling pin." The club reached its peak membership in the late 1920s and early 1930s.

The fact was that many of the women who joined the Club had no idea what debate really involved. They often had little or no experience speaking in public, and many were reluctant to try to learn. In order to get women past this reticence, the club employed several techniques. The first of these was simple instruction in the art and practice of public debate which was accomplished by inviting faculty members to come and give talks on the subject of how to debate.[5]

The second technique used to train the young women to debate publicly was the extempore debates which were a regular feature of Soangetaha meetings. The topics for these debates were assigned by the censors and often focused on issues of campus life such as: Resolved, that the girls should ask the boys for dates . Sometimes the extempore debate would argue the merits of an abstract idea such as: Resolved, that joy brings more happiness than memory or: Resolved, that it is better to have loved and lost than never to have loved at all. Occasionally the topic chosen was designed to provoke laughter such as: Resolved, that the radio is more beneficial to the modern home than the dish rag.[6]

The third approach used to develop logical and analytical skills was the presentation of a prepared debate. An affirmative and a negative team was selected and given a topic which they researched before the next meeting. The two teams would come with developed cases for and against the assigned resolution and present the debate before an audience which was mostly made up of fellow Soangetahans. Normally, there would be three judges who would render a decision as to the winners and losers. However, sometimes the audience would be asked to decide by voting for the winner. According to the various *Echo* reports on these debates, they generated a great deal of excitement and interest. Occasionally, one of the debate clubs announced a topic which was especially timely and a number of students from other debate clubs would come to hear the debate. Such was the case on February 1, 1916 when the Eurekans debated the issue of Women's Suffrage and invited the members of the Soangetahas, and once again on December 9, 1916 when the Eurekans debated the resolution that women should be admitted to the Protestant ministry on equal terms with men. *The Echo* reported that many of the members of the Soangetaha debating club were present.[7]

Between the founding of their club in 1913 and the mid 1930s the Soangetahas debated many issues of significance to the contemporary political scene. In 1914 at the height of the temperance movement agitation they debated: Resolved, that the world wide anti-liquor movement is of more importance than the world wide peace movement. In 1917 during the First World War they debated: Resolved, that President Wilson was justified in severing diplomatic relations with Germany and: Resolved, that the United States is justified in entering the present war. In 1919 they argued: Resolved, that the government should own the soft coal mines. In 1927 they resolved that "a system of old age pensions be established in the United States", and that the "Ku Klux Klan is a profitable organization to the United States." In 1929 the resolution was "that the five day labor week should be adopted by American industries in general."[8]

In 1921 a second women's debate society was formed, the Mnankas—another Miami Indian word meaning "weavers of knowledge." The constitution of this Club declared the purpose to be "to develop oratory, debating, parliamentary drill, leadership, and to promote mental and social development."[9]

The existence of a second women's debate club opened up the possibility for inter-club competitions thus stimulating greater interest in the work of both societies. According to the 1928 *Gem,* within a few weeks after the Mnankas had organized, the Soangetaha Club challenged them to an inter-club debate. In this encounter the Mnankas showed

The Mnanka Debate Club.

their ability to debate by winning the championship banner. However, this banner changed hands from time to time, fostering a spirit of friendly rivalry between the clubs.[10] In 1926 the two clubs met to debate the resolution that the government should own and operate the coal mines. The Soangetahas were the victors in this debate, but in 1928 the results were reversed. The resolution this time was that the Protestant churches of the U.S. should be united, and the Mnankas emerged victorious. The inter-club debate topic chosen for 1934 was: Resolved, that the United States should grant immediate independence to the Philippines.[11]

In the mid 1920s there were some competitions between men's and women's clubs. In February 1928 the Mnankas met the Eurekans for the purpose of debating the resolution that too many students attend college. *The Echo* reported that there was much enthusiasm, that the controversy waged hot with each side making significant points, and that eventually the debate turned on a question of definition which the women's team lost. The reporter concluded, "they [the Mnankas] fought valiantly, and we felt proud of both teams. The Eurekas won."[12]

The following month the Soangetahas met the Eulogonians in a spectacular exhibition of trial by jury enacted in a mock trial. *The Echo* declared: "No better session than this has been held this term." The Soangetahan prosecuting attorney was credited with the winning strategy. "The sensation of the evening, which undoubtedly brought the verdict of guilty was the plea of the prosecuting attorney, Miss Cox. The jury was flooded with her verbiage and visibly moved by her dramatic earnestness."[13]

Another important event which occurred in 1922 was the introduction of intercollegiate debating. The resolutions were decided upon by the Indiana Intercollegiate Debating League which Taylor joined in 1923. This organization was also responsible for scheduling debates between the various colleges which were members. Originally, the League did not segregate men and women debaters. However, during the 1924-25 academic year the League was split into a women's and men's division. Each team had three members, and they debated only one side of the proposition for the entire series of debates in which they participated. The resolution for the women's teams the first year was: Resolved, that Congress should have power to nullify a decision of the Supreme Court declaring a federal law unconstitutional. One negative and one affirmative team participated in this season. They debated against Manchester College twice and against Wheaton College once. All three debates were won by the Taylor women.[14]

Nineteen twenty seven was a particularly good year for the women's negative team consisting of Frances Bogue, Mary Elizabeth Beebe and Merrette Hessenauer. They made *Echo* headlines several times that season. In January they traveled to Adrian College to debate the season's resolution, that Congress should be given the power to enact uniform marriage and divorce laws. They met Adrian's affirmative team and prevailed. In February, the Adrian team came to Taylor's campus for the second match in the series. The same resolution was debated with the same result—Taylor womem won. Also in February, the team traveled to Wheaton College to take on their affirmative team, and the Taylor women won again. Finally, in March Taylor journeyed to Evansville and again returned victorious.[15]

Nineteen twenty-eight appeared to be a less successful year. The resolution for the women's teams that year was that "the United States should grant recognition to Russia." Only two women's debates were reported in *The Echo* that year. The Taylor women lost to Albion College and they defeated Wittenberg. In 1929 the women won three of five debates. The 1930s was a decade marked by change in the involvement of women in intercollegiate debate. The decade began with no women's teams competing, but a revival of interest was exhibited during the next two years, only to decrease once more in mid-decade. In 1937 the concept of separate men's and women's teams was abandoned and one woman joined the coed squad. The decade ended with no intercollegiate debate team.[16]

An obvious advantage which came to women who participated in intercollegiate debate was the exposure to a wider audience. They were forced to test their critical and analytical skills against debate cases they had not heard before and in front of audiences other than their friends. The disadvantage was that not many women were able to benefit from this experience. Only six or eight women each year were accepted as part of the debate squad. In the long run, the women's debate clubs probably contributed more to the intellectual development of women than the intercollegiate experience simply because many more women were meaningfully involved. Perhaps alumnus Lily Leitch summed up this contribution best when she wrote a small essay for *The Echo* answering the question should debating clubs have a place in college life? Leitch asserted:

> When I recall my own experience in the Soangetaha Debating Club, there is not the shadow of a question in my mind as to whether or not the debating club should have a place in college life. It was there we learned to have not NOTIONS, but opinions, a thing women are often accused of never having.

She urged the current members to "stand by their club" because they would find in their later lives that lessons learned there would enable them to be more effective homemakers and citizens.[17]

RELIGIOUS ORGANIZATIONS

When Fort Wayne College became Taylor University the school adopted as its motto "Holiness Unto The Lord", and the whole hearted embracing of holiness theology led to the creation of another category of co-curricular organization on the Taylor campus in the early part of the twentieth century. These were the groups which concentrated on the development of stronger faith commitments in the lives of students. There were three major organizations in this category; the Holiness League, The Volunteer Band and The Prayer Band.

The Young Men's Holiness League was founded in 1902 at Camp Sychar, Ohio. Its purpose was "to secure the conversion and entire sanctification of the young people of the land." The organization grew rapidly by creating local chapters on college campuses including Taylor. By 1911 the national organization estimated a membership of 1500. The Taylor chapter was founded in October 1903. In 1906 a Young Women's Holiness League was started by a senior student Elizabeth Wigglund "to help our young women to maintain the experience of entire sanctification, so that they may become rooted and grounded in love."[18] However, by

The Young Women's Holiness League.

1909 The Young Women's Holiness League had been absorbed into the Young Men's League. *The Gem* for that year indicated that "membership is not confined to the young men, but the young ladies may also become members as auxiliaries."[19] For the next several years the descriptions of the organization which appeared in *The Gem* continued to include women, but the pictures of the organization showed mostly males. For example, in 1911 there were four women members pictured and in 1913 there were three. Finally, in 1916 the name of the organization was changed to Taylor University Holiness League "in order that the ladies might feel welcome to attend the meeting and receive the helpful instruction." By 1919 there were about the same number of men and women members.[20]

The Student Volunteer Band was a part of a national Volunteer Movement. The sponsoring organizations were the YWCA and the YMCA. The Volunteers had four purposes as articulated by Miss Miriam Goodwin, Traveling Secretary of the National Student Volunteer Movement, who spoke at Taylor in 1927. The first purpose was to challenge students to consider foreign missions as a life work. Second, the organization desired to "unite its members for mutual help" and to "permeate the rest of the college with the mission spirit." Third, the organization put students in touch with missionary agencies to insure an adequate world-wide program for Christ. Finally, they sought to convince all Christian students of the need to promote and support the missionary enterprise.[21]

The Prayer Band was the only one of the three religious groups which was not aligned with a national organization. It was organized in 1899 by a group of students for the purpose of praying corporately for the school and for all the needs that were made known to them by alumni and friends. The 1903 *Gem* declared that the purpose of Prayer Band was "to lead people to conversion and the blessing of entire sanctification," and its only condition for membership was "the desire to flee from the wrath to come." The Prayer Band did have a loose organizational structure electing a president, a vice president and a secretary each term. However, the meetings were less structured than the other two organizations in that they did not always have a prepared program for meetings. Meetings usually began with a short devotional message followed by an extended time of shared prayer for the concerns of the community.

All three of these religious organizations provided opportunities for women to develop organizational and leadership skills, partly because all three were open to electing women presidents to lead the group. For example, Martha McCutcheon, Emma Tresler, and Louise Hazelton were all presidents of Prayer Band at various times. Annabel Guy, Alice Eskes, Cora Rahe and Frances Bogue were four women who led the Volunteer Band, and Anna Stewart was president of the Holiness League in 1929.[22]

Obviously, only a few women could serve as officers in the three organizations. However, there were many opportunities for women to exercise their speaking skills within the context of all three groups. Women representing all the different constituencies of the campus community—students, faculty, and staff—spoke with regularity in all three organizations. In addition, many of the outside speakers who addressed the religious organizations were women, thus providing a steady stream of role models for the young women, students. These speakers were usually returned missionaries or Taylor alumni under appointment to the mission field. However, the Volunteers were visited by representatives of the national organization called traveling secretaries. In 1917, 1919, and 1927 women traveling secretaries visited the campus, addressed the organization, and spoke in chapel and other campus venues.[23]

WOMEN'S MINISTERIAL ORGANIZATION

It is certainly true that many more men than women who came to Taylor were preparing for careers in the pastoral ministry. It is also true that some women did come for this purpose, and they pursued the theological course along with their male counterparts. A Ministerial Association had been formed in 1924 for the purpose of assisting aspiring ministers to practice preaching skills and otherwise enable them to prepare for a parish ministry. Some women were involved in this Ministerial Association. For example, on March 8, 1926 Miss Tate, a theological student, preached a sermon before the Ministerial Association in Shreiner Auditorium, and in May the members of Dr. Owen's Homiletics class were in charge of the Ministerial Association's regular meeting. Miss Sara Thompson preached a sermon on the text "Launch out into the deep" from Luke 5.[24]

Perhaps, because of the small number of women theological students, or possibly due to the lack of a suitable faculty sponsor, there was no ministerial association specifically for women until the late 1920s when Miss Madeline Southard joined the faculty as Dean of Women and Professor of History. She was a nationally known evangelistic preacher, editor of a journal entitled *The Woman Pulpit*, and president of the International Association of Women Preachers.

On March 3, 1926 Miss Southard met in Society Hall with a group of young women who were interested in a career in ministry.

She explained the way the International Association of Women Preachers was organized and suggested that they form a chapter which would allow them to become associate members of the organization. They would also receive the paper *The Woman Pulpit* upon payment of the dues. Before the meeting adjourned, the young women present had formed a local chapter and had elected officers. Ruth Lortz, who already was a member of the organization of women preachers, was elected to serve as president. Hattie Seaver was elected vice president and Grace Olson was given the duties of the secretary.

The new organization did not intend to usurp the role of the regular Ministerial Association. Instead, their aim was to cultivate and encourage young women who felt the call to preach. They agreed to meet every two weeks at which time Miss Southard would give talks on practical homiletics and the members would prepare and present reports on the lives of great women preachers.[25]

When Taylor started its student chapter of Women Preachers there was only one other college chapter in existence, and that was located at Asbury College in Wilmore, Kentucky. The organization

The Gem

M. Madeline Southard. Dean of Women and Professor of History.

continued into the 1930s although it underwent several name

The Women's Ministerial Society.
Grace Olson is the fifth from the left in front row.

changes. It began as the Women Preachers and soon became known as the Women's Ministerial Association. Later it became Gamma Epsilon and finally, the Women Evangels. As long as Madeline Southard remained on campus to provide leadership and inspiration, the organization thrived. In 1926 Ruth Lortz represented the Taylor Chapter at the national meeting of the Association and in 1927 Grace Olson, the then current president, attended the national conference where she spoke at the young women's hour. Within the first year the membership had grown to thirty-five, leveling off in the next two years at twenty-five.[26]

The club effectively carried out its announced purposes. They presented programs focusing on practical homiletics by Southard and others including Mrs. Maud Carter Smock, pastor of the Upland Friends Church and Mrs. Faye Pierce, pastor of the Upland United Brethren Church. The latter spoke at a November 1926 meeting giving personal experiences, pointers and hints for the pulpit. A visiting missionary, Mrs. Woodruff Taylor, spoke on "Women's Ministry in Foreign Lands" stressing the need to possess a burden for souls in order to insure that one's ministry would have lasting qualities. An alumnus who had begun a career of preaching, Frances Brown, came back to speak about "The Problems and Delights of the Ministry."[27]

Gamma Epsilon provided young women with opportunities to practice preaching. One such occasion occurred in November 1927 when many students came out to hear "the girl preachers at Holiness League last Friday evening." Three young women presented twenty minute sermons on various aspects of holiness, and *The Echo* reported "the hour was an inspiration and a blessing to all." They conducted an annual preaching contest with Miss Margaret Coghlan emerging as the first winner.[28]

The group occasionally met jointly with other organizations such as the Men's Ministerial Association and The Holiness League. At one such meeting with the latter organization three women presented sermons followed by a concluding statement by Professor Southard. The result of the session was, "all felt that women as well as men have a definite place in God's plan of evangelization from the pulpit as well as the home."[29]

PUBLICATIONS

A third area of student life which lends insight into the actual experience of women students is student publications. Since the turn of the century there were two such publications, the yearbook which was called *The Gem* until 1966 when it was renamed *The Ilium*, and the student newspaper which was originally called *The*

Journal, and was renamed *The Echo* in 1913. *The Gem* made its debut in 1898. The first woman selected to edit the yearbook was Harriet Merrin who was responsible for producing the 1903 edition. Kathryn Hettelsater also served on Merrin's editorial staff. Unfortunately, this did not establish a pattern of women editors, but it did open the possibility for participation on the editorial staff by women. It was not until after the Second World War that a woman again edited *The Gem.* *The Echo* began publication in 1913 taking the name of a regular column which had appeared in the previous publication and using the monthly magazine format already established by *The Journal.* *The Echo's* editorial and business staff was entirely male, a condition which remained until 1952 when a woman was selected as editor-in chief of the newspaper for the first time. The all male staff did gradually yield to the inclusion of women, first as reporters and eventually as section editors. A curious phenomenon which emerged during the publication of *The Journal* and continued with *The Echo* was the annual coed edition. An all female staff was elected by the student body and charged with the responsi-bility of editing a single issue of the newspaper with the assistance of the regular staff.

The discussion of gender issues in the

The Gem editorial staff. Harriet Merrin, Editor, far right. The woman on the left is Kathryn Hettelsatter.

102

campus publications is a strong indicator of the quality of women student's experience at Taylor. During the first two decades of the century the issues of temperance and suffrage dominated many women's thoughts and energies. These issues were of primary importance on the Taylor campus particularly during the presidency of Monroe Vayhinger (1908-1921). President Vayhinger's wife was a strong women's advocate, presenting a powerful role model to the Taylor student body.

Culla Vayhinger was born Flora Columbia Johnson on September 25, 1867 in Bennington, Indiana. She was the second child in a family of six, and her father was a civil war veteran. She was educated at Moores Hill College (today the University of Evansville), earning both a B.S. and an A.M. She met Monroe Vayhinger while she was a college student and he was a somewhat older professor. After the Vayhingers were married, they moved to Chicago and Monroe Vayhinger enrolled in Garrett Seminary. Culla Vayhinger went to work in the Marcy Home settlement house in Chicago where she endeavored to help newly arrived immigrants integrate into the life of that city. It was during this time that she met Anna Gordon, a national officer for the Woman's Christian Temperance Union, and became actively involved in that organization to which she devoted the rest of her life. In her mind the issues of temperance and suffrage were inextricably bound together. She believed that if women were given the power to vote, they would vote against the liquor interests which caused so much needless suffering. In a speech delivered at the Indiana State Temperance Convention held in Indianapolis in December, 1911 she said:

We are told, the hand that rocks the cradle is the hand that

Dr. John Monroe Vayhinger, Woodland Park, Colo.

Culla Vayhinger. President of Indiana Women's Christian Temperance Union.

rules the world, and that woman accomplishes more by indirect influence than she could possibly accomplish with the ballot. Let any man who will exchange places with me and try to get what he wants by indirect influence instead of the ballot, stand to his feet. Not a single man arises. So for the sake of truth never make an assertion of that kind again.

The Vayhingers served several Methodist churches in southern Indiana. Even though Monroe Vayhinger had the seminary degree and was the official preacher in the family, Culla Vayhinger was probably a stronger public speaker. According to her grandson, John Monroe Vayhinger, a psychologist now living in Woodland Park, Colorado, she spoke extemporaneously without manuscript or notes, and was often invited to speak for special services in Indiana's Methodist churches as well as to lecture on behalf of the WCTU. [30]

By the time the Vayhingers arrived at Taylor in 1908, their children were well on the way to adulthood and Culla was President of the Indiana WCTU, a position she held until her death. Taylor was a struggling college very much in need of financial resources. The Vayhingers decided that Culla would earn the money necessary to keep the household going in order that President Vayhinger's salary might be returned to the University in the form of student scholarships. By this time Culla's father had died and her mother came to live with the family freeing Culla from the day to day responsibilities of housekeeping and permitting her the freedom to travel and speak on behalf of Christianity, temperance and suffrage.

Her grandson, John Vayhinger, recalled that when he was a small child his parents moved back to Upland from Chicago to live in the big house with Great Grandma Johnson and Grandma and Grandpa Vayhinger. He said he remembered calling his

grandmother "Grandma Toot Toot" because we were always taking
her to the train or collecting her from the train as she went back
and forth to meet her speaking engagements. He believes that she
spoke in virtually every Methodist Church in the surrounding area
at least once during her years of itinerating for the WCTU's Flying
Squadron.[31] This work also took her far from Indiana to national
WCTU meetings. On November 1, 1921, *The Echo* reported that
"Mrs. Culla J. Vayhinger is attending the National WCTU
Convention at Ocean Grove and will attend the World's Convention
of the WCTU at Brooklyn before she returns. At the recent State
Convention of the WCTU Mrs. Vayhinger was elected as a delegate
to the World's Convention."[32]

     Culla Vayhinger was as revered as her husband by the
Taylor community. She spoke in chapel, as well as in Holiness
League, Prayer Band and Volunteer meetings. She conducted
evangelistic services on and off campus, and she spoke for special
occasions such as the local high school baccalaureate exercises.
Her photograph appeared beside that of her husband in University
publications and her educational qualifications were listed along
with his. *The Echo* declared, "We hear it frequently stated that of
all the lady speakers people have ever heard, Mrs. Culla J. Vayhinger,
State President of the WCTU, beats them all. Well may we be
proud of her as the wife of our College President."[33]

     Given the presence of this undeniably powerful woman on
Taylor's campus, it is not surprising that little evidence of anti-
suffrage rhetoric was to be found in campus publications. In fact,
just the opposite was true. Sometimes the issue was treated
satirically as it was on two occasions in 1914. Both the March 15
and the June 1 issues of *The Echo* contained poems satirizing the

arguments against suffrage—that voting would unsex women, and that women were not intelligent enough to be trusted with the ballot. The first one was entitled "Unsexed", and each stanza presented situations in which women were involved in taxing work in factories, stores and laundries all of which didn't "unsex her." The poem ended as follows:

She's feminine still when she juggles the crockery,
Bringing you blithely the orders you give;
Toil in a sweatshop, where life is mockery,
Just for the pittance on which she can live—
That doesn't seem to unsex her a particle.
"Labor is noble"—so somebody wrote—
But ballots are known as a dangerous article,
Woman's unsexed if you give her the vote!

The second poem appeared in the June 1, 1914 *Echo* and satirized the idea that women were not intelligent enough to vote by suggesting that "many a laddie has the ballot not so bright as I; many a laddie votes the ballot overcome with rye." This poem ended by calling for action on the part of women suggesting that they not "wait for by-and-by" but demand "their woman's right or know the reason why!"

Sometimes *The Echo* reported on news events involving the suffrage issue as in the April 15, 1914 edition after the women of Illinois had been enfranchised and had presumably led the voters to a temperance win in that state. The short news article ended, "The man who will not trade his pet theory against woman suffrage for the destruction of the liquor traffic ought well examine his head."[34]

The 1917 coed issue of *The Echo* is particularly interesting because this represents women students writing about women's issues. There are two very short articles which deal directly with the issue of suffrage. The first article presents "The Anti-Suffragist's Syllogism" The syllogism states that "Everything that takes a woman out of her home is bad." Holding office takes a woman out of her home. Conclusion: Holding office is bad. The writer than draws the legitimate inference that many things that women were currently doing including "evangelistic singing, all religious work, missionary work, and teaching" were bad and should be stopped since these activities took women out of their homes. Immediately following this syllogism and its analysis is a short analogy which argued that voting was a "right" and was like bread, the sustainer of life.

The editorial in this coed edition answered the argument which was still being made by some against the value of educating women. The writer, B. Dancey, began by asserting that "for good or for evil, the power of woman is being felt in the world." She then tackled the oppositions' argument that educating women will destroy their feminine graces and make them masculine. The editorial argued that the reason to educate women was the same as the one for educating men, "to correct their weaknesses, strengthen their strength, and to give them vision." The rest of the article demonstrated how education would help women whatever they did in their lives including returning to the parent's home, entering a profession, entering a Christian vocation of service, or marrying and keeping house. She concluded her essay by asking:

> What then is college for? For the knowledge that makes life richer; for the training that gives power for the difficult task and that makes labor a self-respecting service; for the wisdom that suffers and triumphs, and is strong; for the vision that

will light our way like a pillar of fire; for the truth that shall
make us free.

The Gem

During World War I Taylor women organized a military drill team to
support the war effort.

Unfortunately, the discussion of issues relating to women did
not always remain on such a high level. During the late 1920s the
controversy which found its way into the pages of *The Echo* involved
the length of skirts and hair which a woman might wear and still
identify herself as a Christian. The argument was made in the March
5, 1926 *Echo* that a "professed Christian woman cannot serve God
in the beauty of holiness and have bobbed hair" because several
Old and New Testament texts admonish women against the practice
of cutting their hair. The following week "an Unbobbed Sister"
answered the letter by making an appeal to common sense and
practicality. She asserted that she did not believe in "cutting the
Bible" or in spiritualizing everything that is meant to be literal but

times change and if changes in fashion "prove to be convenient or beneficial to health" we should "be practical and kind in judgment of those who see fit to adopt it." She went on to assert that if the male writer of the previous letter was determined to read Paul's admonitions against women cutting their hair literally, he would also need to extend this logic to areas of men's dress and return to "the loose robe, the long beard and the barefoot sandal of Paul's time and refuse to allow women to teach Sunday school, preach or lead in prayer."

This rather mild, conciliatory letter was followed by another somewhat stronger epistle. This writer argued the interpretations of the Scriptures used by the first letter and ended with a strong defense of the modern woman.

> Woman's sphere in life has greatly changed since that time. In Paul's day they were confined to domestic duties. Today our women are filling positions equal to those men are filling. They are active in public work, in business and in professional life. The spirit of the age is progress and nowhere has this been more apparent than in the activities of women. They have an independence now that was hitherto unknown. It is no longer necessary for her to be married to maintain herself, she now makes her living by her own efforts if it be necessary. Seeing that she has cast off the bondage of former years, is there any reason why she should not likewise cast off the symbolism of the past age. As long hair was the symbol of the subjection of a woman to her husband, so today, bobbed hair is the symbol of the progress of woman, of the shaking off the shackles of social bondage and the stepping out into the light of a new day.[35]

This controversy appeared again in April, 1927 when a preacher wrote a letter to *The Echo* once again decrying bobbed hair and adding short skirts, rolled stockings and knickers to his list of shocking fashion trends which "professedly Christian women" were adopting. This prompted a response the following week from "another student" which was less than cautious in engaging the argument. The writer rejected the use of scripture verses made in the preceding letter and made an argument based on different verses. The letter writer went on to argue that, "it is the use, which determines the classification" of any article of clothing and ended with an admonition to the previous writer to "come to life, and try to adjust your venerable carcass to the time in which you are living."[36]

The February 22, 1928 issue of *The Echo* printed a letter signed "The Royal Order of Billy Goats" addressed "To the Girls." In it the writer expressed disapproval of the wearing of short skirts and rolled stockings because these fashions were immodest and immoral. He declared that when he saw such attire on a girl he immediately discounted "about twenty percent" from the value of her "profession of faith."

The following week a reply from The Royal Order of Nanny Goats was published. In this letter the writer began with a wryly humorous rejoinder. She said she had noticed that "females always seem to need some kind of reforming" and that the male sex has always assumed the prerogative of "telling the female sex what to do and how to do it." Then she changed her tone and asserted that this time she thought he had a point and called for the Taylor girls to take a stand and dress as "women professing Godliness" which she believed could be done "without making ourselves dowdy or conspicuous." She ended with a challenge to the Taylor males to stand with the Taylor women in this decision and not pass them by for women who were dressing according to the fashion trends.[37]

By the 1940s the entire ethos of the campus appears to have undergone a dramatic shift. The coed edition of *The Echo* for

God's Ordinary People:

November 30, 1940 contained no discussion of any serious issues regarding gender. The entire paper was filled with articles about dating practices on the campus. The headline read: *"The Echo Proudly Presents Issue by Feminine Journalists."* The article which was apparently written by the regular editor began with a classic put down of women.

> You know girls, (or do you?) Nine-tenths of the time they like to dabble in everything under the sun. First, they wanted to vote. They worked, and finally after they had ensnared a few male supporters, they received the privilege of the ballot.
>
> Then they wanted to enter business. No use going into the history of how they did it. Suffice it to say, they did. Thus, down through the ages they have obtained just what they want.

The article went on to describe how *The Echo* staff beat the women to the punch and offered them the opportunity to edit an issue before they could demand the privilege.

The other two major articles on the front page dealt with dating. Apparently, there had been a move on the campus to allow women to ask men for dates, and this role reversal was meeting considerable resistance from some males. The author signed the article "President Emeritus of the Hopeful Man Hunters." The third article described the Thanksgiving day festivities held on campus in which the most important ingredient was "that Dan Cupid in the person of Doris Horn had arranged dates for everyone."

The columns continued the tendency to avoid discussion of issues. There was a "Dear Abbey" style advice column in which questions about dating problems were addressed. On the opposite side of the page there was a column which gave fashion advice for coed's wardrobes. There was a gossipy column with inside jokes about people on the campus and another humor column.

Even the editorials did not rise to the level of serious discussion. There were three short two-paragraph articles which appeared in the editorial column. The first one simply praised the chapel program; the second one was a trite admonition to "quit griping"; and the third one suggested that the students should not jump to conclusions about a chapel speaker who held different opinions than they did. This last piece was the most thoughtful one in the entire paper.[38]

This shift in campus ethos continued throughout the 1940s. An interview with three women members of the class of 1948, Alice Rocke Cleveland, Ruth Brose Rogers and Frances Johnson Willert, confirmed that there was little serious discussion of national or international issues on campus. They all agreed that most students paid little attention to the news media including radio and newspapers. All three of them had been members of Soangetaha or Mnanka, but none of them understood the history of these clubs. The young women who called themselves Soangetahans and Mnankans in the 1940s were no longer engaged in any serious intellectual purpose. No debates or parliamentary drills were conducted. No one thought about the necessity for developing the ability to think analytically and critically in the public arena. The clubs were, in Ruth Brose Rogers' words, "social sororities." The same held true for the literary societies. The serious dimension of these organizations had been lost, and the meetings were pure entertainment opportunities for the membership.

This shift in ethos is somewhat mystifying in view of what was happening in the world beyond Taylor during this decade. Perhaps the reality of the war raging on two continents was simply too much for college aged young people to cope with. Rather than confront the fact of their own powerlessness to affect the events in the larger world, Taylor students turned in on themselves and their own small, relatively isolated arena. If they could not stop the guns and the bombs, they could at least drown out the sound by focusing on the purely personal issues of friendship, dating, fashion, and dining hall food.

WOMEN FACULTY ROLE MODELS, THE MOVE TOWARD SPECIALIZATION

Changes in curriculum structure and pedagogical goals during the first two decades of the twentieth century changed the role of faculty members and redefined their involvements in the disciplines which they taught. It was no longer possible to assume that a single faculty member could have his or her teaching load shifted from year to year. Faculty members were obliged to become specialists in one or several related fields of study. In order to accomplish this greater specialization, it was necessary for professors to go to graduate school and earn one or even two advanced degrees.

The first hint of the new trend toward increased specialization in the curriculum appeared in the 1911 Taylor University catalogue which announced a movement towards establishing a divisional structure. The college had been operating under what was termed the elective system for some years. Now the curricular parameters became more defined as courses were divided into six groupings including: languages; rhetoric, literature and Bible; mathematics; science; social science; and physical culture and arts. In order to achieve the A.B. a student was required to be in residence at least one full year and to accumulate two hundred forty term hours, defined as one recitation hour per week for a term. Specific

114

requirements were outlined regarding the number of term hours to be taken from each grouping.[39]

The concept of a major first appeared in 1914. The justification given for this curricular move was very similar to the one given today. Students were still required to take a specified amount of work within each of the six groupings in order to insure breadth of culture and a knowledge of the different fields of learning. In addition, they were to select from among twelve possible fields of study, one in which they would accumulate at least thirty term hours. This would "secure thoroughness and continuity in at least one field of study." The twelve majors offered were: Latin; Greek; German; romance languages; English; a combination major consisting of mathematics, physics and astronomy; biology; chemistry; another combination major in the social sciences; philosophy and education; Biblical studies; and oratory and music.[40]

THE ENGLISH DEPARTMENT

Changes in the English faculty clearly demonstrated the impact of these curricular changes. The first move towards specialization became evident when Miss Belle Corson joined the Taylor faculty in 1905 as professor of Higher English and German. Her only earned degree was an A.B. from the University of Michigan, but "she took special work in the Department of German and Literature."[41]

In 1910 Laura Belle Scott assumed the professorship of English and German at Taylor. She also had an A.B. degree from the University of Denver, but she came with several years experience teaching English and German in a Denver high school where she had also been principal.[42]

In 1915, Marie Zimmerman assumed the professorship of English and German which had been vacated by Scott. Zimmerman was the first woman faculty member at Taylor to hold a Ph.D. She had earned her A.B. from the University of Michigan and the doctorate from the University of Chicago. Possibly because there was only one other Ph.D. on the faculty in 1915, Zimmerman was immediately admired and respected. She was the class sponsor for the seniors of 1916-17 and "her presence wearing her doctor's gown at the annual cap and gown chapel added a new touch to the ceremony of the occasion."[43] Unfortunately, Zimmerman did not remain long at Taylor leaving at the end of the 1918-19 academic year.

The Gem

Marie Zimmerman, Ph.D. Professor English and German.

In 1921, a Taylor graduate, Lula F. Cline, took over the teaching of English. *The Bulletin* for 1923 was the first one to identify administrative heads of collegiate departments and schools, and Cline was recognized as heading the English Department. Cline was the first woman to remain in this position for an extended period of time. She served the University from 1921-1934. During this time she was given two leaves of absence to work on her graduate degrees. Her story illustrates some of the difficulties which were encountered by women in their quest for credentials during the early part of the century. Cline had taken summer work at Harvard, but found it could not be transferred to the University of Cincinnati where she enrolled in the A.M. program during her first leave from Taylor.

She completed the course work toward the Master's degree but ill health prevented her from presenting her thesis. During the second leave in 1928 she was obliged to start the process over at yet another university—George Washington in Washington D.C., and this time she did complete the A.M. The Master's degree was conferred in 1929, and Cline continued to do graduate work during the summers until she left Taylor in 1934.

Cline was a highly respected faculty member who was also popular with students. According to the biographical sketch which appeared in the *Taylor Bulletin*:

> Miss Cline measured up to the rank of a professor when a mere college graduate because of her personal endowments for apprehending our language and its literature. A few years of experience as a teacher enhanced by the friendship and counsel of some of the distinguished English professors of our day, have served to magnify Professor Cline's basic culture and natural endowment as a teacher.[44]

An indication of the esteem in which she was held by students was reported by *The Echo* in June 1927 just before she left for her second stint of full time graduate study. A large number of guests appeared in her Browning class and one of the students presented her with a new brief case "in appreciation of her friendship and inspiration, her faithfulness and patience in teaching them about the artistic and cultural values to be found in English literature."[45]

The description of the English Department's academic objectives which appeared beside her picture in the 1934 *Gem* demonstrated that she was leading the department in a way that kept it abreast of the current pedagogical trends. After affirming the traditional values of training teachers and developing a general understanding of the field, the writer asserted: "In as much as present day training appeals to the culture and aesthetic aspects of the language, the trend of the department is toward the development of the finer arts—self-expression and spontaneity of inward reaction."

Lula Cline was succeeded as head of the English Department by Elisabeth C. Bentley who had earned an A. M. in English from Boston University, an A.M. in Education from Columbia University and a Ph.D. in English from Cornell University. In 1939 she assumed the chairmanship of the Division.

Dr. Bentley was remembered by several former students as a very dignified woman who was highly respected for the quality of her teaching. She also had a habit of expressing her opinion on many subjects in a clear and forthright manner. According to former Taylor Athletic Director and basketball coach, Don Odle, "you knew where you stood with her and you paid attention when she spoke. She was always very much in charge in and outside of her classroom."[46]

Bentley served the University through 1942. Among her students was a young woman from rural South Dakota who had taught high school in her home state and had come to Taylor University to earn the A.B. in secondary education with a specialization in English and history. This young woman's plan was to return to South Dakota and take up her career as a high school teacher where she had left off. She was Hazel Butz, and neither she nor Bentley could have imagined that the latter's position would one day be occupied by the former.

When Dr. Bentley left Taylor in 1942, Professor Edna M. Robinson took over her position. Professor Robinson had an A.M. from the University of Chicago and a Ph.D. from Johns Hopkins. The period between 1944 and 1946 was the only time in the first one hundred years of Taylor's history when the English Department was headed by a male.

In 1946 Florence Hilbish joined the faculty and assumed the chairmanship of the department. She had an A.M. from the University of Pittsburgh and a Ph.D. from the University of Pennsylvania. Professor Hilbish remained head of the department until the end of the 1955-56 academic year. In 1954 her title was changed to Head of the Division of Language and Literature. During these years the number of faculty members teaching in the department increased as the numbers of students grew.

HAZEL BUTZ CARRUTH

Hazel Butz, Bentley's former student, had gone to Indiana University and earned a master's degree after graduating from Taylor. She returned to her alma mater in 1946 to teach English, but she left this position in 1950 to return to graduate school. Upon receiving the Ph.D. in 1955, Butz returned to Taylor and resumed teaching English. Professor Butz was appointed to lead the English Department and the Division of Languages and Literature in 1956, a position she held until her retirement in 1978.

In an interview conducted on July 26, 1996, Butz Carruth (she married in 1967) said that the years of working with Dr. Hilbish were somewhat difficult for her because she "never felt warmly accepted" by her superior and did not believe that she was being given the kind of help a new faculty member needed from a supervisor. Carruth remembered that there were tensions between the two women for a variety of reasons. Hilbish was no longer young and she was burdened by the care of an elderly parent which doubtless contributed to her general disposition to jump to unwarranted conclusions based on limited evidence and to make personally critical and hurtful comments about others.

As a result of her own experience with this strained working relationship, Carruth determined to bring to the department a democratic style of leadership which had been unknown during Hilbish's era. Carruth remembered her own frustration when she had returned with the doctoral degree in hand only to be assigned to teach six sections of freshman composition and to be deprived of teaching any literature courses. She, therefore, determined that she would never load a new faculty member's schedule in this manner. During the years of her administration all members of the department were expected to teach some composition classes but

Hazel Butz Carruth. Professor of English.

120

all were given the opportunity to teach at least one literature course as well.

Carruth focused her efforts on team building as the department grew. She was instrumental in bringing Professors Herbert Lee, (1955), Mildred Stratton (1956), Evelyn Van Til (1958), Charles Davis (1962), Robert Cotner (1963), Frances Ewbank (1964), Hilda Studebaker (1964), Marilyn Walker, (1966), Kenneth Swan (1969), and Ed Dinse (1971) to the department. She also encouraged several of these professors to continue with their studies toward the Ph.D. which was more and more important to insure the professionalism necessary in a college striving to become one of America's premier Christian institutions. It is a tribute to Carruth's leadership that several of these professors including Frances Ewbank and Marilyn Walker remained at Taylor until their retirement. Ewbank continued to teach Literature, and along with her husband William, was deeply involved in the lives of international students. Walker was reassigned to the Communication Arts Department when a Mass Communication major was developed.[47]

Carruth was a respected member of the faculty who contributed greatly to the professionalization and growth of the English Department and to the life of the University. She served on several important faculty committees during her tenure including the Administrative Council, the Academic Affairs Committee, the Faculty Council, and the Fine Arts Committee. She gave the dedicatory address celebrating the opening of the new Liberal Arts Building which was later renamed the Reade Centre for the Liberal Arts. In her capacity as Division Head she played a significant role in the revamping of the curriculum and calendar in 1967-68.

Carruth also enjoyed a reputation as an inspiring and demanding professor. Several of her students went on to earn Ph.D. degrees and to enter the field of college teaching. Included among these are Marjorie Starkweather Terdal, Associate Professor of Applied Linguistics, Portland State University, Portland, Oregon; Marjorie Cook, Chair of the English Department Miami University, Oxford, Ohio; Janet Watson, Academic Dean at Rockhurst College in Kansas, and Kathy Kiel Black, Professor of English, Northwestern College, St. Paul, Minnesota.

During her long service to the University, Carruth received several significant awards including the Alumni Merit Award in 1958, Professor of the Year in 1969, and honorary membership in Chi Alpha Omega. In 1987, the recital hall in the Smith Hermanson Music Building was named the Hazel Butz Carruth Recital Hall in her honor.

MUSIC AND ARTS

In the early part of the nineteenth century music and art were identified as "the ornamentals" and as such operated outside the classical curriculum of Fort Wayne Female College. Prior to the Civil War, music, painting and drawing were offered, but they usually took the form of private lessons for which there was a separate charge. For example, in 1853 music lessons cost an additional $9.00 per term, and drawing or painting lessons cost an additional $5.00. Students taking music lessons had also to pay $1.00 per term for the use of a piano. Given the fact that tuition in the collegiate department was only $7.00 per term, these "ornamentals" were fairly expensive. However, at least among the wealthy class the ability to sketch, paint, sing or play the piano were highly valued cultural skills for women. Each of the surviving catalogues from the early period listed a woman teacher of music, but no one was identified in the Board of Instruction rosters as teaching drawing and painting despite the fact that the catalogue said they were available.

During the 1870s there was a marked change in the way music was integrated into the college curriculum. The 1871 catalogue identified a Musical Department in which instrumental music, voice and singing, harmony and composition were taught. Students were informed that the course in music would occupy three years, more or less according to the industry, natural aptitude and previous advancement of the pupil. They were encouraged to pursue other studies at the same time since the value of music as an element of education, depended upon the other elements of culture acquired with it. If they desired an exclusively musical education, it would be provided. Every student taking the full course was expected to study harmony because "this grammar of music was indispensable." Those who took organ were informed that they would have the use of a "pedal Cabinet Organ, and a large Pipe Organ, one of the finest in the city."[48] The 1888-89 catalogue indicated that there had been considerable growth in the demand for a quality course in music and as a result, several rooms in the college building had been set aside for this department. These rooms contained pianos of a quality superior to those usually found in music schools and were entirely free of interruption.[49]

Throughout the 1870s and 1880s male professors dominated the Music Department, although in most of these years there were women instructors who taught in a single area such as voice or piano. President William F. Yocum's wife taught both piano and organ at various times during the Yocum's tenure (1877-88) at Fort

Wayne College. The students enrolled in the Musical Course continued to be more than ninety percent female. It was during this period that Esther Hanchette, teacher of oil painting, joined the faculty. She remained until the mid 1880s, and nearly one hundred percent of her students were female. The goals of the Art Department were to give the students a thorough course in the science and practice of landscape, decorative and portrait painting. Lessons were given daily for a period of three hours, and students were informed that one or two terms of industrious application would allow for the acquisition of sufficient knowledge to allow him or her to proceed independently.[50]

During the last two years of operation as Fort Wayne College, the Music Department was staffed by women faculty. The first year the college operated as Taylor University no one was listed as teaching music, but Martha Tibbals, who had succeeded Esther Hanchette, continued to teach art.

The first fifteen years in Upland were marked by high faculty turnover—sometimes a professor would stay for only a term or two—and a return to a predominance of women faculty in the arts. May Francis and Mrs. R. R. Ebright Collett are the first women faculty to hold the Music Bachelor's degree. They both came at the same time as Ella Lingo who had an A.M. and taught fine arts and French.[51] Unfortunately, Lingo left in 1898 and no one replaced her. Art was not offered again until 1910 when Mary Snead Shilling began to teach drawing.

In the fall of 1909, Edith Dorothy Olmstead took charge of the school of vocal music. She had studied with a private teacher in New York City, at Ithaca Conservatory and at Cornell University. Olmstead was apparently a competent and popular professor. The

1911 *Gem* declared, "Her teaching at Taylor has never been excelled and she deserves great credit for the way in which she has built up her department." The Vocal Department was described as one of the most important in the University as evidenced by the fact that nearly one-fourth of the student body was taking private lessons and many were involved in chorus work. In addition to the many recitals given throughout the year, two large works had been performed, one by a double quartet and another by a large chorus. The department sent out two quartets each summer to sing in camp meetings, prohibition meetings and on the Chautauqua circuit. In the summer of 1909-10 Olmstead had been a member of the Ladies Quartet.[52] Olmstead remained at the University through the 1917-18 academic year. This was the longest time any music faculty member had remained at the institution until that point.

In 1917 Arthur Verne Westlake, who had a Music Masters from Beaver College Musical Institute and who had spent a year studying in Vienna, was brought in from Pennsylvania for the purpose of developing a Conservatory of Music similar to The Extended Conservatory of Pittsburgh, which he had opened on his return from Europe. He taught piano, composition, counterpoint, analysis and fugue. Interestingly, nearly all of the other professors in the new Conservatory were women, several of whom had been his students and teachers in Pittsburgh. Westlake expanded the program in terms of its courses. Particularly, two new courses were added to the traditional conservatory music core—evangelistic piano playing and evangelistic singing. The main thrust of these courses was to teach students how to elaborate and embellish the ordinary hymn tune , and to train pianists and singers for the summer camp meetings and other revival meetings which were always in need of trained musicians.

God's Ordinary People:

THEODORA BOTHWELL

Theodora Bothwell came to Taylor in 1923-24 the year Vern Westlake left, and in 1924-25 she became Director of Music, a title which she held until 1939 when the concept of a conservatory was replaced with a Division of Fine Arts. She was Chair of this division until 1948 when another male with a Music Doctorate came to the department. He stayed for two years, and upon his departure, Bothwell returned to the Division chair-manship and held this position until her retirement in 1954. In addition to serving in this administrative position, Bothwell also served on several faculty committees including the Commencement Committee, the Lyceum and Museum Committee and an extended term on the Library Committee.[53]

Although Bothwell did not have a Music Doctorate, she was a thoroughly trained, highly competent musician. She had a Music Bachelors from Syracuse University, a

Theodora Bothwell. Professor of Music.

126

Music Masters from Chicago Conservatory and she had completed additional work at the American Institute of Normal Methods, Columbia University, and Chicago Musical College. In addition to her teaching, she played the organ for chapel and regularly led the chapel worship which normally interspersed music with devotional thoughts. One such chapel was described in the October 26, 1935 *Echo:*

> Miss Bothwell, keeping up her reputation for pleasant surprises, treated the faculty and student body to a most unique chapel service on Thursday, October 17. The theme of nature was predominant in the short, formal worship service which included responsive readings, prayers and hymns. Following the service, the group was dismissed to go out and enjoy the nature for which they had been giving thanks to God. At first the students were uncertain about the use of their unexpected freedom, but soon all were strolling about the campus thoroughly enjoying the autumn scenery. The bell, recalling students to classes, ended the spell of the hour all too soon.[54]

The students chose to dedicate the 1948 *Gem* to Theodora Bothwell in honor of her having completed twenty-five years of teaching music at Taylor. In their dedication they characterized Bothwell as "an active person" who took the time to "take a personal interest" in those she associated with. They stressed the fact that her interests were not limited to music, and credited her with a diversified knowledge which encompassed such things as seventeenth century drawing-room manners and modern architecture. Her ability as an interesting conversationalist contributed to her talents as a gracious hostess who loved to entertain amid the family heirlooms which she treasured. They ended their tribute to her by enumerating the reasons why they chose to honor her:

Because she has done more than any other individual in
making a cultural contribution to the campus and to the
hundreds who have passed through her studio; because of the
zeal and enthusiasm which she has shown in her work; because
of the high esteem in which she is held by those who know
and work with her; and because this is her twenty-fifth year
of teaching at Taylor University, the 1948 *Gem* is respectfully
dedicated to professor Theodora Bothwell.[55]

Alumni remember Bothwell as an extremely cultured person
who was interested in and knowledgeable about all the arts,
particularly music. Alice Holcombe who knew her as both student
and fellow faculty member, said, "She inspired me quite a bit. I
remember her as a truly scholarly woman who spent her meager
resources on good books which she often ordered from England.
When Penguin Books became available, she was among the first in
the Taylor community to buy these inexpensive editions of the
classics, and she was extremely knowledgeable in the field of
literature."[56] Don Odle, who also knew her as both student and
faculty peer, characterized her as "the most dignified woman" he
had met up to that time. The Odles also remembered that she had
a dog named Ebenezer who had the status of a much loved family
member and was walked every day on the campus.[57]

On the occasion of her retirement it was noted that beyond
teaching and contributing to the chapel worship, Bothwell had also
established and built up the record library, been responsible for
many fine lyceum series, and, "most of all Miss Bothwell has done
much to increase the general culture of the school."[58]

SADIE LOUISE MILLER

Another woman who was a member of the Taylor University
Department of Music faculty for an extended time was Sadie Louise

Miller. She came to Taylor as a student in the Music course in 1908. According to the 1913 *Gem* she was already an experienced teacher, having taught large classes of piano forte, voice, and sight reading, in Carbondale, Pennsylvania and neighboring towns. She completed two music degrees at Taylor, graduating from the Instrumental Departmental and the Vocal Department. Miller became a full fledged member of the faculty upon her graduation in 1910. Her career as a piano teacher spanned seventy years, forty of which were spent at Taylor.[59]

She began by teaching piano along with courses in harmony and voice. Eventually, she developed the piano preparatory department into a first class enterprise. The 1934 *Gem* stated:

> Miss Sadie Louise Miller has profited from many years experience in teaching beginners, and it is her desire to keep abreast with the latest improved methods for her particular line of work. The recitals given by the children of this department are among the most interesting programs which are held during the college year.[60]

The Gem

In addition to teaching piano, Miller used part of what must have been a meager salary to establish a scholarship prize providing full tuition for the freshman year of college to be awarded to the student in the Taylor Academy who made the highest GPA.[61] She was also the

Sadie Louise Miller. **Piano Preparatory Department.**

Preceptress (the modern term would be Dean of Women) for several years. Miller was a very active member of the WCTU and often spoke at campus organizations such as Prayer Band, Holiness League, and The Volunteers, and occasionally in chapel. When she spoke in public she often did so by reading poetry she had written for that particular occasion. An example of this is the poem she wrote for the fifteenth anniversary celebration of the Soangetaha Debate Club.

SOANGETAHA HISTORY

BY

SADIE MILLER

One time, well 'twas just fourteen

Years ago this very night,

a few of us weak maidens felt,

If we could work it right,

That we perhaps could learn to speak

As well as T.U. Boys,

And if we didn't say so much

We at least could make a noise.

So, we met in Speicher parlor

Before the hour grew late

And dared to organize a club

To learn us to debate.

She was a poet of good reputation in the tradition of James Whitecomb Riley, publishing several collections of her poems in booklet form. In addition, many were published in various religious magazines and at least two found their way into an anthology of poems by American women. In 1936 she won the Ida Mohn Landis Prize contest for a temperance essay sponsored by the WCTU, an organization in which she was active most of her life. Who's Who of American Poets published by Avon House in 1933 carried a biographical sketch and a poem by Sadie Louise Miller.[62]

Sadie Miller was instrumental in convincing her sister Alberta Abbey to bring her son, Vere and her daughter, Iris to Upland to complete their education at Taylor. Alberta's husband, M. O. Abbey, eventually followed the family to Upland. He was hired to oversee the construction of the new Helena Music Building and stayed on as the Superintendent of Buildings and Grounds. Mrs. Abbey did not have an official position, but she was a well known mother figure on the campus acting as hostess for many campus social events, and she ran a boarding house where students and some faculty members lived at various times. One of these students, George Fenstermacher, married the youngest Abbey daughter,

Iris Abbey's Senior Piano Recital — the first one to be held in Shreiner Auditorium. Iris is in the center.

Eloise. When he graduated from Taylor he joined the faculty as instructor in German and violin and later became the Dean of Men. Vere entered the Academy and Iris continued to study piano with her Aunt Sadie because as she said in a recent interview, "music was my life then."[63]   Both Iris and Vere earned A.B. degrees from Taylor. Iris became a Latin instructor, teaching first at a college in Kentucky and later in South Carolina. She went to the University of Michigan and earned another A.B. in Secondary Education with an emphasis in Latin. She ultimately returned to Upland where she taught Latin in the local high school until her retirement. Vere became a Methodist minister and then a missionary to India and Burma. His story is told in Chapter Four.

THE LIBRARY

During the early part of the nineteenth century the only mention of a library is the following: "These Literary Societies have each a well selected Library, to which the members have weekly access."[64]

The catalogue for 1871 was the first one which mentioned the existence of a college library. The reader was informed that there were a number of Religious and Scientific Periodicals kept on file for the use of the students. The same catalogue indicated that the Literary Societies possessed "a library of about one thousand volumes."[65] Apparently the first books to be collected in the college library were various encyclopedias and dictionaries including the new British Encyclopedia as far as published and Webster's and Worcester's Dictionaries as well as some specialized dictionaries and historical, biographical and scientific reference books. Students were encouraged to use these materials in the preparation of their lessons. There was also a textbook circulating library from which students could rent text books.[66]

During the 1880s, the catalogue began its description of the college library resources with the disclaimer that, "the library of the institution is not large." This was somewhat compensated for by the fact that students had access to the books of various teachers, and attempts to improve the situation were being made. Reading rooms were added in the early part of the decade. These were supplied with "church papers, several secular dailies, many of the best quarterlies and monthlies, and occasional pamphlets which students could use during all proper hours."[67]

The first mention of a librarian occurred in 1888-89. "Professor Rogers, our Librarian, will give special attention to both the library and reading room, and see that the latter is well supplied with church and secular papers and many of the leading monthly periodicals of the day." However, Professor Rogers' main responsibilities were the teaching of Latin and Greek which must have left little time for functioning as a librarian.[68]

For the first two years in which the institution operated under the name of Taylor University no mention was made of the library. Then, in 1893, when the College moved to Upland, an announcement was made that "Reverend G. W. Mooney of New York City proposes to secure large donations for the Library... and to forward the books rapidly as soon as provision has been made in the new building." The library would be named for him in honor of his work on this much needed improvement.[69] By the mid-1890s, progress was being made on the collection of books for the library. More than 1,000 volumes of history, science, literature and theology were accessible to students by 1896. The reading room with numerous periodicals and newspapers and its "Unchangeable Law:

No Talking" was also maintained for student use.[70] By the turn of the century, thanks to generous donations from many interested friends of the college, there were 3000 bound volumes in the Mooney Library, but there was still no professional librarian.[71]

As late as 1923, a group of women faculty and students staffed the library. A small photograph of eight women who are identified as library staff was shown in *The Gem,* but there was no explanation given as to their qualifications or their responsibilities. Presumably, they were assigned this task in addition to their teaching loads or as student employment, following the pattern developed in the 1880s.[72] The 1924 *Gem* indicated that Professor Adeline Stanley who was the Director of the Department of Education was also the Director of the Library. She was assisted by a 1923 Taylor graduate in Romance languages, Ivel Guiler.

IVEL GUILER

Ivel Guiler was appointed Head Librarian in 1924, a position she held until her untimely death in 1944. She was the first trained librarian Taylor University had ever had. At the time she assumed the post, the Mooney Library had grown to about 8000 volumes and it was obvious that it needed major reorganization if it was to serve the growing needs of the University. During the summer of 1924 Guiler began attending the University of Michigan where she received technical training in the art of library science and eventually earned the A.M. degree. Upon her return to the campus, she set about the formidable task of cataloging the collection using the Dewey Decimal System. She was also involved in the reorganization of the space on the second floor of the Wright Building, separating the two large rooms allocated to the library, and utilizing the wide central hallway between the two rooms as a space to locate the card catalogue and the librarian's desk. The stack area, circulation desk, and periodicals were placed in the room to the right of the card catalogue and the large room on the left became the reference area and reading room.[73] The brief biographical sketch which appeared in the 1925 *Taylor Bulletin* said, "Her interest in the library and her helpful attitude toward those using its facilities make her a valuable factor in the institution."[74]

There is evidence that Guiler did indeed care about books, libraries and especially students. She believed that the purpose of the library was to supplement the class work with additional material and to give breadth and inspiration to students in their quest for knowledge. She taught students "that books were like friends to whom we should be able to return again and again for they will never fail us, never cease to instruct."[75]

Bonnie and Don Odle, alumni of the University, remember Miss Guiler with special affection. Bonnie worked in the library as a student and she characterized Guiler as "an agreeable person to work with, quiet, not aggressive." Don said he still remembered going to the library one day to try to find

Ivel Guiler.

some information for a class assignment. He was obviously not succeeding and after Miss Guiler observed him for awhile she came over and asked him if she could be of some assistance. When he explained what he was looking for, she kindly informed him that he was in the wrong part of the library and then took him to the right area and helped him find what he needed to complete his assignment.[76]

During her administration, Guiler worked tirelessly to build a credible collection which would meet North Central accreditation standards. Her first task was to weed out the books which had little value in a college library. She then set about acquiring the kinds of books that were valuable, especially good reference books. After just ten years the library could boast of 13,000 volumes, a large number of pamphlets, and a good selection of general and scientific periodicals. The senior class of 1932 gave their class gift to the library for the purpose of purchasing reference books. The money was used to acquire *The Dictionary of American Biography, Encyclopedia of the Social Sciences, The Dictionary of Applied Chemistry*, and *The Cambridge Modern History*.[77]

As Taylor's one hundredth birthday year approached, plans were made for a capital campaign and a new library building was placed at the top of the list of proposals. Guiler threw her energies into helping to plan for this event. Unfortunately, she became ill and died quite suddenly in 1944. She left in her will a gift of slightly more than $1000 to be used toward the new library building. According to today's standards, this would seem to be a very small amount indeed, but as Burt Ayres wrote, "He who judges in righteousness and equity and counts in the currency of Eternity would say: She hath cast in more than they all."[78]

For several years her friends lobbied the administration urging them to create a suitable memorial to this quiet woman who had given so much to the institution for two decades. Finally in 1951, a committee consisting of Bonnie Odle, Ruth Lindell, Olive Draper, James Charbonnier, and John Lamey was appointed by President Clyde W. Meredith to decide on a memorial and to plan for raising the necessary funds. The committee decided that the East Reference Room of the new Ayres Memorial Library should be designated the Ivel Guiler Room, and that a bronze plaque should be placed there in her memory. The campaign was launched to collect the funds, the plaque was apparently made but for some unknown reason it was never placed in its designated spot.

During her life at Taylor she had been the sponsor for the Holiness League, and she often spoke at this organization's meetings. During this period, the Holiness League was one of the largest most active organizations on campus. The 1945 *Gem* contained a memorial page which gave a good indication of the quality of her life as she lived it and as it was perceived by the students whose lives she touched.

> All of us who were privileged to know Miss Guiler were impressed by the beauty of her life whether it was in library administration, in social fellowship, or in devotional leadership. We recall her pleasant, ready smile as we sought her help—and she was always ready to do more than we asked of her. None of us can recall a single instance when she spoke an unkind word or did anything other than that which is consistent with true Christianity.

Several of her colleagues joined in expressions of gratitude and appreciation for the years they had spent with Ivel Guiler. Burt Ayres, to whom the new library building was dedicated, believed that, "it would have been more fitting to have her name where mine is." Irma Dare who was also a Taylor graduate and head of the Home Economics Department and a close friend wrote, "Although most worthy, Miss Guiler never sought praise or laurels; rather with the utmost humility and consecration she was constant to her Christ, her work and to those she contacted in every day living." Theodora Bothwell another close friend and colleague, offered this reflection. "Her sincerity and integrity of life, her kindness and loyalty to her friends, her generosity to noble causes and her clear sense of duty made her a great influence for good on the campus and a person not to be forgotten." Finally, Sadie Miller wrote the following memorial poem.

SHE WALKED WITH GOD

She learned to walk with God. She started out
While young to travel on the upward path
Of the abundant life with Him to guide.
He brought her to our midst, and by His side
She trained her fertile mind in truth and lore;
Then after reaching higher heights, returned
To our own school to join glad hands with us;
And sought through books to guide the growing mind
Of honest youth in eager search for light.
And then, one day, He led her from our sight.
They crossed the river to the other side
Where grows the Tree of Life, whose fruits abound
And whose unfading leaves bring healing touch
To those who dwell among the happy throng.
There weeping is unknown, and close beside
The throne she dwells at rest, her hand still held
Forevermore within the tender clasp
Of her beloved Guide.[79]

ALICE HOLCOMBE

The second professional librarian to head Taylor's library was Alice Holcombe. She had come to Taylor as a student in 1934 after hearing a Taylor Quartet sing in her Methodist church in Newark, Ohio. At Taylor she majored in secondary education with English and Latin as her subject fields.

Upon graduation, she discovered that there were few opportunities for secondary teachers. Therefore, she decided to pursue her equally strong interest in library science. According to Holcombe, her interest in libraries went back to her childhood in Ohio where she carried arm loads of books home from the public library every week. She had also worked in the Taylor library during her senior year. As a result of not locating a teaching position, the fall of 1939 found her at Ball State University pursuing library science courses for secondary teachers. Following completion of this course she took a job at the Pine Ridge Methodist Mission School in Kentucky. After working for only one semester, she became seriously ill and returned to her home in Newark to recuperate.

After regaining her health, Holcombe began working in the public library in Newark which she had visited so often as a child. There she

Alice Holcombe.

139

encountered a librarian who had studied at the University of Michigan, and Alice was inspired by the possibility of pursuing a B.A.L.S. degree. Accordingly, she applied for admission to the program in Michigan, was accepted and spent the next three years at that institution working in the University library and earning a full fledged degree in library science.

Faced with the need to fill Ivel Guiler's position so suddenly and unexpectedly vacated, Dean Milo Rediger contacted Holcombe. They decided that she should complete her work at Michigan and then come to Taylor as Head Librarian which she did in September 1946 for a salary of $1900. When Holcombe arrived, she found the library in surprisingly good condition for a college as small as Taylor was in those days. The reference collection was particularly impressive, and Holcombe was surprised and delighted to find the *Oxford English Dictionary*, a reference which was seldom to be found in small libraries in the mid-1940s. It was obvious Guiler had understood that placing money into reference books was a good investment in the future of the institution. The biggest problem Holcombe faced was the cramped space. The shelves had been raised to the ceiling and one had to climb a ladder to reach books on the top level. However, the plans were already in place to build the Ayres Library which made the tight quarters a tolerable situation. The second problem was the lack of trained staff. Holcombe was the only librarian and her assistants were retired women who were interested and willing but unqualified for many of the tasks.

In 1950, Holcombe resigned her position and went with Milo Rediger to the University of Dubuque in Iowa. However, when Rediger returned to Taylor as Dean at the invitation of President Evan H. Bergwall in the fall of 1952, she returned with him. During her absence the move into the new facility had been accomplished solving the space problem. However, the lack of adequate trained staff continued to be a concern.

One day in the fall of 1953, Holcombe looked up from her work to see a young woman whom she recognized as one of her former student assistants walking through the library with a group of high school students she had brought to Youth Conference. The young woman was Lois Weed, and Holcombe decided she had found her assistant. At the time Weed was working in the public library in Marietta, Ohio, but she did not have a library degree. After conversations with Dean Rediger, it was agreed that Weed would come to Taylor as Assistant Librarian and that she would begin work on a library science degree the following summer.

Weed took the position and enrolled in the University of Kentucky where she earned the M.L.S. Holcombe and Weed complemented each other in terms of their personalities and in the particular library tasks which interested them. Both women functioned as reference librarians, staggering their hours so that each worked two evenings a week. Holcombe assumed the duties of acquisitions librarian and cataloger, and Weed became responsible for managing circulation and periodicals. The third professional position was added when Marcella Fuller came as cataloguer. Fuller was followed in this position by Audrey Berendt. Laurie Wolcott currently occupies this position. David Dickey was

Lois Weed.

the first full time library secretary, a position he assumed in 1964 while finishing his B.A. In 1972, after completing his M.L.S. at Western Michigan University, Dickey became the fourth full time librarian and the first Reference Librarian on the staff. In a recent interview, Dickey the current Head Librarian, said he believes that one of Holcombe's "most important strengths was her ability to choose staff who shared her service mentality."[80]

In addition to building a quality staff oriented to serve, Holcombe also continued the task begun by her predecessor of building a notable undergraduate research library. Holcombe enjoyed very positive relationships with the faculty, especially with department heads who both appreciated and respected her. As a result, she was able to convince them to use their expertise in selecting and ordering the books most valued in their disciplines. When she assumed the position of Head Librarian in 1946, the collection was approximately 23,000, and when she left in 1983 it had grown to 145,000. Holcombe was not only concerned with the number of volumes in the library, but also with the quality of the collection. She believed that the collection needed to be balanced, that there should be resources which reflected a multiplicity of viewpoints on all issues, and she worked toward that end.

The third major area in which Holcombe influenced the future of Taylor's library was her willingness to acknowledge the trend toward technological innovations and to embrace this trend. In 1975 Robert Pitts, who was then Academic Dean, wrote Holcombe a note asking if she thought that Taylor should join O.C.L.C. which at that time stood for Ohio College Library Center and was the first attempt to create an on-line library data base. Holcombe turned the question over to Dickey to research since he had recently been involved in graduate study. In his report, he said he felt the University could justify the continuing cost of the system but the cost of the hardware needed to implement the system was prohibitive. The following week the Kellogg Foundation offered to fund hardware for any small college library who wanted to join O.C.L.C. Taylor was ready to accept this propitious offer due to Holcombe's foresight, and it became the first college in Indiana to accept a computer from Kellogg.

Dickey remembers one particular day in 1975 when he was teaching Holcombe how to use the new computer in her first floor office in Ayres Library. They were testing the system to find out if it could help them answer some of the apparently unsolvable cataloging questions which they had shelved for later consideration. They were both caught up in the excitement of the exercise and did not notice that the rain outside had turned into an Indiana flash flood. In those days, rain of this magnitude always meant there would be water on the floor in Alice's office, and there was in fact an inch of water soaking their shoes before either one of them became aware of this potentially dangerous situation.[81]

In 1979, Taylor began to use the O.C.L.C. system for inter-library loans, a move which revolutionized this process. Prior to this time, if a librarian wanted to locate a book in another library she or he would have to guess who might have it and make a request to borrow the book not knowing for sure if it was available from this source. After the advent of O.C.L.C., everyone knew where books were located. In the pre-O.C.L.C. days, Taylor was a borrower of books from other libraries and never a lender. Since the advent of the on-line system, the situation has equalized so that

143

Taylor lends almost as many books as they borrow in any given year.

The process of applying for the first Lily grant to do retrospective conversion making Taylor Library's catalogue machine readable began before Holcombe's retirement. Today ninety-nine percent of the collection is on-line and by next year the periodical collection will be added.

A fourth area in which the foresight of Holcombe can be seen is the Taylor Archival collection. Early on in her career she had received the Ayres Collection of books and artifacts from Burt W. Ayres. She also maintained a rare books collection, but it was housed in a largely inaccessible closet. When Dwight Mikkelson joined the faculty, Holcombe began working with him to develop a true archival collection. Mikkelson was never a part of the library staff; his interest was that of an historian. Nevertheless, he and Holcombe worked together to lay the foundation for the day when a new library would be built which would contain a space where archival documents could be stored safely and accessed by researchers under controlled conditions. When Mikkelson retired, Bonnie Houser was hired as the first trained archivist librarian.

Over the years, Holcombe had many student assistants who worked in the library. It is a testament to the quality of the library staff and its sense of mission that many of these young people have gone on to become professional librarians. Lois Weed, Audrey Berendt, David Dickey, Laurie Wolcott and Bonnie Houser all fall into this category and all share her vision for what a professional librarian should be and how a first class undergraduate research library can best meet the needs of college students and faculty.

While the areas of literature and language, music and art and the library have been led by women faculty for significant periods of time, most women faculty have worked in departments and divisions where they have been in the minority. Several extraordinary women have made significant contributions to the academic life of the institution in these other fields.

OLIVE MAE DRAPER

The area of natural science and mathematics at Taylor owes much to a woman, Olive Mae Draper. According to Elmer Nussbaum, Physics Professor Emeritus, "she probably did more than anyone else during her active years to develop the Natural Science area of the curriculum."[82]

Draper was born in Iowa in 1888. She attended Central Holiness University in Iowa before coming to Taylor in 1911. She completed her A.B. degree in 1913 and stayed on to study for her A.M. in chemistry and physics with Professor Robert E. Brown. Brown was leaving Taylor and he suggested that Draper replace him as professor of chemistry. The Board agreed and she was appointed to the faculty in the fall of 1914. Later she earned an A.M. in mathematics from the University of Michigan. In addition, she did graduate work over several summers in various institutions including The University of Iowa, Columbia University and Indiana University. Nussbaum speculated that she probably was unable to complete a Ph.D. because of a lack of financial resources. In

Olive Mae Draper.
Professor of Science and
Mathematics.

145

the absence of a published salary scale it would be difficult to document, but it is unlikely that she ever earned very much at Taylor. The testimony of several other women faculty members of the same period established that single women were paid less than men as a matter of policy.[83]

From all accounts Draper was an extraordinary teacher. Her reputation was that of being a demanding teacher who called forth

the best in her students.[84] At the same time, her winsome smile and sparkling dark eyes made friends of the students and assured their lifelong regard. Don Odle, remembered that when he came to

Chemistry Laboratory. Olive Mae Draper is on the far left.

Taylor in 1938 he was ill equipped to handle a course in mathematics, but he had been scheduled to take one. After a couple of days, Professor Draper approached him and said, "Mr. Odle, you don't belong in this class." Then she took him in hand and helped him to switch to a course which he could handle. Odle said this was strong evidence that she cared about him as an individual.[85]

Nussbaum, who was one of her students, said:

Olive Mae Draper was very much at home in her classroom with several chalkboards and mathematical models which were the tools of her trade. In the physics laboratory she was not quite at ease with the electrical meters and other measuring instruments. She was grateful to the students, usually male, who suggested practical applications for the fascinating devices.[86]

One indication of the magnitude of her intellectual capabilities can be observed in the fact that her teaching responsibilities were constantly shifted among several disciplines including chemistry, physics, mathematics and astronomy. Finally, at the end of her career she was teaching mathematics, which according to Nussbaum, was her main area of expertise, along with astronomy. The only apparent reason why her teaching load was changed so much was that various male faculty members with different areas of expertise came and went, and Draper seemed to be a sort of swing faculty member—one who could be called upon to teach whatever was left over. Don Odle remembered her teaching a course in surveying. He said she was always taking the students out to do surveys or taking them to the county court house to check surveying records. She apparently was committed to providing students with field experiences as the best way to learn mathematical and scientific concepts. She did the same thing with her astronomy classes. She would bring them out on a starry night to view the heavens through the telescope which she had set up for the purpose. Odle said, "she had the knack of understanding nature , and she had the ability to communicate her own sophisticated knowledge in a way that an average student could understand."

The fact that the students chose to dedicate the 1942 *Gem* to Draper is an acknowledgment of the impact she made on many of their lives. The dedicatory paragraph reads in part:

To You Miss Draper who has become an integral part of the

147

university both academically and spiritually, who has proved
herself a friend to those who needed friendship and a counselor
to those who might need help, who has so loyally upheld the
standards that have made Taylor so well known, and who, by
both faculty and students is honored and loved, the Nineteen
Forty Two *Gem* is respectfully dedicated.[87]

During her long tenure, Draper was a model who quietly and
effectively demonstrated that a woman could exercise leadership
in the academic arena. In addition to her leadership in her classroom
and in the Division of Natural Sciences, she also served on many
important faculty committees including the Administrative
Committee, the Academic Affairs Committee, the Religious
Services Committee, and the Student Organizations and
Publications Committee. In 1944 the position of Academic Dean
was not filled, and President Robert Stuart created an Academic
Committee made up of three faculty members including Draper to
assume the responsibilities of this position. [88]

Alumni who knew her described a profound appreciation for
the quality of Christian faith which Draper daily demonstrated as
she moved about the campus and encountered students and faculty
who were in need. She had come from the Holiness tradition of
Methodism, and as a student herself she had been active in The
Holiness League, as well as in the Prohibition League, and Prayer
Band. She wrote in the 1913 *Gem*: "We pray because we believe
that prayer is an effectual working force in the kingdom of God"
and went on to assert that "even though prayer was an unseen force
and one that could not be measured in volts and amperes it was no
less powerful."[89]

Elmer Nussbaum remembered an occasion when Dean Rediger
was near death from pneumonia, and Draper talked to her classes

about the necessity of prayer warriors to bring him through this crisis. Bonnie Odle remembered that Draper was always in the chapel praying with students who were in some kind of spiritual crisis, talking and counseling with those who sought her help. Don Odle characterized Draper as an encourager. He then went on to tell of the night in 1938 when he knelt in the chapel to get his life straightened out. The person who came to pray with him was Draper. She stayed with him for at least an hour, sharing the truths of the gospel in a simple comprehensible way. It was an evening and a touch from a woman who did not even know him that he has never forgotten. Draper retired from Taylor at the end of the 1954-55 academic year having served Taylor for forty-one years.

Some of the people who remembered her in the years following her retirement found her difficult to understand. Her natural quiet nature and tendency to not talk much apparently deepened into reclusiveness. David Dickey told the story of coming to Taylor as a student from a farm in Pennsylvania and smelling goats on the streets of Upland. He had raised goats and was intrigued enough to search out the source of this pungent odor. He found the goats in Draper's back yard. She apparently had always kept and milked goats and raised her own garden. Her house was surrounded by an imposing wall of shrubbery and few people tried to make personal contact with her. Dickey is not sure, but he believes that their common interest in goats may have allowed Draper to let him into her life. On several occasions she asked him to go with her to buy the sacks of feed she needed for the goats. He remembers that she drove a red car because she explained that black cars were the same color as the road in summer and white cars were the same color as the roads in winter. Therefore, driving a red vehicle was the safest way to insure being seen by other motorists. She also did not haul the sacks of feed in the trunk because it would unbalance the car. Instead she had holes drilled in the four fenders and tied one sack of grain to each fender.[90]

The last decade of her life was tragically unhappy. She became unable to live alone and had to enter a nursing home in Marion. According to Nussbaum, the care she received there was substandard. She was often tied in her chair and left for long periods of time. Draper died on February 3, 1982 at the age of 94.[91]

Perhaps the paragraph which appeared in the *Taylor University Bulletin* on the occasion of Draper's retirement best sums up the life of this extraordinary woman:

> If all the lives of the Taylor family which have been touched by Miss Draper's Influence throughout the past forty-one years were to be gathered together, it is quite obvious that a great host would be present. To the persistency and consistency of Miss Olive Mae Draper, Taylor University is surely indebted.[92]

GRACE OLSON

Although in recent years, men have generally served as social science faculty, however, this was not always true. One of the most influential professors in that division from the mid-1940s to the early 1970s was Grace Olson.

Olson was born in Pawtucket, Rhode Island, but she grew up in various cities in the midwest including Detroit, Chicago and Cleveland. After graduating from East High School in Cleveland, she came to Taylor University. While an undergraduate, her majors were English and history. Her leadership abilities were evidenced by the fact that she held several elective offices and actively participated in a number of organizations while a student. She was president of the Mnanka Debating Club, president of the Women's Ministerial Association, president of the Associate Quill Club, a member of the Holiness League, served on both *The Echo* and *The Gem* staff and was a member of the Philalethean Literary Society.

During Olson's junior year, Professor M. Madeline Southard joined the faculty as Dean of Women and Professor of History. Southard was a leading Women's Christian Temperance Union evangelist and President of the Association of Women Preachers. During her short tenure at Taylor, Southard wrote and published a book entitled, *The Attitude of Jesus Toward Women* and organized a student chapter of the National Women Preachers. This group was open to all young women students who felt called to any form of Christian ministry.

Southard was a strong female presence on the campus. She regularly spoke in chapel— sometimes two and three times in one week—and addressed the Holiness League, Prayer Band and Student Volunteers, in addition to carrying on her speaking engagements in local and regional churches. As president of a national organization, she had a great deal of visibility. For example, in the winter of 1926, *The Echo's* front page carried a banner headline about the meeting of the Student Volunteer Convention telling how Dean Southard gave the "Climactic Address of Convention."[93]

During her senior year Grace Olson, in her capacity as president of Taylor's Women Preacher's chapter accompanied Southard to the national meeting of the Association of Women Preachers. Even though Olson did not do a great deal of public speaking while a student, it would seem reasonable to assume that Southard had some influence on her developing awareness of her own leadership potential.

After her graduation from Taylor, Grace Olson went to the University of Michigan where she began work on her A.M. in history with a cognate in political science. After finishing this degree she returned to her family home in Cleveland and took a position teaching history in Cleveland Bible College. While teaching there she continued to pursue additional graduate work at Western Reserve University, accumulating about two years of study toward a Ph.D. She continued to teach at CBC for eight years, but she apparently did not lose interest in her alma mater. In fact, it was while she was visiting Taylor with a group of students during Youth Conference in 1944 that she met the Chairman of Taylor's Board and first discussed the possibility of returning to Taylor to teach history.[94]

Grace Olson. Professor of History.

Olson was appointed Professor of History at Taylor in the fall of 1945. Her contract specified that she would be paid a salary of $1800 and she would teach a total of sixteen credit hours per semester. During the 1946-47 academic year, she assumed the position of Chair of the Division of Social Sciences which she held until she was caught up in an unfortunate set of circumstances in 1950. During the four years of her tenure, she had been steadily contributing to the life of the Taylor community by serving on several faculty and faculty student committees, the most important of which was the Academic Affairs Committee chaired by the Academic Dean Milo Rediger.

Rediger's relationship to President Meredith had become increasingly strained. According to Alice Holcombe who was the Head Librarian at the time, the strain was caused by the fact that Meredith was not very competent in his position and was deeply threatened by Rediger who was effective and who had the confidence of the faculty.[95] Whatever his underlying motivations may have been, the record indicates that Meredith began to behave in a paranoid manner which led to his removal of Rediger from the Deanship replacing him with Leland Forrest and eventually demanding that key faculty members pledge their personal loyalty to him.[96]

Confronted by this paranoia, Olson was unwilling to meet Meredith's demands. However, she did write a letter to the Board carefully outlining the situation as she understood it, articulating her points of difference with Meredith, and affirming her loyalty to Taylor University. The points on which she disagreed with the President's policies were the introduction of varsity football, a decline in the teaching of the doctrine and experience of holiness, the extreme disparity in salaries between administrators and faculty members, discrimination against staff members in the matter of salary and apparent duplicity on the part of Dean Forrest especially in his communications regarding tenure status. She ended her letter by arguing that it should be possible to disagree with the President and Dean in the matter of policies without having one's loyalty to the institution called in question.[97]

On June 20, 1950 Professors Olson and Butz received identical letters from President Meredith stating that he was convinced that they had taken both a defiant and a derogatory attitude toward his administration. He demanded the surrender of their contracts and the severance of their relationship with Taylor University effective at the conclusion of their summer school responsibilities. Rediger was also relieved of his contract, and Holcombe resigned her position in protest.[98]

With encouragement from Charles Shilling, who was a member of the Board and a personal friend, Olson and Butz requested a hearing before the Board of Trustees. According to Carruth, they received a hearing, but it was very short, and while the Board listened to their presentation the decision was made that Meredith's action was justified.[99]

Olson left Taylor, returned to Cleveland and was immediately hired by the Cleveland Bible College to teach history. However, her years of exile from Taylor were short. By 1952 the membership of the Board of Trustees had shifted; Meredith was fired; Evan Bergwall assumed the Presidency and Milo Rediger was brought back as Academic Dean. Holcombe returned with the Redigers and picked up her tasks as Head Librarian, and Grace Olson was offered the position of Registrar and Director of Admissions with the opportunity to teach one or two history courses a semester. Olson resigned her position at Cleveland Bible College and accepted Bergwall's offer even though she wrote, "The concept of such an administrative position with all its responsibilities quite overwhelms me."[100]

Olson remained in the position of Registrar and Director of Admissions until the spring of 1959 when she was offered a new faculty contract. Under the terms of this contract she would be Professor of History, Head of the History Department and Chair of the Division of Social Sciences. Her salary would be $4,800 for ten months. She held these positions until the Division structure was abandoned as a part of the curricular reorganization in 1967-68. She remained as History Department Chair until her retirement in 1971.

During her tenure at Taylor, Olson served on several faculty committees including Academic Affairs, Scholarship and Student Aid, Student Personnel Services, and the Administrative Council. When she occupied the post of Director of Admissions, she chaired the Admissions Committee.

Olson enjoyed the respect and appreciation of her students. When asked about the woman faculty member they looked up to most as a role model, Alice Cleveland, Ruth Rogers and Frances Willert, all graduates of the class of 1948, answered immediately, "Grace Olson! We flocked around her." They remembered with warmth the many evenings which they spent with Miss Olson in her apartment. They knew even at the time that she had very little money, but they related how she always had something to share with them— a cup of tea, a dish of fruit, some crackers and wonderful conversation. They said they often talked about their boyfriends with her, and Alice Rocke Cleveland told the story of how Will had given her an engagement ring before they were ready to announce their plans. Alice was afraid to keep the ring in the dormitory, and she asked Olson if she could leave it in her care. Olson agreed, and then Alice proceeded to bring an endless string of girls up the stairs of the Abbey house to see the ring that no one was supposed to know existed; a fact which greatly amused Olson.

Olson gave them more than easy friendship and female camaraderie. She also engaged their intellects in serious conversations about many issues. When they would get into a discussion about some controversial issue, Olson would normally not reveal her personal bias. She had the ability to stand outside of the heat of the argument and to present and evaluate many ideas and multiple viewpoints.[101]

Don and Bonnie Odle remembered that she would always bring the events of the campus into her classroom. If there had been a concert, a lecture, or an athletic event Grace Olson would have been there and she would have something to say about it the next day in her classes. She also had a public presence on campus speaking in chapel on occasion and addressing other student groups.[102]

Professor Phil Loy, currently Associate Dean for the Division of Social Sciences, was a student of Olson's in the early 1960s. Loy classified Olson as one of the five best teachers he had ever had in his life. She was always well prepared for classes, and she expected the same of her students. She called on students to answer questions, and "you came to class prepared because if she called on you and you didn t know the material she could make you feel about six inches tall." According to Loy, Olson was a "truly scholarly person" in that she read widely across many disciplines, sought to integrate her knowledge with other disciplines and encouraged the same habits of intellect in her students. She left her mark on a whole generation of history majors including several who currently serve on Taylor's faculty.[103]

Olson was apparently a woman who was not given to much speaking about her religious faith, but one who was deeply committed to God. She acted on this commitment in quiet, unobtrusive but decisive ways. One outstanding example of her commitment to missions is found in the fact that after her parents' death, she and her brothers and sisters undertook to build a primary school in Keyero, Urundi (Burundi) in cooperation with the National Holiness Missionary Society. When the school cost a great deal more than was anticipated, the Olson family did not give up. Instead, they increased their pledges and paid for it in its entirety. Later, when an annex was needed, they also underwrote this construction. The school was dedicated as the Olson Memorial School on February 12, 1950 and a beautiful bronze plaque which Olson had had made and shipped to Urundi was installed. The inscription was written in French and Kirundi and read: "In memory of John and Maria Olson of Cleveland, Ohio. Because I live, ye shall live also." The school was nationalized in the 1980s, but a representative of World Gospel Mission, the successor to the National Holiness Missionary Society, reported that the building was still there and still serving as an educational institution for African children.[104]

One of the great ironies in Taylor's history surely is that the year Meredith fired her, the students chose to dedicate *The Gem* to Grace Olson. In 1966 she received the Teacher of the Year Alumni Award, and in 1974 a woman's residence hall on Taylor's campus was named in her honor.

The dedicatory page of the 1950 *Gem* provides a fitting tribute to her beautiful life.

To you, Miss Olson
In recognition...

> of the position in the world which you represent,
> the Christian approach to man's problems, in opposition
> to any force or ideology which would
> destroy the dignity of men.

In Appreciation...

> of your own scholastic achievement which continues
> in a life of loving service

In Honor...

> of the example which your life affords, radiating
> an intriguing personality, a genuine concern for
> fellow men, and a vital relationship of prayer with
> your Lord and Savior.

MARY OSEE SNEAD SHILLING

All of the other faculty women who have made substantial contributions to Taylor University are too numerous to be mentioned in an essay of this size and scope. However, there are several more extraordinary women who need to be acknowledged.

Mary Osee Snead Shilling is one such individual. She first joined the faculty in 1899 as instructor in elocution and physical culture. During the summer of 1899, she and John Shilling, the Dean of Reade Theological Seminary, were married in the University chapel by President Thaddeus Reade. She continued on the faculty for the next two years teaching in the areas of elocution and physical culture.

John Shilling was appointed Acting President of Taylor following the unexpected death of Thaddeus Reade in 1903, and

No Ordinary Heritage

Mary Shilling left the faculty and concentrated on raising their two sons, John and Charles. Widowhood came to Mary Shilling precipitously in November, 1904 while John was pursuing further academic work on the East Coast. Left to raise her two sons alone, Mary Shilling returned to Upland and set about the task of upgrading her credentials in hopes of continuing her teaching career.

She had previously studied art with the International School and had taken private work in Canton, Ohio and in Newark, New Jersey. In 1906-07, she began teaching drawing in the Upland Public Schools. In 1912, she attended the Art Institute of Chicago, and in 1913, assumed the position of professor of art at Taylor University while continuing her work in the Upland Public Schools. While doing all this, Shilling also managed to earn an A.B. in expression from Taylor.

Mary Shilling.

During her tenure as Director of Art, Shilling instituted the practice of presenting an annual exhibit of the work executed by her students. *The Echo* for June 13, 1928 reported on one of the last such exhibits:

> The novel array of beautiful pictures, most of them depicting sea scenes caused delight from everyone that saw them. Many people were surprised at the unusual talent shown by the young artists. Much credit is due Mrs. Shilling whose untiring patience and artistic ability has made the department one of the most progressive in the college.

Shilling continued as Director of Art and the only professor in that area until she suffered a severe heart attack early in 1930 which forced her into retirement. She continued to live in her home on the campus until her death in December, 1952. Following her death, her two sons established a scholarship in their parents' honor.

FLORENCE COBB

Two other women whose names should not be passed over also taught in the general area of the arts during the first two decades of this century. They were Bessie Foster and Florence Evelyn Cobb. Bessie Foster is notable because she was the first director of the College Orchestra.

Florence Cobb became professor of the School of Oratory in 1909. She was the second woman to come to this position from the Curry School of Expression in Boston, and she set about developing the School of Oratory using Curry's methods. The 1911 *Gem* declared, "She is a first class teacher, a reader who charms all her hearers, and one who acquires and retains the friendship of all."

Cobb remained at Taylor for ten years, and during that time she developed the basic curriculum of the Expression Department. The Curry Method "sought to develop the mind, body and voice in order to call forth an individual's innate powers to think and express the self." The course could be studied as part of the A.B. or separately as a diploma course. It required thirty-six term hours of class work in the Expression Department, five term hours of psychology, six in private work and three or four in logic and argumentation. Those who were studying for the ministry were encouraged to do at least some work in the department because of the emphasis on platform work, and there were many joint recitals and programs between Expression and Music students.[105]

Cobb attracted large numbers of students both male and female.

When she came, the department had far more males than females, but by the time she left there were an equal number of men and women studying expression. By 1915, the department was one of the largest on the campus. One of her students was Barton Rees Pogue who became head of Taylor's Expression Department and achieved a degree of fame as a Hoosier poet in the tradition of James Whitecomb Riley.[106]

The Gem

Florence E. Cobb.

Cobb left at the end of the 1918-19 academic year to take a position at Eastern Nazarene College in Boston. An interesting twist occurred in 1927 when she was teaching at Wheaton College in Illinois and brought her women's debate team to Taylor. The question debated was: Resolved, that Congress should be given power to enact uniform marriage and divorce laws. Taylor took the affirmative and Wheaton the Negative, and the Taylor women won.[107]

JENNIE ANDREWS LEE

Jennie Andrews Lee is a name which looms large in the history of the Education Department. Andrews was a native of Iowa, but she came to Marion College in Marion, Indiana to earn her A.B. degree in education. Her A.M. was earned at the University of Iowa and she took additional graduate work at the University of Minnesota

161

and the University of Arizona. She taught secondary school in Iowa and was a high school principal for nine years before coming to Taylor in 1951 as Assistant Professor of Elementary Education.[110]

Andrews made many important contributions to the Education Department during her more than twenty years at Taylor, but one of the most important changes was the introduction and development of the professional semester for elementary education majors. Andrews had attended the National Education Association convention in Chicago where she had learned about this new direction in teacher education. She realized that Taylor would have to change its curriculum to match this trend or the education major would become outdated and possibly lose its accreditation. After the convention, she returned to campus, discussed the concept with Dean Rediger, and the two of them then set to work developing a proposal whereby the professional semester could be implemented at Taylor.

Andrews developed good relationships with principals and superintendents because she knew this was important if her students

were to have optimum field experiences. She did this in part by developing a no-nonsense approach with her students. They were expected to abide by the rules she set out including where they were to live, how to dress and how to style their hair. Students who were unwilling to accept this reality knew they would not be allowed to student teach. Even though she gained a reputation for being a tough lady, she still enjoyed strong positive relationships with her

Jennie Andrews Lee.

The Gem

students. She recalled many instances when student teachers invited her to their apartments for dinner after she had visited them in their classrooms. She was known to have a good sense of humor, and if a student like Robert Freese pulled a practical joke on her she was liable to respond in kind.

Perhaps the strongest legacy which Andrews Lee left when she retired from Taylor in 1975 was the large number of excellent elementary teachers, principals and school superintendents she trained to be quality educators. Several of those young people came back to teach in Taylor's Education Department including Jane Hodson, Nancy Moller, Dave Hess, Robert Freese and Steve Bedi. Jennie Andrews Lee's home remains one of the most visited faculty residences in Upland on Taylor Homecoming Saturdays.

It is clear that there has been a continuous stream of significant women faculty in a variety of disciplines who have contributed largely of their talents and resources to Taylor University. Several important curricular areas bear the marks of their leadership and dedication. They functioned as significant role models for the young women and men who sat in their classrooms and came to know them as friends. The example of their commitment to God, to their students, and to the University community influenced the kind of campus environment in which young women studied, and thus, affected the quality of experience which these young women had as students at Taylor University.

The Gem

Volunteer Band - 1909 (John Wengatz - back row, fifth from left, Susan Talbott Wengatz - second row, fourth from left)

Chapter Four

TO THE CORNERS OF THE EARTH:
IN BISHOP TAYLOR'S FOOTSTEPS - THE MISSIONARY QUEST IN AFRICA AND ASIA

*S*ince the 1890s, Bishop Taylor's life and ministry has had a profound influence on Taylor University students. His missionary zeal inspired the founding in 1900 of the Volunteer Band or Student Volunteer Movement on the campus. This organization was under the sponsorship of the YMCA and the YWCA, and was international in scope. The Volunteers held a regular weekly meeting on Monday evenings where the topics of "God's call to the field and God's subsequent leadings in that direction" were discussed. Members were encouraged to sign commitment cards and to work toward a life of service on the foreign mission field. During each school day from 12:00 to 12:15 there was a missionary prayer meeting in which the "Cycle of Prayer for missions was used." At least once a month there was a special missionary meeting on Sunday afternoons often with a visiting speaker. The Volunteers maintained a table of literature with "the leading missionary periodicals of Methodism and of inter-denominational interest, and they collected the missionary offering." Their motto was "The Evangelization of the World in this Generation", and they confidently expected to make this a reality.[1]

The 1911 *Gem* noted that:

> Taylor is a missionary school, as is proved by the fact that
> nine of her people have sailed from here to foreign fields

within the last year and a half, more than have gone from all
the other schools in the state of Indiana during that time. At
the present time thirty-six of the students are members of the
Band, six of whom God has called to the mission fields this
year.[2]

Through the decades many Taylor alumni have gone into
mission work as evangelists, administrators, teachers, and medical
workers. William Ringenberg in *Taylor University The First 125
Years* noted that about 10% of all Taylor graduates in the period
before 1949 worked on a mission field.[3]   Of the 160 students in
1895, 30 were ministerial candidates and 9 missionary trainees;
these two categories totaled some 25% of the student body. In
1915, some 39% of the student body were preparing for the ministry
or as missionaries. In 1953 37.2% were heading for the ministry
in one form or other, 8.5% in missions, and 2.5% in religious
education, for a total of 48.2%.[4] At least up to the early 1950s the
greatest number were involved with the Methodist Episcopal Church
(now The United Methodist Church).

As far as can be determined, the first alumni went out as
Methodist overseas foreign missionaries in the 1880s. But it was
in the first decade of the twentieth century that many students
responded to the missionary call. Not surprisingly because of
Bishop Taylor's work, Africa caught the imagination of the student
body. This chapter will focus on a selected number of early
Methodist missionaries who followed Taylor's footsteps to Africa,
and to Asia where the Methodist Episcopal Church had its largest
overseas involvement.

OLIVER MARK MOODY

The first student who felt the call to Africa and specifically to

Angola was Oliver Mark Moody. Much is known about Moody because his father, Hale J. Moody, a high school principal, wrote a ninety-seven page booklet entititled *Life Story of Oliver Mark Moody* following the tragic death of his son in Angola approximately a year after he arrived on the field.[5] Oliver Moody was born in 1882 in South Evanston, Illinois. When he was two years old, his family moved to northern Nebraska where he lived until 1896. The family again moved, this time to Tennessee. He entered Cumberland Normal College, graduating from there in 1898. The family moved a third time, to Greensburg, Indiana where "he [Mark] received the experience of Holiness." He entered Taylor

Oliver Mark Moody
missionary to Angola

University in 1901 where he pursued the Greek Theological course and graduated in June 1904. At the graduation he gave an oration and sang a solo, the hymn being "Master take me through the gate."[6]

While at Taylor, Moody as a member of the Volunteer Band felt led to become a missionary to Africa. In April 1904 at the annual Methodist conference, he met Bishop Joseph Hartzell who had replaced William Taylor as Missionary Bishop of Africa, and according to his father "a mutual attachment was formed which was continued till Oliver's last breath."[7] After graduation, Moody

Moody in Angola with a man
identified as Sanji

was in constant demand preaching in various Indiana churches. During the summer of 1904, a letter from Bishop Oldham arrived offering him the superintendency of an English speaking school in India. He declined this offer saying "God wants me for Africa." At last a telegram came from Bishop Hartzell asking if he would be ready to sail from New York on November 19. Moody sailed to Liverpool, England on that date. From there he spent a week sightseeing in London, and then boarded the "Biafra" for Luanda, Angola, the same ship that took Bishop Taylor and his first missionaries to Africa in 1885.

Moody's first African experience was to travel up the Congo River to Matadi, to Leopoldville, and then on to Boma. He spent time with various missionaries and visited Vivi where "Bishop Taylor had his headquarters and made the greatest mistake of his life trying to found his line of Congo self-supporting missions."[8] Apparently Moody found the Congo to be "very wonderful." But he also commented about:

> ... the horrible Congo Free State atrocities. These Baptist brethren told me of things that they had heard and seen that would almost freeze one's blood... I have two photos that Rev. Jos. Clark gave me, taken by himself, of four natives whose hands had been cut off because they did not bring in

enough rubber. Of course the government and commercial agents deny all this for they are mixed up in it; but these missionaries are telling what they have seen and know to be true. Old King Leopold will have some things to answer for.[9]

In a letter written January 19, 1905 from Luanda, Moody described the city:

> We have a fine property very nearly clear of debt-nice big house in big grounds, overlooking the city and the beautiful harbor... The biggest need here is more workers. Brother and Sister Shields, Mrs. Shuett (a widow), and Florinda Bessa, a native girl and a marvel - truly a miracle of grace. These four are carrying on the work here. They have a school that is drawing from the best families in the city and this must be kept in the hands of competent teachers. Also there is a start for a girls' boarding-school.... Brother Shields is holding revival meetings now and last night I preached, Florinda Bessa interpreting for me. The Lord blest the word and two native men came to the altar and prayed through. 'Twas blessed indeed.[10]

On February 3, 1905, Moody wrote a letter to his father and mother from the interior station of Pungo Andongo, Angola which had been founded by Bishop Taylor and where he was slated to become its superintendent. He commented on the spectacular rock formations in the area:

> I fell in love with Pungo... Those mammoth rocks three hundred feet high, some standing like great shafts that never have been scaled, others big enough to put your farm on. I never saw such rocks before... It is said that Livingston climbed the one across street in front of our property and prayed that God's people might some day have a strong-hold there, He passed through Pungo twice we know and for eight or ten miles I tramped the same path that he did fifty years ago. Ah those rocks![11]

Moody commented that:

Brother Herbert C. Withey has been here since he was twelve
years old, with only a one year furlough. He must be thirty or
past. Truly a noble young man and one of the corner-stones
of the work here in Angola. His father and mother labored
here for years and are now in America. He is a wonderful
student and knows the Portuguese and Kimbundu better than
any of the other missionaries here. Has done some translating
and longs to do more but is overloaded with other work so
that he cannot. O how we need more workers![12]

In his last letter home written October 17, 1905, Moody noted
that he and another missionary "were accepted into Conference on
trial, were elected to Deacon's Orders and on Sunday A.M., Bishop
Hartzell ordained us."[13] After the annual conference, Moody
accompanied Bishop Isaiah B. Scott of Liberia on a tour. However,
they ran into a heavy rainfall, and Moody caught a severe cold. On
October 31, 1905 he died in the presence of Bishop Hartzell.

His passing was a great shock not only to his family but also to
the other missionaries and to the student body of Taylor University.
For many years Taylor University remembered Moody and his tragic
passing. Three people who were particularly affected by Moody's
sacrifice were John C. Ovenshire, John Wengatz, and Susan Talbott
Wengatz.

Ovenshire entered the Commercial Department of Taylor
University in the fall of 1902. *The Gem* (1907) noted that he was
an instructor in the Commercial Branches while pursuing the
English Theological course. He was a member of the Volunteer
Band during the same time as Moody, and was preparing himself
for missionary work in Japan. It can be surmised that with Moody's
death, Ovenshire decided on Africa as his mission field. While at
Taylor he married Ethel Bowles. Shortly after their graduation in
1908, they went to Africa. There they worked for three years until

Ovenshire, like Moody, tragically died. Ethel Ovenshire stayed in Africa for several years before returning to the United States where she married James McCosh, a Methodist minister.

JOHN AND SUSAN TALBOTT WENGATZ

Both the tragedies of Moody and Ovenshire encouraged John Wengatz and Susan Talbott to consider missionary work in Africa. Susan Moberly Talbott was born in Coatesville, Indiana in 1885. Her grandfather was a Methodist preacher, and her father, W.H. Talbott, was a lawyer and member of the Indiana State Legislature. In 1898 she had a conversion experience and five years later became a member of the Methodist Episcopal Church. Against the wishes of her parents, Susan Talbott entered Taylor University in the fall of 1905, "from religious convictions."[14] Shortly after entering Taylor, she joined the Student Volunteer Band and signed a declaration card of her intent to go into foreign mission work. She was obliged to work during her Taylor years. She had taken courses in a shorthand training school in Indianapolis which enabled her to become the private stenographer to the President. Despite having to work, she was a student leader at Taylor. She was secretary of the Student Volunteer Band, president of her junior class, and traveled with the Taylor University Ladies' Quartette. She took time from meals and free hours to tutor

The Gem

Susan Talbott as a student at Taylor University

English to three Puerto Rican students.

Talbott became committed to Africa as her mission field upon learning of the death of Oliver Moody. According to biographer Sadie Louise Miller in her booklet *In Jesus' Name Memoirs of the victorious life and triumphant death of Susan Talbott Wengatz,* during the memorial service for Moody in the college chapel, when the leader prayed:

> that God would raise up someone and send him to Africa to fill Mr. Moody's place, definitely the Voice spoke to her [Susan Talbott] that she was to be that one. She did not even know just where in Africa Oliver Moody had been buried, but years later when actually reaching the field herself, she found that she was stationed within sight of his tombstone - so definite was God's call to her.[15]

While at Taylor, Susan Talbott met John Wengatz who was born in 1880 of German-American parentage. During his childhood in Steuben, New York, Wengatz initially attended a German Lutheran congregation, but in 1898 he joined the Methodist Episcopal Church. When he was seventeen years old, a sermon that he heard made him decide to become a missionary. While studying at Cazenovia Seminary in the first few years of this century, Wengatz signed a declaration card of the Student Volunteer Movement. After spending two years in the Methodist Episcopal ministry for the Central New York Conference where he was known for his singing and evangelistic messages, Wengatz entered Taylor in 1906, graduating in 1909 from the Greek Theological course.

In June 1909 John Wengatz and Susan Talbott were married. For a year John Wengatz was pastor of a church in McCordsville, Indiana while they waited for a missionary appointment. On July 19, 1910 Bishop Hartzell appointed them to mission work in Angola.

They sailed the following month and for twenty years the two labored in central Angola in Luanda, Quiongua, and Malange. He became the superintendent of the Malange district. John Wengatz learned the Kimbundu language, was engaged in industrial work, an evangelist, and organizer of churches. He always wanted to explore the possibilities of expanding the mission field like his hero, David Livingstone, had previously attempted to do. As a missionary in Angola and later in Liberia, John Wengatz is reported to have constructed 36 churches, 44 schools, 12 parsonages, and baptized over 44,000 converts.

John and Susan Wengatz in Angola

Wengatz reflected some of the first generation missionary paternalistic approaches to missions and attitudes towards Africans. Taylor alumnus Paul Kasambira has noted that from his own experience growing up in Zimbabwe, Western missionaries went through three stages—the paternalistic period, the transition, and the modern missionary.[16] Characteristics of the first group included eating and living separately from Africans, seeing African culture as inferior to Western culture, frequently not learning the African language fluently, and being on close terms with the colonial power. When touring the country, they brought their own food and slept separately from the Africans. Modern missionaries, on the other hand, have related to Africans as being their equals, eating and socializing freely with the African nationals, and maintaining a distance and even hostility toward the colonial power. In his book *Miracles in Black Missionary Experiences in the Wilds of Africa,* Wengatz demonstrated many of the characteristics of the older missionaries. "The mind of the African is simple and childlike. It has never been clouded or sidetracked by anything but sin and ignorance."[17] Wengatz was paternalistic. He addressed many Africans as boys, natives, and referred to Africa as "dark" with sorcery, witchcraft, and magic. He was opposed to the mixing of races.

> We believe that, according to God's holy ordinances, the white man was always to be white, and the black man was always to be black. It is, indeed, a beautiful scene and a gratifying feeling possesses one when we find a place of pure unspoiled African life, in all the simplicity and chastity of primitive uncontaminated black ideals of the best; and also when, once in a while, we find a white family in the far interior that gives one an impression of real pure, holy, chaste European family life. Finding them crossing their blood, crossing their habits, crossing their sins, and crossing and debasing everything that either side possesses as God-given and good always gives us a sort of nausea, a sick feeling, a feeling of wanting to withdraw from the place. I am sure that from such cases God Himself has long withdrawn His smile and favor.[18]

At the same time, Wengatz exhibited characteristics of the transitional stage. He learned the indigenous language and recognized that the Africans must be in charge of their own church.

> We believe it should be the aim of every true and farsighted missionary to work himself out of a job as soon as possible...
> To build up a native leadership that would withstand coming storms and persecution has been our aim all through our

work; secondly, we have tried also to build up a church that would be self-supporting in its own field and finally be able to take up the task of sending out preachers and teachers from its own ranks to the farther interior tribes. This can be done only by allowing them to make at least as many mistakes as we have made.[19]

He was very critical of the Portuguese colonial government's support of contract labor being used in Angola, calling it an evil policy (see Chapter Two) He changed some of his personal views about Africans.

Upon going to Africa, our thought was that the low, base African must have many years spent on him to civilize and uplift him in order that he might understand the Gospel. We thought his mind too dense to understand what sin was, what salvation was; but after spending several years at this, we reached the conclusion that we were wrong, and as an experiment we went out into a tribe hitherto untouched by the Gospel or civilization, and found, to our surprise, that often a single Gospel message was enough, with the power of the Holy Spirit, to bring conviction on them.[20]

John and Susan Wengatz in Angola

God's Ordinary People:

Wengatz clearly had some respect for African culture and art as shown by his extensive artifacts collection which he generously donated to Taylor University. Unfortunately much of the collection was lost in the 1960 Administration Building fire. In a letter (May 2, 1934) to Dr. Thos. S. Donohugh of the Mission Board in New York City, while on furlough in Marion, Indiana, Wengatz wrote:

> I firmly believe that older missionary ideas of tearing down and destroying all that the native has and then offering him a completely new and strange religion in its place, is a great mistake. We must be patient with him, long suffering and kind. Perhaps to exalt our Christ and the more refined and wholesome things in our religion would gradually give him time to study it and then make up his mind that it is better, and desire it in that way, rather than to be threatened and frightened into it. The native of any land have given ages of thought and study to their religion and its form, and no doubt there are many things that do not need to be relegated to the pit, even though they do not agree with our opinions and creeds.
>
> We [missionaries] must keep in mind that he [the African] must increase and we must decrease.[21]

In the same letter Wengatz made the following comments about recruiting new missionaries:

> He must have a 'Call' to the ministry. This gives him the urge and passion that is needed to withstand persecution and hardships. Those who do not have a definite call frequently fall out before long, and sometimes bring reproach upon the cause.[22]

Susan Wengatz had a gift for languages, learning both Kimbundu and Portuguese. Herbert E. Withey noted that "she was especially owned of the Lord in evangelistic work, and undoubtedly, thousands have been turned to Christ by the influence of her life

Taylor University Archives

Susan Wengatz teaching Angolan students

and work."[23] She was a musician, translating more than 50 songs into Kimbundu. She was John's secretary and helper while he was District Superintendent. She was also sub-editor of the *South African Missionary Advocate* and "kept that paper well supplied with bright and telling articles representing various phases of the [Angola] work."[24] Mr. and Mrs. Wengatz initiated camp meetings in Angola. Her call was to evangelistic work, but more and more she became involved in teaching. In 1928 she was a major mover in founding a Bible training school in Quessua, Angola, named the William Taylor Bible Institute. The Quessua mission station, located some ten miles from Malange, had been founded by Bishop Taylor who described it as an "Angola Eden in the Garden of the Gods." "Mrs. Wengatz oversaw the making of the brick and bossed the mason work" in the construction of the Bible school. She also taught several classes.[25] H.E. Withey noted:

Mrs. Wengatz worked and prayed much to get a new building at Quessua for a Bible School, with conveniences for institute work, special instruction and training of native workers. Thanks to her labors, with those of other faithful souls, the staff of native workers at the present time [1930] are better equipped spiritually and educationally than ever before. Her last earthly resting place is close to this building, and one feels that she must be glad to have it so.[26]

The Quessua mission station became the heart of Angolan Methodism and was the largest Methodist mission in Africa. By 1934 the mission station had a girl's school built by the Woman's Foreign Missionary Society; a church; three missionary residences; boys' dormitories; shops for carpentry, blacksmithing, auto repair work, shoemaking, and tailoring; a hospital; and the Bible school.[27] Bishop Ralph Dodge taught at the Taylor Bible Institute in the late 1930s and he recalled having 15-20 students at the time. The school continued to expand through the decades. But during the middle of 1992 and also in March 1993, students and teachers left the campus because of civil war. The mission was bombed, invaded, and people were kidnaped. As of February 1994, nobody was living there. But plans are being discussed to rehabilitate the facilities.[28]

The *New York Herald Tribune* reported (January 21, 1930) that Susan Wengatz died on January 16 after being bitten by a rabid dog on December 13, 1929 in the mission yard at Malange. H.E. Withey noted that serum arrived from South Africa, but apparently it came too late and was not effective.[29] She was buried near her Bible school in Quessua. This tragedy had a great effect on her alma mater. Sadie Louise Miller was inspired to write *In Jesus' Name,* and a detailed account of Susan Wengatz's death was noted in *The Echo* (January 29, 1930).

John Wengatz returned to the United States and spoke frequently at Taylor University between 1931 and 1934. During that time, he met and married Miss Helen Barton, a registered nurse and a missionary of the Woman's Foreign Missionary Society of the Methodist Episcopal Church who was sent to China in 1924. Alice Holcombe recalled that John Wengatz met Helen Barton at the Board of Global Ministries in New York City where she was working. He noted that she was

The Gem

John Wengatz in the 1950s

wearing flat shoes which to him was a sign that she could do well in Africa.[30] Mr. and Mrs. Wengatz went to Liberia as missionaries in 1934 where they served for ten years. Then in 1946 they were sent to the Congo and in 1949 to Angola. John Wengatz spoke several times in the 1950s and 1960s to Taylor students and faculty. He received an honorary Doctor of Divinity degree, and was a member of the Board of Trustees beginning in 1952. In 1954 he wrote *Sammy Morris The Spirit-Filled Life* (published by Taylor University). In the fall of 1965, a new residence hall for men was dedicated in honor of Mr. and Mrs. Wengatz; they were present for this event. They retired to Winter Park, Florida where John died in 1977 and Helen passed away in 1990. John Wengatz's influence on the lives of many Taylor graduates has been very significant.

179

Professor Jane Hodson remembered that "when Wengatz prayed it was like a hotline to heaven - he was really talking to the Lord." He had a deep burden for all peoples. Alice Holcombe noted that Wengatz was a tall man with a booming voice, genial, always with a smile..

In 1993, for the first time funds from the John and Helen Wengatz Endowed Scholarship Fund were distributed to twelve sons and daughters of missionaries. The mace used in important University ceremonies was John Wengatz's African walking stick.

RALPH E. AND EUNICE DAVIS DODGE

Two students at Taylor University in the early 1930s at the time of Susan Talbott Wengatz's death were Ralph and Eunice

Bishop Ralph Dodge as a Taylor University student.

Dodge, both of the class of 1931. Ralph Dodge was born in Terril, Iowa in 1907. He intended to become a farmer, following his family background, but in 1925 was converted during a revival in the local Methodist church and felt the call to the Christian ministry.[31] At the urging of some young people in a neighboring community, Dodge applied to Taylor during the summer of 1926. He had little financial backing, and so during his five years as a student Dodge worked first in the school's greenhouse, and then later on the farm, rising every morning at 4:00

A.M. to milk the cows and bring the milk to the cafeteria in time for breakfast. Dodge recalled earning .35 cents an hour.

Academically Ralph Dodge worked closely with Barton Rees Pogue, his favorite professor who taught him public speaking. Dodge confesses he was a very shy student, but Pogue gave him confidence. Dodge claims he took every course Pogue offered. Dodge was a popular student. He was President of his junior class as well as the Philaletheans, Holiness League, and Student Volunteers. He was also a debater and a member of the Philalethean basketball team. During his junior year, he and Eunice Davis of Little Valley, New York began a relationship which eventually led to their marriage in 1931. She had a double major in French and English, was President of the Thalonians and the Mnankas, Vice President of the sophomore class, and news editor of *The Echo*. Eunice Davis was very definite about overseas mission work. As a girl she had been impressed by a missionary serving in China.

The Gem

Eunice Davis Dodge as a student

Following graduation from Taylor, Ralph Dodge earned a graduate degree from Boston University's School of Theology, and the S.T.M. degree from the Hartford Seminary Foundation. Later in 1944 he earned a Ph.D. from that Connecticut institution. He held two pastorates in Massachusetts and North Dakota. At a church conference in North Dakota he became acquainted with overseas mission opportunities. In 1936 the Dodges learned that the Methodist Episcopal Church was looking for a young couple to take over the work in Luanda. They arrived in Luanda just before Christmas 1936, and they remained missionaries in Angola until 1950, interrupted only by World War II when they returned to the United States. Ralph Dodge was plagued by tropical diseases, particularly black water fever and malaria, and his doctor suggested he return to the United States for a furlough to regain his health. This was during the Second World War. Upon returning to Angola in 1946, the Dodges worked in northern Angola with the Dembos people who had not been Christianized. From 1950 to 1956, Ralph Dodge was the Executive Secretary for Africa, Board of Missions of The Methodist Church, New York City. In 1956 he was elected Bishop of Southern Africa with jurisdiction over Angola, Mozambique, and Southern Rhodesia. Dodge is proud of the fact that he was the first bishop to be elected by the people. Prior to that time the bishops were elected in the United States. His position between 1950 and 1956 had given him the opportunity to travel widely and to become well-known in southern Africa.

Dodge wanted to become involved in the lives of the people he was serving. While the early missionaries took their own food and provisions with them when making the rounds, Dodge accepted the hospitality of the Africans. This made a great impact on the people, and demonstrated the confidence he had in them. Dodge believed that the time had arrived when the church needed to turn over administrative responsibility to Africans. This had major repercussions in white-ruled Southern Rhodesia. If Africans could have leadership in the Church, why not in politics and economics? Dodge went against the status quo by sending a number of Africans to the United States for university degrees, and making Jonah Kawadza, father of future Taylor student John Kawadza, his administrative assistant. Although Dodge was reelected bishop in 1964, he was expelled by the Rhodesian white minority government led by Ian Smith.

Dodge is the author of three books which had a significant impact on the church in Southern Rhodesia (Zimbabwe) as well as in the United States. They were *The Unpopular Missionary* (1964), *The Pagan Church* (1968), and *The Revolutionary Bishop (1986).*[32] This last book is his autobiography and has an introduction by Bishop Abel Muzorewa, Dodge's successor, and political leader of Zimbabwe Rhodesia prior to the country's full independence in 1980.

Dodge represents the modern missionary with his/her emphasis on equality for Africans and a greater sensitivity to their culture and heritage. In *Rise Up and Walk,* the autobiography of Bishop Abel Muzorewa, the following comments about the impact of this famed Taylor alumnus appear:

> In 1956 we welcomed Dr. Ralph E. Dodge as our new bishop... From the start we knew he wanted to change things. As he spoke to the pastors, he said, 'I would like to visit all of you, my brothers, in your circuits and get to know the people and the Church well. But I am going to be radical. I will not carry any food when I come to visit you. I will come and stay with you in your homes, wherever you are. I know that is the African custom and we will observe it.'...
>
> Bishop Dodge's radicalism continued to be manifested in his sermons, teaching, conversations and above all in his example. In former years missionaries and African Church workers ate in separate dining-rooms during Church conferences, only joining together for worship and discussions. Saying nothing,

God's Ordinary People:

Bishop and Mrs. Dodge merely went to eat with the African ministers and laymen. One day the Annual Conference delegates were going to the dedication of a new church. Missionaries jumped into their cars while Africans boarded a hired bus. Many were embarrassed as the bishop boarded the bus with his African pastors.

I, and many others, will never forget that it was Bishop Ralph Dodge who had the vision and determination to crash through the barrier to higher education for Zimbabweans. He secured funds so that more than one hundred of us could go to Europe or America for study. It was he who encouraged those selected to train not only for teaching, journalism, law and medicine, but also for Christian ministry.[33]

In commenting about Dodge's deportation from Southern Rhodesia in July 1964, Muzorewa observed:

His [Dodge's] words to us at Old Umtali reminded me of Jesus' final words to his disciples, as he encouraged us to continue with the fight for justice and peace. In reply the people said to the beloved bishop: Deportation has only taken your flesh, but not your spirit. You have speeded up the educational, medical, and African leadership in church work. We wish you a speedy return to take up the unfinished task.

At the airport farewell I met my old friend Darius Jijita who had, like so many others, drifted away from the Church as he became active in politics. He was there not because he loved the Church but because he admired what Bishop Dodge stood for. Upon seeing the bishop again and the support of the people for him, Jijita resolved to return to the Church and today [1978] he is a staunch leader.

Little did the white regime realize what was happening in those days. Although they expelled anyone who spoke out courageously for justice, by that action they stimulated hundreds of churchmen to take up the torch in the struggle to end discrimination.[34]

No Ordinary Heritage

Dickson A. Mungazi, Professor of Education at Northern Arizona University and originally from Zimbabwe, has written a book entitled *The Honoured Crusade Ralph Dodge's Theology of Liberation and Initiative for Social* Change *in Zimbabwe.* Mungazi noted in his preface that:

> Few individuals have had a greater impact on social change in Zimbabwe than Ralph Edward Dodge. The fourteen years that he spent as a Methodist missionary in Angola from 1936 to 1950, and the eight years that he spent as the episcopal leader of the Methodist Church in Zimbabwe from 1956 to 1968, were destined to help alter the structure of the colonial society and pave the way for the advent of a black government that Ian Smith, the last colonial prime minister, vowed to stop from becoming a reality in his life-time.[35]

Dodge saw his main contribution to encourage Africans to get an education. Dodge encouraged Muzorewa to study in the United States. He also was instrumental in persuading and arranging for William James Humbane, his secretary and chauffeur, to come to Taylor University for his education. Dodge was present at the Taylor commencement in 1971 when Humbane received his degree. Humbane then went on for his Ph.D. at Ball State University. He returned to Africa where he is currently Executive Secretary of the Methodist Church's Africa Church Growth and Development Project. Other Zimbabwean students who were encouraged by Dodge to study at Taylor were Josiah Njagu, and Paul and Silas Kasambira.

Dodge also maintained contact with many African leaders. Agostinho Neto, former President of Angola, was a friend. Dodge noted that his father was a Methodist pastor in a Luanda church. Dodge bemoaned the fact that Neto was forced to seek aid from the Eastern bloc because the American government did not support his government.

After 1964, Dodge served as chaplain at the Mindolo Ecumenical Institute in Kitwe, Zambia. Mrs. Dodge served as field treasurer for the World Division of the Board of Missions in Zambia. From 1974 to 1976 he headed a church-wide Bishops' Call for Peace and Self-Development of People. This involved a trip around the world. Later, for nine months in 1979-80, Dodge replaced Bishop Muzorewa in church administration while he was a leader of Zimbabwe Rhodesia.

Eunice Dodge died in 1982, and Bishop Dodge remarried in 1984 to Elizabeth (Beth) Law. They live at the Christian Advent Village in Dowling Park, Florida. Two of Bishop Dodge's sons attended Taylor as well as a grandson and granddaughter. In 1957 he was named Alumnus of the Year, and in 1989 he received the Legion of Honor award from his alma mater. Dodge expressed his gratitude, "Taylor helped me to grow up. It gave me a sense of a certain amount of independence. I found my wife at Taylor."[36]

In an interview conducted with Ralph and Eunice Dodge by the editor of the *Taylor University Magazine* in 1981, Bishop Dodge made the following observations regarding what he might have done differently:

> I would say the biggest mistake... was that when we went out as new missionaries we did not buck the tide and learn the indigenous language of Angola. The Portuguese did not allow us to use it at all, and therefore we learned and used the Portuguese language. As I see it, that has been the main weakness in my missionary career in that I understood a certain amount but never really became conversant in the language of the people. In other words, we ministered mainly through the European media of the colonial empire of that era.[37]

Dodge also noted in the interview that "without realizing it, one can weaken his or her personal Christian witness by completely identifying with any culture." That also includes the American culture. In answering what was his most rewarding experience, Bishop Dodge said:

> Historians may evaluate differently but one of the most creative things in which we participated was the opening of the Dembos region in Angola to the Gospel. I had the privilege of actively assigning the first pastors and evangelists to the region in the late thirties. The whole region was evangelized with literally thousands (mainly youth) coming to the Church through a meaningful encounter with Christ as Lord and Savior. Personal lifestyles changed as the Gospel made its impact on the people.
>
> The most rewarding experience for any missionary is in witnessing the change that occurs when an individual commits his life to Jesus Christ. To have had a part in the positive changes which have taken place in Africa through the development of responsible leaders is most rewarding. [38]

MARSHALL AND LOIS NEES MURPHREE

Earlier missionaries than the Dodges to southern Africa who represented some of the earlier views towards Africans were Marshall and Lois Nees Murphree from the class of 1917. Marshall Murphree was born in Oneonta, Alabama in 1890.[39] His father was a minister. Marshall spent one year at the University of Chattanooga, two years at Taylor University (1916 and 1917), and from 1918 to 1920 studied at the Boston University School of Theology where he received the degree of Bachelor of Religious Education. His wife, Lois (Azalia) Nees, was born in Terre Haute, Indiana in 1898. She spent two years (1914-16) at Olivet University, two years at Taylor (1916 and 1917), and then studied at the Boston

Marshall and Lois Murphree and son,
Marshall W. - missionaries to Southern
Rhodesia (Zimbabwe)

University School of Theology (1918-19). She was a gifted pianist and vocalist. In 1920 Marshall and Lois Murphree were appointed missionaries of the Methodist Episcopal Church and began service in Southern Rhodesia (Zimbabwe).

Rev. Marshall Murphree was principal of the Hartzell Training School and the Hartzell Theological School at Old Umtali. He and his wife served 37 years in Southern Rhodesia. He was also superintendent of the Old Umtali district of the Methodist Church, director of Christian education for the Rhodesia Methodist Conference, manager of the Rhodesia Mission Press, and director of programs for strengthening Christian family life. He was known by the Africans as "Baba" ("Father") Murphree, and was viewed with awe and even some fear by the Africans.[40] In his obituary (he died in 1966 in Oneonta, Alabama) it was noted:

> Dr. Murphree's name was almost synonymous with Old Umtali Mission for he served there as a missionary for almost all of his 37 years of service to the Rhodesia Annual Conference. For many years he was its principal. But probably he will be best remembered for his great work in

188

ministerial training. He founded the Hartzell Theological Seminary which has produced most of our active ministers in Rhodesia. Students came also from the Congo and from Mozambique... One of Dr. Murphree's great loves was the camp meeting, and these became one of the most distinctive features of Methodism in Rhodesia.[41]

Today Old Umtali (Mutare) is the site of the recently established Africa University.

Mrs. Murphree was described as a quiet woman.[42] She was a teacher in the mission schools of Old Umtali. She sang, wrote a number of hymns in the vernacular and set them to African music. In recognition of her contribution to Christian hymnology, she was elected a member of the Hymn Society of America.

The Murphrees had a daughter and two sons. One son, Dr. Marshall W. Murphree, was a renowned professor of sociology at

Lois Murphree teaching in Old Umtali.

189

the University of Zimbabwe, and an authority of the independent church movement in Zimbabwe. He is the author of *Christianity and the Shona* (University of London, Athlone Press; New York, Humanities Press, 1969). A daughter, Mrs. Verna Culver, was a missionary in Zimbabwe; her daughter, Tara, taught with the English Department at Taylor University and was also Dean of Instruction in the early 1980s. Other members of the family have attended Taylor as students.

Bishop Abel Muzorewa in *Rise Up and Walk* recalled several interesting anecdotes about the Murphrees. Like many early missionaries, Murphree was not fluent in the indigenous language and thus from time to time had to rely on African translators. Muzorewa sometimes was cast into that role. He related a humorous incident involving Murphree:

> I [Muzorewa] bear a marked resemblance to my father. Laughingly, my father likes to relate the story of the church gathering which he attended when I acted as interpreter for a senior missionary, the late Dr. M.J. Murphree. At the end of the meeting many people gathered around my father to congratulate him on his brilliant performance as an interpreter![43]

As a boy, Muzorewa loved to imitate other people:

> My parents tell how about the age of four I became an accomplished mimic, imitating their actions and those of others with hilarious accuracy. Dr. Murphree, the missionary preacher, was one whom I loved to imitate. My congregation would be dried twigs stuck in rows in the sand. The double-bladed leaves of the *musekesa* tree served as my Bible. Remembering his sermon about the parable of Dives and Lazarus, I would stand before my 'congregation', and my childish voice would ring out in Shona in the characteristic tone of Dr. Murphree, 'Are you rich up there, Dives?' When other children came near the scene, I would immediately insist

that they join my 'congregation'-grateful for a live audience!
Others marvelled at how I could remember and repeat every
syllable of the preacher's words over and over again.[44]

Muzorewa showed how the earlier missionaries, perhaps without
realizing it, could cause misunderstandings and bitterness between
the Africans and themselves. He related such an incident with
Murphree. After his graduation from the Hartzell Theological
School, Muzorewa's first appointment was as Assistant Conference
Evangelist to Murphree, and then as a pastor. Muzorewa recalled
that the people of his congregation were scattered over a wide area:

> I realized immediately that careful and systematic visiting
> from church to church would be required if I were to serve
> effectively as a pastor to so many. All I possessed for transport
> was a bicycle. I remembered with some bitterness the day
> when I asked Dr. Murphree to sell me one of his three cars,
> only to have him refuse, saying that I could not afford to
> maintain it. Probably that assessment was correct, but I would
> have preferred to make it myself![45]

Yet Muzorewa also acknowledged his indebtedness to the Western
missionaries:

> Today [1978] it is the living example of my teachers more
> than their formal teaching that remains impressed on my
> memory. Dr. M.J. Murphree, our principal, was a conservative
> but exceptionally well-experienced man. His wife Lois gave
> us a love for music and Christian education which was later
> to become my field of graduate study.[46]

OTHER TAYLOR ALUMNI SERVING AS METHODIST MISSIONARIES IN AFRICA

Several other Taylor alumni began serving as Methodist
missionaries in Africa before the 1950s. N. Leota Ratcliffe Hapgood
was an early Methodist missionary to Liberia (see Chapter Five).

Other single women missionaries have included Ila May Scovill (class of 1924) and Marguerite Deyo (class of 1931). In more recent times the list includes Rev. and Mrs. Charles Melvin Blake (class of 1940) and Kenneth D. Enright (class of 1945). An example of a Free Methodist missionary to Africa is Marie Heinemann (class of 1938) of Huron, South Dakota. (See Appendix for brief biographical sketches of these missionaries). In more recent times scores of Taylor alumni have or are serving as missionaries in Africa mainly with denominations or groups other than the Methodists. A future study needs to be conducted with this group. The unique relationship between Africa and Taylor University continues.

TAYLOR UNIVERSITY ALUMNI AS METHODIST MISSIONARIES TO ASIA

The Methodist Episcopal Church in the early years focused on China, India, and Latin America, and to a lesser extent Japan and the Philippines, and these areas attracted several Taylor alumni.

CHINA: Dr. and Mrs. Robert Ellsworth Brown

More Taylor alumni went to China as Methodist missionaries than any other area of the world. Early Methodist missionaries to China included Mr. and Mrs. Horace Robson, Clara Carris, Martha McCutheon, Cora Rahe, Clara Sauer, Floy Hurlbut, Ethel Householder, Jessie Edwards, and Rev. J. Theron Illick.

Perhaps the most famous Taylor alumni to serve as Methodist missionaries to China were Dr. and Mrs. Robert Ellsworth Brown. Robert Brown was born in Lyons, Kansas in 1886 but attended public schools in Illinois including Danville High School.[47] He joined the Methodist Episcopal Church in 1900. He came to Taylor

University in the fall of 1905 but then taught school for two years, reentering Taylor in 1907. He then went on to the University of Illinois and in 1910 graduated from that institution. During his senior year he taught zoology. Brown returned to Taylor, taught chemistry and physics for five years (1910-14) and was chair of the science department. Burt Ayres, Dean of the College, recalled that Brown was also the school's Registrar. He referred to Brown as a man of "genuine human kindness."[48]   B.R.

General Commission on Archives and History - UMC

Dr. and Mrs. Robert Brown and two sons

Opper, a student at Taylor at the time and a future missionary to India, noted that Brown "was a good teacher, humble and godly."[49] Brown then left Taylor to finish his medical training in preparation for missionary work in China. He received his M.D. degree from the University of Michigan in 1916. The Browns would later make Ann Arbor, Michigan their home.

While at Taylor as a student, Brown married Carrie Mae Willis in 1907. She was born in Danville, Illinois in 1888, and joined the Methodist Episcopal Church in 1902. She had one year of business training as well as Bible training. She attended Taylor University in 1907-8 and was a Student Volunteer. Carrie Mae Brown also taught Latin and music. In 1908 and 1909 she studied at the University of Illinois.

In 1917 the Browns were accepted as missionaries of the Board of Foreign Missions, and sailed for China in June of 1918. They worked in China until 1946. Dr. Brown worked at the Wuhu General Hospital and by September 1924 was its Superintendent General, serving in that position into the late 1930s. Carrrie Brown was involved in evangelistic work in Wuhu.

Under the leadership of Dr. Brown, the Wuhu Hospital situated on a hill overlooking the Yangtze River became famous. It was in an area plagued by famine and floods for decades. For his work he was decorated by the Chinese government of Chiang Kai-shek. In the fall of 1931, Colonel and Mrs. Charles Lindbergh visited the hospital. The January 30, 1932 issue of *The Echo* ran an article about this visit featuring a photograph of the Lindberghs with Dr. Brown and other members of his hospital staff. During the invasion of China by Japan in the 1930s, the Browns witnessed Japanese atrocities, and they cared for thousands of war victims. In an address at Christ Methodist Church, New York City on February 25, 1941, Dr. Brown gave a detailed description of the Japanese atrocities in China. The Browns faced hostility from both communists and the Japanese invaders. *The Toronto Daily Star* in its October 19, 1940 edition carried an article with photographs entitled "White Doctor Carries On Under Fire, Defies Jap Troops at Bayonet Point, Makes Pals of China's Toughest Warriors." In the article Brown recounted his attempts to save Chinese women from Japanese soldiers. The article noted:

> The women had sought the mission compound as a refuge against Japanese soldiers. It was while protecting these

women that Dr. Brown experienced the bayonet incident. For
two hours he stood firm while a ring of soldiers held bayonets
to his body, demanding that the women be given up to the
soldiers...

Brown noted that "much of my time was spent in rescuing women
and bringing them to the hospital. A man would sneak past the
Japs and tell me where his wife was hiding under a bed or some
place and I'd go out with my car and get her and bring her safely
past the Japanese." *The Toronto Daily Star* article continued:

Dr. Brown's exploits have won him the reputation in China
of being the man who tackles and does the impossible. He
speaks in modest and sweepingly casual generalities. He's to
a large extent responsible for the fact that the Burma road is
running today for part of the Burma road cuts through a part
of Yunnan province.

And that part of Yunnan province ... was badly infested with
malaria when the Burma road began operating. It was so bad
that nine out of 10 men who stayed there any length of time
during the rainy season got malaria...

Now thanks to Dr. Brown who went there at the request of
Generalissimo Chiang Kai-shek and a staff of other doctors
and specialists ... it is rapidly becoming safe...

The New York Times (December 1937) ran an extensive article with
the headline "Nanking Prepares to Resist Attack." The article noted
that "Dr. Robert Brown of Wuhu, American medical missionary,
has arrived in Nanking to present to Chinese authorities a plan for
a Wuhu safety zone... Dr. Brown heads the foreign safety zone
committee at Wuhu, where there are now more foreigners than in
Nanking..."[50]

In the late 1930s Dr. Brown was called upon by the Chinese
government and by various international bodies to survey health,

sanitation and hospital needs in western China. He traveled as a liaison officer to coordinate the work of the medical missions of the 268 mission hospitals with the medical work of the Chinese Red Cross, the army medical service, the International Red Cross, and the American-British Relief funds in order to see how the relief work could be enlarged. He was also made Director of the Medical Center in Chengtu (Chengdu), west China, an area still unoccupied

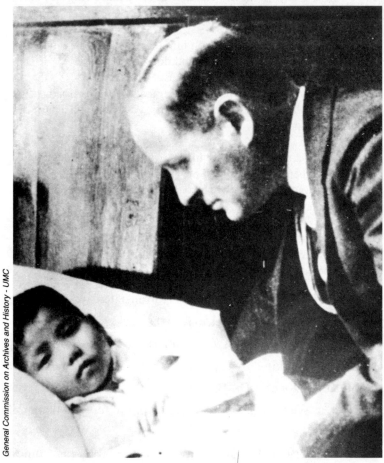

General Commission on Archives and History - UMC

Dr. Robert Brown and young Chinese patient

by the Japanese but subject to repeated bombings. This was a significant position because a number of universities and schools were forced to move to this city with the onslaught of the Japanese military.

The Browns remained Methodist missionaries until 1943 when they withdrew from service. After that time he served as medical officer of the China Travel Service, with the United States Army, and as medical advisor to the Chinese government in 1945. In 1946 the Browns moved to Los Angeles, California, where he served on the staff of the Pacific Home until his death in 1948.

The Browns kept in touch with Taylor University. They were close friends with Dr. Burt W. Ayres and Miss Sadie Miller. Brown also wrote to Dr. Robert Stuart, Taylor's President (one of the letters appeared in the *Taylor University Bulletin,* September 1931). Dr. Brown spoke at Taylor in the spring of 1930, and in 1934 Taylor conferred upon him the honorary degree of Doctor of Science.[51] Again in 1941 Dr. Brown spoke to Taylor's students and faculty about conditions and needs in China.

JAPAN: Dr. Epperson Robert Fulkerson

Japanese Christians and the Taylor University community has also developed a special relationship. Through the decades a number of Japanese students have studied at Taylor. Two of the earliest Taylor alumni or faculty members serving as overseas missionaries were Leonora and Mabel K. Seeds (see Chapter Five) who worked in Japan for a number of years. An affiliation was developed between Taylor and The Chinzei Gakwan Seminary in Nagasaki between 1898 and 1902. The four Taylor University catalogues between those dates contained descriptions similar to the following 1898-9 entry:

God's Ordinary People:

E. R. FULKERSON

FORMERLY OF JAPAN

A PENNSYLVANIAN by birth; educated at Simpson College and Taylor University; licensed to preach at 20.

SERVED as pastor in Arkansas and Nebraska.

FOR 20 YEARS a missionary of the Methodist Episcopal Church in Japan—Educator and preacher.

PROFESSOR in Anglo-Japanese College, Tokyo.

DEAN of Chinzei Gakuin and Principal of Chinzei Gakuin Academy, Nagasaki.

U. S. VICE-CONSUL at port of Nagasaki during Spanish-American War.

CHARTER MEMBER of South Japan Mission Conference.

HONORED by degrees of Ph.D., LL.D. and Litt.D. by American colleges.

HAS TRAVELLED extensively through the East—Studied, written and lectured on conditions and problems of Asia—In great demand as a speaker.

IN 1928-29 visited the Far East and studied the new political, social, economic, and religious conditions.

RECOGNIZED as one of America's leading authorities on the Far East, and as a speaker of unusual ability.

DR. FULKERSON speaks on these subjects: "Facing the Issue", "The Unfinished Task", "Religion's Broken Witness", "Woman's Contribution to World Redemption", "Christianity or Communism in China", "Old Wine in New Bottles", "Japan's Contribution to Modern Civilization", "Potential India", "The Next Great Fight", "The Rising Church in Non-Christian Lands".

COME AND HEAR HIM

Advertisement notice of an address given by E. R. Fulkerson

No Ordinary Heritage

The Chinzei Seminary

We believe that Taylor University is the only Methodist School that has an associated College in a foreign country. The Chinzei Gakwan (Seminary) is the largest Methodist school in Japan and began last year [1897] to receive diplomas from our University. It maintains a comprehensive course of study and the enrollment for the past term has been 125 students. The report comes to us that every boarding student in the past year has sought and found Christ. Rev. E.R. Fulkerson, Ph.D. Litt.D. is the President of the Seminary.

This relationship was no doubt fostered by Dr. Epperson Robert Fulkerson (1859-1940), a missionary of the Methodist Episcopal Church in Japan for more than twenty years, nearly all of the time in connection with educational work.[52] He was born in Newcastle, Pennsylvania, and did his educational work at Simpson College and Taylor University, the latter institution granting him the degree of doctor of philosophy in 1897, and doctor of literature in 1898. Accompanied by his wife, Fulkerson first sailed to Japan in 1887, and after a few months in Yokohama, joined the faculty of the Anglo-Japanese College in Tokyo. Two years later he moved to Nagasaki where he took up work in Chinzei Seminary which was considered the most important Methodist school in south Japan. From 1894 to 1906 he was Principal of the Seminary and Dean from 1906 to 1907. During the Spanish-American War, Fulkerson served as Vice-Consul for the United States in Nagasaki.

Fulkerson left Japan in 1907 mainly due to health problems (he also lost his first wife; she died in Nagasaki in 1903). By this time the special relationship between Taylor and Chinzei Gakuin had ended. But it is interesting to note the seminary's early history and the tragic events that were to take place in its future. Chinzei Gakuin (also spelled Chinzei Gakkwan) or Methodist Academy

199

and Biblical Training School began in October 1881 with twelve male students and three departments (preparatory, collegiate, and theological). Its 1896-7 catalogue noted Fulkerson to be the principal and chairman of the faculty and with the following objective:

> The object of the school is to furnish a liberal education on Christian principles, particular attention being given to the formation of right character. The design is to meet the needs of the Japanese and to fit young men for the highest usefulness.[53]

On the other side of the road in Nagasaki there developed a school for girls known as Kwassui Jokakko. There was much faculty exchange between the schools. In 1908 the middle school department of Chinzei Gakuin corresponding to an American high school was given full recognition by the Japanese government. Thus graduates of Chinzei Gakuin had the doors of all government colleges and universities open to them. When the school lost its buildings in a fire in 1924, it moved to the northern suburbs of Nagasaki where a spacious campus allowed for it to expand its student enrollment. In the 1930s, thanks in part to gifts from supporters in the United States, it had a modern four-story facility with 25 classrooms, well-equipped laboratories, and an auditorium with 800 seats (the student enrollment by this time was 400). Tragically the school lost everything in the atomic bomb attack on Nagasaki on August 8, 1945. Five teachers and 130 students perished instantly from the blast and additional people died as a result of radioactivity. Many of the surviving teachers and students lost their entire families. Principal Taneo Chiba, a graduate of Ohio Wesleyan University and Garrett Biblical Institute, was seriously wounded and finally died from the effects of the bomb in 1950.

The school then moved to Isahaya in the spring of 1946, some sixteen miles to the north of Nagasaki. By 1950 it had a student enrollment of 700 including some 250 girls.

Dr. Fulkerson returned to the United States in 1907 and served as a field representative of the Methodist Board of Foreign Missions until his retirement in 1935. During that time he traveled throughout the United States and was in demand as a speaker. An advertisement noted that some of the subjects on which he spoke included "Christianity or Communism in China", "Japan's Contribution to Modern Civilization", "Potential India", and "The Rising Church in Non-Christian Lands." He visited Taylor in 1933. The October 20, 1933 issue of *The Echo* noted that Fulkerson spoke in the college chapel, explaining Japan's importance in world relations. The same year Fulkerson founded the American Institute of Applied Psychology in his home town of Canon City, Colorado where he remained until his death in 1940.

Another Taylor Methodist alumnus who served in Japan in the 1920s was Mark R. Shaw (see Appendix).

THE PHILIPPINES: Dr. and Mrs. Joshua Frank Cottingham

A number of Taylor students have come from the Philippines, and have returned as missionaries. These individuals will be discussed in the last chapter of this book, but two significant Taylor alumni prior to 1945 who were missionaries to the Philippines deserve mention. Dr. and Mrs. Joshua Frank Cottingham were in the class of 1908. Rev. Cottingham was born in Butler County, Kansas in 1874.[54] He received his education at Moore's Hill College (now University of Evansville), and Taylor University. Mrs. Cottingham (Bertha D. DeVer), from Milan, Indiana, was born in

1878. They had been married eight years before entering Taylor, and decided to mortgage their home in order to do so. While students at Taylor, they signed cards of the Student Volunteer Movement with the intention of becoming missionaries to the Philippines.

The Cottinghams left for Asia in 1910. For ten years they labored in rural parts of the Philippines before being transferred to Manila where in 1920 Rev. Cottingham became superintendent of the Manila district with 250 preachers under his auspices. The total Methodist church membership in that district at the time was 11,500 people with some 41 churches. He was also Professor of Greek at Union Theological Seminary, Manila, from 1926 to 1928. Mrs. Cottingham was Dean of Women at Union Theological Seminary, Manila. She also served as Vice President of the Women's Conference of the Philippine Islands Mission of the Methodist Episcopal Church.

Dr. Joshua Frank Cottingham, missionary to the Philippines

According to an *Echo* article in 1934 (April 13), "...thousands of souls have been won for Christ through their ministry and their work has been one of lasting impression upon the people of the islands." The *Taylor University Bulletin* of December 1934 noted some 22,000 were won to Christ and baptized by the Cottinghams. He was described as a gifted speaker.

The Cottinghams kept close contact with their alma mater by speaking at the University during furloughs. In 1934 at a special meeting of Taylor's Board of Directors of the Alumni Association,

Rev. Cottingham was elected its Executive Secretary and field representative. His desire was to make the 1935 commencement a great gathering of alumni, particularly focusing on the class of fifty years earlier and all students of the old Fort Wayne College. Cottingham was a member of the faculty of the Biblical and Religious Education Department in the mid-1930s and was popular with the student body. He frequently was invited to give addresses as for example the interdenominational youth conference which was noted in the April 13, 1934 issue of *The Echo*. The fall 1933 revival meetings were led by President Robert Stuart and Dr. Cottingham. Cottingham died in Spiceland, Indiana in 1939; Mrs. Cottingham continued to live in Indiana until her death in Indianapolis in 1951.

INDIAN SUBCONTINENT: Vere Walford Abbey

Several outstanding alumni have served as Methodist missionaries in the Indian subcontinent including Emma Knowles, Charles and Elizabeth Hastings Scharer, Vere Abbey, Cora Fales, Olive Dunn, L. Chester and Emma Tanner Lewis, Kathryne Bieri, Arthur and Esta Herrmann Howard, Alice McClellan, J. Wascom Pickett, and Mrs. Marybeth Smith Hunt. Several of these missionaries are included in either Chapter Five or the Appendix along with two non-Methodist missionaries, Burt R. Opper and Paul Clasper.

Vere Abbey (1894-1943) was born in Carbondale, Pennsylvania, the son of Mr. and Mrs. Merritt O. Abbey (Merritt Abbey was for years the head of the maintenance department at Taylor).[55] Vere Abbey's sisters are Iris Abbey and Eloise Abbey Fenstermacher, both of whom are presently residing at the Warren

Home. Vere Abbey joined the Methodist Episcopal Church in 1902, and entered Taylor University the fall of 1910. He was in a variety of student activities including The Student Volunteers, President of the Philalethean Literary Society, President of the Prayer Band, violinist in the University Orchestra, Holiness League, on the *Echo* staff, bass in the Male Quartette and Mixed Quartette, President of the junior class, and an excellent debater. He was a chemistry major and received his AB degree in 1916. It can be said that Abbey showed enthusiasm in whatever he undertook.

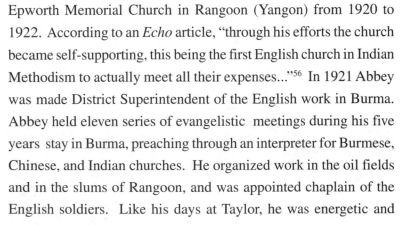

The Gem

Vere Walford Abbey, missionary to Burma and India

Following graduation, Abbey taught high school for one year in Minnesota and then pastored a Methodist Episcopal Church in Colman, South Dakota from 1917 to 1920. In 1917 he married Jessie Woodward Norman. Vere Abbey's heart was in overseas missions. In 1920 he and his wife sailed for Burma (Myanmar). He served as pastor of the Epworth Memorial Church in Rangoon (Yangon) from 1920 to 1922. According to an *Echo* article, "through his efforts the church became self-supporting, this being the first English church in Indian Methodism to actually meet all their expenses..."[56] In 1921 Abbey was made District Superintendent of the English work in Burma. Abbey held eleven series of evangelistic meetings during his five years stay in Burma, preaching through an interpreter for Burmese, Chinese, and Indian churches. He organized work in the oil fields and in the slums of Rangoon, and was appointed chaplain of the English soldiers. Like his days at Taylor, he was energetic and enthusiastic.

Abbey kept up a steady stream of correspondence with Taylor, particularly with *The Echo*. In a letter which appeared in The *Echo* in the February 28, 1925 issue, Abbey noted:

> Dearest Folks:
>
> You will be thinking that I've forgotten entirely that I have a family to write to, but such is not the case. This last month has been an awful rush and strain... This has been the best year of our work anyway. There had been more evangelism and greater results..... Our after dinner meetings around the tables as we all ate together were times of real power and blessing. Seemed like Taylor.

Abbey then went on to state his concern about financial cutbacks.

> I doubt if the home church ever realizes what this is meaning to us out here. We who were sent out to the field by the church at home, assured of a living and enough to carry on the work, now left in a position where we have to give out of our pittances to carry on the work that has to be done.
>
> I know this is plain speaking, but if you had been through this past two weeks with me you would feel as I do. Can't you put this on the hearts of the people there? Can't some one send out a couple of hundred dollars to keep the Burmese preacher in the field where he can win his hundreds to Christ? He has the gift and vision of evangelism. I've worked with him and I know, and yet for lack of funds we have to close the doors of opportunity. But above all, please get the folks there praying for us. Our situation in India is going to be desperate. I can't see any way through except in God. Forgive me if I seem harsh. I'm not, but the load is greater than we can bear alone. Although I could get my full allowance, as mine comes from the church here, I don't feel like taking what the others can't take, and so we put all in the pot together. It doesn't leave us very much to go on. However we are doing the best we can and we are leaving the rest to God. We got the word

from the Board that no one could go on furlough this year, nor could any one at home come to the field. That makes my furlough an impossibility.[57]

Vere Abbey also expressed the view that his wish was to be an evangelist, not an administrator as he was required to do as District Superintendent.

Abbey was disgruntled with the state of Methodist missions, and this came to a critical point when the Abbeys returned to the United States on furlough in 1925 and withdrew from the service of the Methodist Board of Foreign Missions in December 1927. While on furlough, Vere Abbey took graduate work at Drew Seminary and received his Master's degree at the Hartford School of Missions in Connecticut. It was while there that he formed contacts with the Indian Christian Endeavor Society. He became actively involved with the Christian Endeavor Society, and lectured extensively on their behalf throughout the eastern part of this country. In 1929 the Abbeys returned to the Indian subcontinent under that Society. He was General Superintendent of the Christian Endeavor work in India, Burma, and Ceylon. The same year *The Echo* staff elected Vere Abbey to its Hall of Fame.

The Echo in its November 27, 1929 issue printed an excerpt of a letter written by the Abbeys soon after their return to India:

> We completed our first month's tour a few days ago... We traveled 1,920 miles by train, lorry, Ford, and tonga (a two-wheeled contraption). We slept (?) in eighteen beds, three nights on trains, and one night on the benches of the waiting-room of the railway station. We have held twenty-six rallies, one convention (provincial), and eleven officers and leaders meetings. We have had an attendance of about 2,600 at the rallies, 300 at the leaders' meetings, and about 600 at the convention. As a partial result of our contacts, we know of at least ten societies in process of being started. So our time has been fairly well spent.

It's a great job and we are enjoying it every bit.

Unfortunately this hectic pace broke his health, and in 1938 after ten years in India, Abbey was forced to return home. He accepted a Presbyterian pastorate in Freedom, Pennsylvania but never fully regained his health. Less than a year after being installed as pastor of that church, he died in 1943 at the age of 49.

CONCLUSION

Since the 1950s, some Taylor University graduates have continued to serve as Methodist overseas missionaries. However, more significant numerically have been alumni working with non-Methodist Church groups. The experiences of their extraordinary contributions in Christ's mission will be left for a future research project.

Brief biographical sketches of other Taylor alumni who have served as overseas Methodist missionaries including Ila May Scovill and Marguerite Deyo (Zimbabwe), Rev. Charles Melvin Blake and Mrs. Doris Brown Blake (Angola), Kenneth D. Enright (Zaire), Marie Heinemann (Free Methodist missionary in Burundi), J. Theron Illick (China), Mark Shaw (Japan), LeRoy Chester and Emma Tanner Lewis (India), Arthur and Esta Herrman Howard (India), Walter and Anna Skow Oliver (Panama), and Charles Raymond and Lois Allen Illick (Mexico) as well as non-Methodists Burton Raymond and Hazel Newlon Opper (India), and Paul and Helen Aleshouse Clasper (Burma and Hong Kong) are included in an Appendix at the end of this work.

Chapter Five "To the Corners of the Earth: In Bishop Taylor's Footsteps - Women in Ministry" will explore the experiences of several additional Taylor women alumni who served as early Methodist missionaries in India, China, Japan, and Liberia.

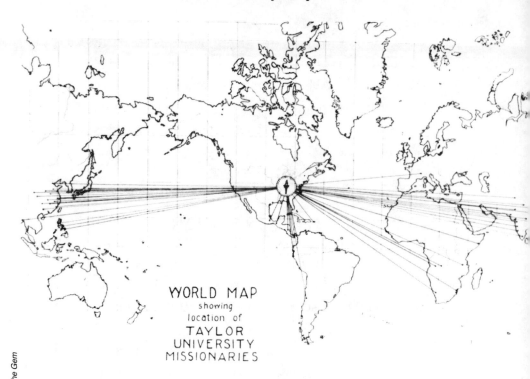

WORLD MAP
showing
location of
TAYLOR
UNIVERSITY
MISSIONARIES

The Gem

A map showing the location of Taylor graduates who served on the
mission field was placed in the front of the chapel in the early 1920s.

TO THE CORNERS OF THE EARTH:
IN BISHOP TAYLOR'S FOOTSTEPS - WOMEN IN MINISTRY

he college constituency which has the greatest potential for impacting the world beyond the borders of the institution is the alumni. In the past one hundred fifty years a large number of women have left the halls of Fort Wayne College and Taylor University eager to contribute their talents in the larger world.

They have literally journeyed to all the corners of the earth. Married and single they have taken with them a strong faith in God and a deep commitment to serve humanity. Many of them became servant leaders in their homes, churches and professions.

During the first few decades of the twentieth century, Taylor University was a place where the cause of world wide evangelism was constantly kept before the student body. A large map of the world showing the places where Taylor graduates served had been placed in front of the chapel following a visit to campus by Ethel Householder, a missionary alumnus who was on furlough from China. She suggested that this would be a way for the students to stay in touch with the Taylor alumni who were presently serving as missionaries. Professors Olive Draper and Sadie Miller had directed the students in the creation of the map, and the day it was put in place there was a special chapel service. All the Taylor missionaries were identified by name and a brief description of their work was given. Students and faculty were encouraged to adopt one of these missionaries and pray particularly for that person. In addition, there was a constant stream of missionary speakers in chapel. Many of these were connected in some way with the Methodist Episcopal Church. It is small wonder that many women as well as men chose to make missions their life work.

A significant number of women who were associated with Taylor either as students, graduates, or faculty members became missionaries with the sponsorship of the Methodist Episcopal Church. Those who were single normally went out under the auspices of the Women's Foreign Missionary Society (WFMS). The purpose of this association was "to engage and unite the efforts of Christian women in sending female missionaries to women in the foreign mission fields of the Methodist Episcopal Church, and in supporting them and native Christian teachers and Bible readers in those fields."[1]

EMMA L. KNOWLES

The earliest identified Methodist missionary to be associated with Taylor was Emma L. Knowles who was Preceptress and Instructor in Literature and Elocution at Fort Wayne College in 1879-81. During the summer of 1881 she read an advertisement asking for a woman teacher to volunteer to come to India and open a girl's school. Miss Isabella Thoburn, an early Women's Foreign Missionary Society appointee to India, had placed the advertisement in the *Christian Advocate*. Even though she was forty-one years old, Miss Knowles answered the advertisement. The two women met, and instead of returning to Fort Wayne, Miss Knowles sailed for India with Miss Thoburn at the end of 1881.

Knowles' first assignment was to the Kumaon District at Naini

Emma L. Knowles. Missionary to India.

Tal. Dr. and Mrs. Humphrey of the General Missionary Society had begun work in this region and Mrs. Humphrey had brought a few little girls who were old enough to learn to read to Naini Tal to educate them. She described the girls as "bright and promising" and said she believed that "the work of educating the children of native Christians is now our most important work." When Knowles arrived, her first task was to visit the *zenanas*, the part of an Indian household in which the women and girls of the family were secluded. The purpose of these visits was to establish trust and develop relationships with the girls and their mothers.

At the end of the first year of the school's operation, Miss Blackmar, another WFMS missionary, whose responsibility it was to make annual reports back to the home office, wrote:

> Miss Knowles has had a hard time for the first year, but has managed well, and came out nobly. I rejoice greatly that she is succeeding, but we knew she would. This year she has had nineteen boarders. This is the way all of our schools have been made, by degrees; and Miss Knowles' school will be one we shall be as proud of as we are of Miss Easton's. She must have a building.[2]

Knowles remained at Naini Tal until her first furlough in 1888. During those years, she succeeded in building a high quality educational institution for English-speaking Indian girls which provided education from the primary grades through high school. This was not an easy task beginning as she did with no suitable buildings and with a relatively small group of girls. However, by 1885 the WFMS had succeeded in purchasing a fine property in which to house the school, and Miss Knowles reported that though she had had "many discouragements" she was "now rejoicing in the prospect of great future usefulness."[3]

No Ordinary Heritage

Two years later enrollment had grown to such an extent that the school, which she had named Wellesley, was again suffering an overcrowding problem. The school numbered forty boarders and ten day pupils, but Knowles said the attendance could be increased if there were more space, and she expected to have part of a new building ready for occupancy before the rainy season set in.[4]

Buildings did not occupy all of Knowles' time and energy. She also expended considerable effort in making the curriculum strong. In her report to the WFMS in 1886, she stressed the quality of the education being provided. "Great importance" has been attached to "thorough primary work." The "Government Inspector's examination showed good attainment by the scholars and several were promoted to the higher grades." She was also able to report that there was a "good degree of religious interest," and the school had maintained "a high moral tone" which she predicted would provide "permanent strength of character" to the students.[5]

As she left on furlough she was able to report: "There has never been a year when teachers have done such good and faithful work here, nor when scholars have been more appreciative. I think every year finds them inclined to higher aims in life, finds them more true, more womanly." During the six years she had been in charge of the school, she had supervised the construction of several good buildings and had increased the enrollment by two-thirds. She had also improved the quality of the education the girls received and had provided a strong Christian witness which included the girls, their mothers and other women of the *zenanas*. It would appear that the WFMS confidence in her abilities was entirely justified.[6]

Although Knowles did not return to Naini Tal and Wellesley High School after her furlough, the school continued to prosper. A report filed with the WFMS in 1918 indicated a steady rise in enrollment and staff. There were ten class teachers and six music teachers, a principal and vice principal. Two years of college classes were added for a period of three years in the early part of the century. Since 1888 there had been an average of five per year who passed the Government High School examinations. Many of the girls had gone on to college to study medicine, become nurses, teachers, clerks, government school inspectors and missionaries. The school now had six buildings one of which was named "Emma Lodge."[7]

Until her death in 1924 at the age of 84, Knowles stayed in touch with the alumni of Wellesley who had been her students. Every year on June 28, Knowles' birthday, these students would gather at Wellesley's "Old Girl's Day" to write her a letter sending birthday greetings, and she always acknowledged their communication.[8]

When Knowles returned to India following her furlough she was sent to Calcutta to the Girls' High School where she was principal from 1890 to 1895. Miss Knowles kept this institution to the same high educational and spiritual standards she had developed at Wellesley. In writing of the school she said, "I think it safe to say that hundreds are either blessing the home, instructing the young, or serving in places of business, having received their preparation here."[9]

In 1895 Knowles left Calcutta to found her second school, Arcadia, located in Darjeeling. She remained there until her retirement in 1917. Knowles felt deeply that "it was God's plan for her" to start this school, and the WFMS gave their approval but had no money to contribute to the cause. Therefore, she borrowed one thousand rupees for furnishings, used her salary to pay the rent on a building and opened the school on the eleventh of March 1895 with thirteen pupils.[10]

In the spring of 1899 Knowles found herself in failing health and had to return to the United States. While she was gone Miss Stahl, another missionary took charge. At first, the work of the school seemed to prosper as before. There were forty girls in attendance, and one of these passed the matriculation examination of Calcutta University at the head of the list of all the girls' schools. However, that spring disaster struck. "Heavier rains than usual deluged the hillsides and simultaneously shocks of earthquake made it almost impossible for the teachers to get the children up the hill. All were saved except nine." Six of the children who died were from a single family. When this news reached the Executive Meeting of the WFMS in Cleveland, it was immediately moved to appropriate $20,000 to rebuild the school.[11]

Knowles returned to this devastation and though she must have been heart broken at the loss of life and property, she immediately set about putting Arcadia, now renamed Queens' Hill, back together. New property which already had two good buildings was secured at a cost of $20,000, and the Annual Report for 1900 indicated that the school was "coming back to its former status and prestige."[12]

In 1905 Knowles wrote an extended report on the school. She stressed the fact that the school was extremely healthy by all standards. Its enrollment had recovered and stabilized at about sixty boarders and twenty day students. The school had successfully added a small boys' department limited to no more than twenty at a time. She wrote "we think it is an advantage to have the stimulating influence of boys and girls in the classes." She hastened to add that they had separate living quarters and even separate playgrounds. Queens' Hill was under scrutiny by a number of different government agencies, but everything was proceeding normally, and Knowles was confident they would more than pass the examining officials' evaluation. Students continued to do well in examinations at all three levels. In addition, five students had taken the Trinity College Theory of Music Examination and all had passed with good results. Knowles noted, "These facts show that our school is keeping pace with the requirements of the Educational Code." She concluded her report with a statement of the purpose of the school:

> The aim of our school is higher than the secular work marked out for us. It is Christian culture. Ruskin [the English philosopher] speaks of Truth as one of the choicest materials in the building of character and upon this we try to found our daily work. Out of it surely grow natural courtesy, obedience, consideration for others, and all those graces which are so valuable to a noble womanhood.... So leaving the past, we enter upon the opportunities and responsibilities of 1905.[13]

In the 1906 report, Knowles included several testimonials from parents which demonstrated the high esteem in which the school was held. One man had had his daughter in Queens' Hill for six years and wrote he had no desire to change her. "We regard the school as a place where not only a good sound secular education is given, but also one in which the teachers seek to train children committed to their care, to be followers of Christ." These sentiments were representative of the other statements from parents. After informing the members of WFMS of the growth in the library and several other important curricular developments, she turned to the debt problem. She was encouraged by the fact that it had been reduced by half of the original purchase price, but she was concerned because only the operating expenses could be met from tuition and fees leaving no money to pay towards the interest and principal.[14]

Emma Knowles gave thirty-seven years of her life to the cause of educating young girls in India. She sought to give them an education which would enable them to become responsible for their own conduct, to provide an education which would strike deep into their moral and religious natures, and to teach them not merely to do right things but also to enjoy them. She loved Wellesley and Queens' Hill deeply and after she retired at age seventy-seven and went to live with a niece in New Jersey, Knowles continued to stay in touch with the work in India. It was her desire to give all the meager financial resources she had to this work, and her niece reported that "she was sometimes hard put to get Aunt Emma to provide for herself."

Several moving tributes to Emma Knowles' life of service and faith appeared in *The Indian Witness* and *The Woman's Missionary Friend*. One of these was written by C. J. Stahl, the missionary who had taken over for her when she went home to rest. "Miss Knowles' religious experience was like a steady deep flowing stream. She instinctively shrank from any excessive expression of religious emotion, but lived every day with a consciousness of and a firm reliance on God's power and guidance."[15] Fort Wayne College lost an outstanding educator when Emma Knowles did not return, but Indiana's loss was demonstrably India's gain.

LEONORA AND MABEL SEEDS

Leonora and Mabel Seeds were sisters who grew up in Delaware, Ohio near Columbus. Although Leonora was born in 1867 and Mabel in 1869, they both graduated from Ohio Wesleyan University in 1889. Immediately following her graduation, Leonora

Leonora Seeds. Missionary to
south Japan.

The Gem

was appointed by the Women's Foreign Missionary Society of the Methodist Episcopal Church, Cincinnati branch as a missionary to Japan. She arrived at Fukuoka Mission Station on February 20, 1891 where she assumed the position of principal of the Eiwa Jo-Gakko [girl's school] and took on the responsibility for the evangelistic work with the women in the district. Mabel stayed in the United States where she taught in various public high schools including one in Montezuma, Iowa. In 1896 she joined the faculty of Taylor University as a professor of Latin and rhetoric. That same year Leonora took her first furlough, sailing from Japan October 6, 1896. Leonora chose to spend her furlough as a student at Taylor University, graduating with the class of 1898. Following her graduation, she again sailed for Japan where she took up her duties as Principal of Eiwa and district evangelist. Mabel remained on the Taylor faculty for three more years.

In November, 1901 Mabel was appointed to Japan by the Women's Foreign Missionary Society, Northwestern Branch. She joined Leonora in February, 1902 in Fukuoka and took on the duties of Principal of the School, thus freeing Leonora who was the District Superintendent of the Kyushu District, to devote most of her energies to the work of evangelism and supervision of the Bible Women. The two sisters worked together in this place until February 1905 when Leonora returned to the United States for what became a prolonged furlough. Mabel remained in Fukuoka as Principal of

Eiwa and took on the responsibilities for evangelism and supervising the Bible Women in the large Kyushu District until her furlough which began after the Annual Conference in 1907. Mabel returned in 1909 after a two-year furlough and resumed her responsibilities as Principal.

The WFMS work began in southern Japan in 1879. It was an area of the world where "persecution had been most bitter, and where no door seemed open to receive the brave pioneer women missionaries." A school named Kwassui was opened in Nagasaki that year with a single student in attendance.[16]

Fukuoka is a city about seventy miles northwest of Nagasaki. As the result of a revival held in the city in the fall of 1884, a number professed conversion and soon after began to seek Christian education for their daughters. They petitioned the WFMS missionaries in Nagasaki to open a branch of Kwassui in Fukuoka. Finally, one of these missionaries, Jennie M. Gheer, was able to reach the town and opened Eiwa Jo-Gakko June 1, 1885 in a small building with an enrollment of thirty girls. Since it did not have space for boarders, it operated as a day school.

In 1888 through funds secured by the Northwestern Branch of the WFMS, land was secured and a comfortable building was erected which contained a chapel, dining room, several recitation rooms, and dormitory space for fifty students. There was also a wing in which the women missionaries lived. A church with a seating capacity of two hundred and fifty was built next door. Jennie Gheer stayed on as principal for only one year. She was relieved of this responsibility when Lida Smith came in 1886. Leonora Seeds took over this position from Smith in 1890.

Establishing mission schools in Japan was not an easy task,

and Eiwa encountered many obstacles. In 1894 the local Government officials demanded that the school give up the teaching of the Bible or forfeit the opportunity to teach primary students. Of course, Leonora Seeds had only one option, and she gave up the primary division. At this point the school was left with a preparatory department and an academic department. A young woman graduating from the scientific course in the academy was qualified to continue her education at Kwassui in Nagasaki if she chose to do so.

Despite opposition, the school prospered. When Leonora Seeds returned in 1898 after her first furlough, she found the attendance had increased so that it more than made up for the five young women who had graduated the preceding term. The political climate had also improved so much that Fukuoka was declared by the Conference to be "ideal, the school authorities and pupils and members from the city working together most harmoniously." [17]

In her report to the Conference in 1900, Seeds rejoiced in the changed circumstances in Japan which now allowed for as many as thirty five percent of Japanese girls to attend school. Since the objections to educating girls were less than in the past, the Government was proceeding to erect female schools. In fact, a large government school was in the process of being constructed in the street next to Eiwa. As a result, its enrollment was not growing as much as had been expected, but the positive side was that Christian teachers were now being sought after by the government schools. Four of the graduates from Eiwa were employed in government schools and even some of the undergraduates were being urged to accept positions without examination. Several of Seeds' teachers and her school nurse had been offered positions.

The nurse was to teach nursing students, and Seeds wrote, "believing that a little leaven leaventh the whole lump, we have loaned her for a time. The Bible woman will follow her, and thus gradually is the gospel of the Kingdom spreading."[18]

When Mabel Seeds arrived in Fukuoka in 1902 enrollment in the school had reached ninety, half of whom were boarders. At the end of her first full year as Principal, she reported that the most important purpose of the school, evangelism, was being met.

> All our boarders at present are Christians, and all, except one, have been baptized. Many of the day pupils have become earnest inquirers, and some have become Christians.

Mabel K. Seeds. Missionary to south Japan.

She also reported that Leonora Seeds, who was now completely devoting her energies to the evangelistic work in the District, was using all of the older girls very effectively in the city Sunday school work. Some girls were mature enough to be placed in charge of these mission outreach programs. In addition, all of the present teachers in the school were Christians.

Mabel Seeds' time was given to what she considered to be the second objective of Christian mission schools, providing a good academic experience. One of her first tasks in this regard was to change the curriculum to bring it in line with the course of study at Kwassui. This new course was one year higher than the school had previously pursued. She had encountered some problems in doing this and, in fact, had to drop five girls from regular to irregular status because they refused to study Latin. She reported that the course was going well now, but a new problem had come about with its introduction—the need for more efficient teachers especially in the areas of science and mathematics. The unfortunate fact was that she did not have sufficient funds to pay the necessary salaries to attract this higher quality teacher. She had also introduced some areas into the curriculum which had not previously been there including "foreign drawing", physical culture, organ lessons, and a singing class. She concluded on an optimistic note: "We realize the merits of the new course, and that in time the results may prove the wisdom of its adoption in Eiwa Jo Gakko."[19]

During Mabel Seeds' entire first term in Japan, Eiwa continued to prosper. Seeds' priorities of evangelizing the girls and giving them a top quality education remained in that order. By the time she was ready to go home on furlough at the end of 1907, the school had an enrollment of 150. Of this total, 119 girls were Christians, the largest percentage the school had ever attained. Increased attention was given to grounding these new converts in the faith, a work which Seeds believed to be as important as winning new souls for the kingdom.

On the educational front, she rejoiced in that "the standard of scholarship of the school is in high estimation by the public." There was a proportionate decrease of irregular students and an increase in those taking the full course of study, a change which she attributed to the greater confidence in the course of study offered. The library was growing following several appeals made by her to the WFMS. Eiwa had received several large gifts—one for $50 in gold was used to purchase standard reference books in English — other smaller cash gifts, and collections of Japanese language books.

Staffing the school was still somewhat problematic due to the disparity in salaries she was able to offer compared with the government schools. However, she was able to report that all the departments were functioning effectively.

She ended this report by writing, "To have a part in helping to mold the character of the future Christian womanhood in Japan is a privilege that angels might envy, and our prayer is that God may count us worthy of that great blessing."[20]

When Mabel Seeds returned from her furlough one and half years later, the fortunes of the school had again shifted. There was now an enrollment of seventy-four girls, half that of 1907. Most of the girls who had left were now in attendance at the new government schools. Even in the face of these discouraging statistics, Seeds remained courageous and optimistic about the future. Since Fukuoka was fast becoming a center of education for southern Japan, she believed it was doubly important that the mission "take the lead in making it a center for Christian education as well as secular." She acknowledged that the school "was somewhat embarrassed" by the lack of teachers, but asserted that this need along with all others would be met in due time.[21] The year 1910 was one of significant and far reaching change in the educational system in Japan and the mission schools such as Eiwa. Japan was making great strides in upgrading its system of government schools, and Seeds was one of the people in the Christian Church who saw the changes as opportunities. In addition to her annual report on the state of Eiwa, she wrote an extended essay entitled, *"The Present Educational System in Japan and our Relation to it."* Essentially she argued that in the past the mission schools had been in the position of leading the educational enterprise, but that time was gone. Now Christian schools must "get in step" with the indigenous educational work. She declared, "it is ours not to fit the Japanese to our educational ideas, but rather to fit our educational ideas to the Japanese." To refuse to do this would, in her opinion, effectively close the door of opportunity to influence Japan for the Gospel. The ability to influence depended on the presence of students, and if the Christian school was not offering the same or better educational product as the government schools, parents would no longer choose to send their daughters to a private mission school.[22]

She took the opportunity of her Annual Report to inform the Conference that she was taking her own advice and Eiwa was poised on the threshold of the second major curricular shift in its two decade history.

> Our course of study is to be adjusted soon to the Government girls' high school grade, above which will be a special English course, the length of the curriculum being about as before, but in its nature radically different. This change is to meet a present demand, and also, by thus getting in line with Government schools, to gain the greater favor and popularity, and the resultant greater opportunity to impart Christian instruction and influence. Our advance may not be marked at first. A change often means a backward step. But in making this change we feel assured of our ultimate and successful progress in our Christian educational work in Fukuoka and in North Kyushu.[23]

In addition to being responsible for Eiwa, both Leonora and Mabel Seeds were at various times responsible for the district work in Kyushu. The Methodist missionaries organized national churches the same way they organized the conferences and districts in the States. Thus Kyushu was a large district within the Southern Japan Conference. Women missionaries worked with women and children in the districts, using Japanese Christian women to aid them in their touring and visitation. These Japanese Christians were called Bible Women and they received a salary by the WFMS, a strong indicator of this organization's ability to raise money for missions. The District Superintendent was responsible for recruiting Bible Women, training them, and enabling them to carry out the work of evangelism. Each Bible Woman was assigned one of twelve small circuits located within a city and the surrounding area. She would then work with local pastors in identifying women who might be open to receiving a call from her. A Bible Woman might make as many as 1200 personal calls on other women in their homes during the course of a Conference Year. The missionary in charge would visit each Bible Woman's circuit at least once a year and usually twice or three times to give support and encouragement.

Leonora Seeds explained this system in the report she made to the conference in 1904. She first affirmed that she had found the women very receptive to being visited in their homes, and after a few visits, "a way to the heart of most of the women is gained." According to Seeds, "much of the evangelization of Japan must come through sitting on the floor while talking with the Japanese around their hibachi [stove]." The missionary accompanied by a Bible Woman or the Bible Woman alone would come to a woman's house by invitation. After the preliminary ceremony around the hibachi, hymn books and Bibles would be produced and the visitors would conduct a service of song, prayer and Bible lesson. Often the woman of the house would invite other friends who were interested either because they were already Christians or because they were inquirers. If there were a local pastor in the city, the missionary and Bible Woman might be asked to lead a service to which men would be invited, but for the most part their work was confined to exclusively women's meetings. In this way the gospel was spread, inquirers were identified and nurtured, and converts made.

Another aspect of district work was the organization of street Sunday schools for children. The goal was always to use the children to find a way into their homes and make contact with the parents. Each child who attended a Sunday school was given a memory card and a lesson leaflet and told to take them home. Starting Sunday schools was often the way that churches were planted. As adults became interested, arrangements would be made to bring in a pastor, and the Sunday school was turned into a "preaching place." Bible Women and students from Eiwa were used to teach these Sunday schools. By 1906 there were twenty-two street Sunday schools located in Kyushu District with nearly two thousand children attending regularly. When the teachers arrived at the appointed place, they would often find as many as one hundred children gathered varying in age from the very young to about ten or twelve. Older people would often crowd around the doorway to listen. At Christmas time, the missionaries would hold a special meeting in the local church. The children from the various Sunday schools would supply the program with songs and recitations. Afterwards, each child would be given a special treat of some kind. A bag of cakes or an orange were typical gifts.[24]

A third way in which the District work was carried out in Kyushu was through a cooking school. An American missionary, Mrs. Fretz, conducted the classes twice a month. She had an attendance which varied from fifteen to twenty-five women. Meetings were divided into two segments, with the first half devoted to Bible study and the second half to the cooking lesson.

Most of the women who attended the cooking school came from a class of women unlikely to be reached by any other method. [25]

Since District work required extensive touring as well as constant involvement with large numbers of people, it must have been extremely taxing. It is incredible to even think that at various times both Leonora and Mabel did the work of evangelism simultaneously with the work of directing a boarding school. However, the limited number of missionaries available to south Japan necessitated such heavy work schedules, and the two Seeds sisters more than rose to the challenge.

During the last two years she spent in Japan, Mabel Seeds was in charge of six day schools in Yokohama. She reported in 1911 that there were 252 children enrolled in the six schools throughout the city. In connection with the day schools, Seeds also was responsible for a bi-monthly mother's meeting. At this informal meeting, tea was served and the women engaged in sewing, knitting and other needlecraft. "Gradually, the way opens for singing, prayer, and Bible talk. It is wonderful how these people open up their hearts and freely talk of their trials and afflictions."[26]

The following year the enrollment in the schools had more than doubled, reaching a total of 645. Seeds wrote, "These are truly Christian schools, with daily Bible

General Commission on Archives and History - UMC

Leonora Seed near her retirement
from missionary service.

lessons. The pupils carry home with them the truths learned; they can not help but do so." The schools were used as distribution centers for Bibles and New Testaments in cooperation with The American Bible Society, and the children were encouraged to share Bibles with friends who were not Christians. At the end of 1912, Mabel Seeds was compelled to give up her work and return to the United States due to the illness of her mother. [27] She retired in 1914 and died in the United States in 1924.[28]

Information in Leonora Seeds correspondence file in the Methodist Archives in Madison, New Jersey, is sketchy. Apparently she did return to Japan, presumably after her mother's death, because she did not retire from the mission until 1934. Probably she returned home to Ohio upon her retirement. No obituary could be found.

By all accounts, both Mabel and Leonora were remarkable women with multiple talents. They understood their own strengths and they worked together effectively to maximize each sister's potential in the work they were called upon to do. Together, they contributed immensely to the education of young women and the evangelization of women and children in southern Japan.

LEOTA RATCLIFFE

Unfortunately, not all the stories of young women who left Taylor University to work in foreign misions were as positive as those of Emma Knowles and Leonora and Mabel Seeds. The story of Leota Ratcliffe is one of the more unhappy ones to be found in the General Commission on Archives and History of the United Methodist Church in Madison, New Jersey.

Ratcliffe was born in 1877 near Olney, Illinois. She was converted to Christianity when she was eight or nine years old and joined the church on probation. She came into full membership when she was eleven or twelve. She said that "her thoughts when young were turned toward mission work."[29]

She had a desire for education, and despite serious family difficulties she was able to graduate from Olney High School. Ratcliffe taught public school for a term, but sensing the need for more education herself, she enrolled in Westfield College, a United Brethren school located in Westfield, Illinois where she remained for two years. She taught again for several terms, attended the Normal School in Charleston, Illinois, and went to North Dakota where she worked among the foreign speaking children, teaching them English, for several terms. She finally came to Taylor

Leota Ratcliffe.
Missionary to Liberia.

The Gem

University where she was "sanctified." She studied at Taylor for two years, and was apparently doing well. A letter of reference sent to the Methodist Board from Dr. A. R. Archibald indicated that she had an average of ninety percent, and though she was a bit deficient in languages, she made up for it in other areas. He further stated that her greatest asset was her ability to teach young children.[30]

During 1906-07, the years Ratcliffe was a student at Taylor, interest in Holiness and missions was constantly kept before the student body through the auspices of the Student Volunteer Movement. Ratcliffe was a part of this organization.

At some time during these two years, Reverend J. M. Harrow of Toronto, Canada, who had spent many years in Africa, spoke at Taylor, probably at one of the Saturday afternoon missionary meetings. Ratcliffe spoke with him about the possibility of going to Africa, and he gave her Bishop Isaiah B. Scott's Address. At this time Scott was Bishop of Liberia. Ratcliffe wrote Bishop Scott directly on September 11, 1907 expressing a desire to go to Africa. Bishop Scott wrote her back saying "he was glad to know of her desire to join our forces in the effort to redeem Africa." He instructed her to write Dr. A. B. Leonard, the Corresponding Secretary for the Board of Managers of Methodist Missions, and ask for an application blank which she was to fill out and return. He also recommended that she have a thorough physical. He concluded by saying "my plan will be to have you work at Monrovia for at least a year until you become acclimated...Afterward, of course I would feel safer to have you go back into the country." He added a postscript asking if she "could be ready to sail by January 20 next."[31]

When A. B. Leonard received the letter from a young woman he had never heard of living in Upland, Indiana telling him that Bishop Scott "desires that I send to you for an application blank and that if possible to be ready to sail for Africa by the 20th of January", he was mystified since he had heard nothing of the sort from Bishop Scott. He did, however, answer her letter asking that she send him a copy of the Bishop's letter to her. He enclosed an application blank which he said she would need to return before the next Board meeting on December 17. Probably the only sentence she actually read carefully was the one which said "If the way is clear we shall be very glad to do everything we can to get you on the way to Africa by the date named."[32]

After Ratcliffe sent in her application accompanied by a letter giving an account of her call to missionary service, Leonard again wrote her saying that since Bishop Scott had not comunicated with him, he felt "it would be safer to wait until the arrival of the Bishop." He concluded his short letter by saying "I take it for granted that you will receive an appointment. Perhaps a few months delay will not in any way be an inconvenience to you." This was all the encouragement she needed. She left Taylor and began to make plans to embark for Africa. However, Bishop Scott's arrival in New York was delayed until April. Ratcliffe received another letter informing her that her case would be brought to the Board of Managers on April 21st for final action. There was no question that she would receive an appointment. The Bishop desired her to sail as soon as possible. On April 22, 1908 Leonard again wrote Ratcliffe stating that she had indeed been accepted and that she should plan to be ready to sail in June after the Annual Conference.[33]

No actual sailing date or date of arrival in Monrovia appears in the Ratcliffe correspondence, but she did arrive and was assigned to the College of West Africa which at the time was under the supervision of John H. Reed who had been appointed to this post by Bishop W. F. McDowell in January 1905.[34]

From the beginning, Ratcliffe and Reed had a different understanding of what constituted her responsibilities as a missionary. As far as Reed was concerned, she was a teacher and her work was to teach in the day school. Ratcliffe believed a missionary was to be engaged in the work of evangelism, and she wanted to be involved in the Kru church and village as well as teach her classes in the college. Probably, Ratcliffe did not see this desire as a challenge to Reed's authority, but he did, and he immediately began to treat her as though she were a major threat.

In late July Ratcliffe wrote A. B. Leonard in New York voicing her concerns about "the situation as she found it in Monrovia." She was aware that she was a newcomer and that she might not "be considered justified in making a statement so early," but she saw the issues as serious enough for the Board to be concerned. She spent considerable time in the letter detailing an incident in which Dr. Reed had appropriated a letter addressed to her. Even though the letter was sealed, he had opened it and then sought to conceal his action by placing the letter in another envelope, re-addressing it and finally returning it to her. She ended her description of the incident by saying "I approached Dr. Reed on the subject in a Christian spirit but he was not inclined to discuss the matter. I tried to show him how wrong it was for him to open my mail. He declined however to make any explanation concerning his actions with the letter."

Her next paragraph details "some underhanded work in Krootown" which Dr. Reed did while she was visiting another nearby mission. According to her understanding of what had transpired in her absence, Reed had called a meeting in Krutown and told the people that Ratcliffe had left because she was afraid of them. He explained that she had run away because she was white and a coward. Reed then allegedly went to the Kru pastor who had been working with Ratcliffe and denounced her to him saying that she wanted to be " teacher, pastor, and everything else."

Ratcliffe went on to say that she had gone down to Krutown to carry out her work only to discover that Dr. Reed had been there before her and had instructed Nimley, the Kru pastor, that he was to take charge of the service. Later on in the day, Reed himself had appeared at the Sunday school service and requested to address the meeting. In his address, Ratcliffe asserted Reed talked only about himself and how he had done so much for the Krus, " how so many were working against their church to break it up and how he had come there to save it. He never mentioned Christ. " Reed then told the assembled Krus that they were to treat Nimley as their pastor, that Miss Ratcliffe was a day school teacher and they should treat her as such.

The thrust of her letter was that she could work with anyone who was honest, but she could not work with one who was "dishonest and hypocritical hindering the cause of Christ just because he is bitter against the white people." She alleged that she had been prevented from doing the work she was sent out to do by both Mr. and Mrs. Reed. Since she could not "live in the college" she had moved out and taken a house near Krutown "so that I could help the people more, have a place to pray with them, and work as a real missionary of God." She detailed her plans for taking in children, having Bible classes and training Kru teachers and asked for the Board's financial support. She asked that he write her, but she said until she heard from him she would act as she deemed best because she believed this was God's will.[35]

Apparently Ratcliffe wrote a similar letter to Bishop Scott the following day since she received a reply directly from him dated September 1, 1908. In the letter he expressed sorrow and concern that things were not going well. He reminded her that he and Reverend Harrow had told her that there were problems in Monrovia. He then commended her for her fine Christian spirit

233

and the "splendid impression for noble Christian purpose" she had made on him. He explained in detail the structure of the work in Krutown and his intentions for her work. She was to assume that she was principal and teacher in the day school and render any assistance she could to the local pastor including teaching a class that would train new converts so that "they might become intelligent Christians and Methodists." He explained Dr. Reed's role as "having general oversight over all educational interests in that part of Liberia" and his relationship to the Kru church. He also indicated that he was sending a copy of the letter to Reed to prevent any further misunderstandings between them.[36]

Ratcliffe received a reply from Leonard as well. He expressed his regret over the "differences existing in the mission", but told her that he did not see that "there is anything for me to do to adjust things." He told her that the matter would have to be referred to Bishop Scott who would come to Liberia probably before the end of the year. He also informed her that the Board had taken no action on her request for money to pay the rent on the house she had taken in Krutown. He thought the Bishop would take care of the matter when he came to Liberia. The only specific concern he addressed was the opening of the letter. He agreed that Reed acted inappropriately "if he opened her letter," and indicated that he was writing Reed about the matter.[37]

Throughout the next three months the situation worsened. Reed was able to call upon friends in high places, especially Dr. Ernest Lyons, the American Consul, to support his actions and vouch for his integrity and character. Ratcliffe built a power base within the Kru village, and several other Americans including independent missionary Mary Sharp, took her side. Sharp wrote to Leonard,

"Miss Ratcliff [sic] is altogether the best missionary worker that has been here abouts. Dr. Reed has tried to kill our influence with the Kroo people... He goes into the town and says such hateful things of Miss Ratcliff and myself to these people with whom we work. Miss Ratcliff has felt it keenly."[38] Letters crisscrossed the Atlantic between the Methodist Board in New York and Reed, Lyons, Sharp and Ratcliffe, each one telling the story as she or he saw it. Finally, in December 1908, the quarterly Conference met and Ratcliffe was present when both Reed and Lyons arose and made speeches against her. This caused the Conference to dissolve into confusion and factionalism. One Liberian pastor from another village said if he had Ratcliffe in his village "he would cut off her head." But many others from Krutown supported her. She was not allowed to speak in her own defense because she was not a member of the Conference.

Four days after the Quarterly Conference meeting, Ratcliffe again wrote an appeal to Leonard presenting a detailed description of the way things had unfolded since July. She said her financial means were almost gone. Even though she had spent very little on personal needs, resorting to treating herself when she became ill with fever to spare doctor's bills, she now had only five dollars left. At the same time, she asked for song books and supplies for the Sunday school, offering to have them take it out of her salary if the Board could not make the necessary appropriation. She acknowledged that Reed and Lyons wanted to remove her and she denied the charges which were being brought against her by these two men. She hoped that she would not be "removed from this work" until " I have put the Kroo workers in their right places. I only hope Bishop will give me a chance here. I have had no chance so far."[39]

The chance that Ratcliffe pled for in her December letter was not forthcoming, and on February 16, 1909 she wrote Leonard informing him that she had written to Bishop Scott, requesting that she be released from the work in Liberia. She said she would leave for America in a few days and she requested that she be granted an interview with the Board.

It is unknown whether she was granted a hearing or not. In any case she did not return to Africa nor did she remain with the Methodist Board. She returned to the United States and married a Taylor alumnus, Maurice T. Hapgood [sometimes spelled Habgood]. He was a Methodist minister, and together they served churches in the South Dakota and Colorado Conferences.

It appears from the available evidence that Ratcliffe was a naive woman who had almost no understanding of organizations and the political realities which permeated even religious groups such as Methodist missions. If she had had some knowledge in these areas, she would have realized that Reed was a powerful and influential male and that her actions would likely be interpreted by him as power moves on her part designed to undermine his authority. If she had recognized that relationships in organizations are often necessarily negotiated based on status and position within the organization, she would have developed appropriate strategies of dealing with Reed rather than immediately appealing to the Corresponding Secretary and the Bishop. As soon as she made her grievance known to these men, she had sealed her fate. Reed was not the kind of person who would allow himself to be embarrassed before his superiors by a young white woman, and he was bound to destroy her.

It also appears that she knew very little if anything about the history of Liberia. She does not appear to have grasped the fact that there were deep divisions in the Liberian society caused by the tensions between the indigenous people and the freed slaves who had come from the United States and were known as Americo-Liberians. It does not seem to have occurred to her that an American black like Reed had a paternalistic feeling toward both the indigenous Liberians and the Americo-Liberians, or that he could possibly see himself as greatly superior to the Krus. She saw the issues arising because of differences between white and black missionaries regarding how to best relate to Liberians. It is also possible that she did have some personal feelings about American blacks and their competence and character which made her quick to render moral judgment of Reed's actions. It is equally possible that she was right about Reed, and that he did harbor anger against white women.

It also seems evident that she had a strong personality and an independent spirit. At least two of the letters of reference which were sent to the Board of Managers allude to these qualities. Her pastor in Souris, North Dakota wrote "I don't know of anything that she undertook that she didn't go thru with. She will always get to her goal." Another pastor friend from her days at Westfield College said, "I know of no one more persevering and determined than she. She is not headstrong or impulsive but very thoughtful of God as her most worthy adviser and leader." These characteristics manifest themselves in Liberia. She came with a clear idea of what "true missionary work" was—probably an idea she had developed in the many Volunteer Band meetings at Taylor—and she was not about to compromise her vision.

It appears that the Board of Managers must bear some

237

responsibility for things going awry with Ratcliffe. The very fact that she was never actually interviewed and never went through any training in New York, would seem to indicate weaknesses in the system. Had there been some orientation to the country prior to her leaving and some communication about the way the organization worked, it may have enabled her to navigate through the system more effectively. One wonders what kind of missionary she would have been had she gone through the normal appointment process with the Women's Foreign Missionary Society. She did not lack zeal or vision. Nor did she lack a heart for the enterprise of missions. She was physically healthy and was in Liberia long enough to demonstrate that she had adjusted to the climate. Liberian Methodism lost a good friend when they lost Leota Ratcliffe

CORA FALES

Although Ratcliffe's story is certainly a dramatic one which reaches a regrettable climax in her departure from the mission field, it is not the only instance of a Taylor missionary encountering serious conflict with the Methodist establishment. Olive Dunn and Cora Fales, both evangelistic missionaries in India, were sent out under the sponsorship of the WFMS, and both had personality clashes with authority figures which threatened their ability to remain on the field.

Fales had been involved in Deaconess work in the United States for a number of years before applying for foreign missionary service in 1918. At the age of thirty-eight she was appointed to Sironcha, India where she did medical and educational work. Later she was transferred to the

Cora Fales.
Missionary to
south India.

238

South India Conference where she served in Belgaum, Madras, Bangalore, and Dhupdhal. She was fluent in three different Indian languages including Kanarese in which she developed the greatest facility. She was in charge of a small boarding school during her third term, but she also did a great deal of touring for the purpose of evangelizing some parts of the district which had not yet been reached.

At the conclusion of her third term in 1938 she received mixed evaluations from her superiors on the field. One recommended she be allowed to return for short term service, one said she should be allowed to return for a fourth term, and a third said no. The first recommendation was made by fellow missionary Esther Shoemaker who wrote an extended set of reasons for her opinion which provide considerable light on the situation:

> I know there is division of opinion in the conference with regard to her return. In spite of this I still feel that there may be a field of service for her in India. There could be complaints about all of us perhaps. I should like to list reasons for my opinion even taking into consideration the listed difficulties.
>
> Assets for evangelistic or educational work on the mission field in South India Conference.
>
> Persistence in work in spite of all obstacles.
>
> Keen interest in spreading the printed word. She has perhaps the highest record in the conference for selling gospel portions...
>
> General knowledge far above average. We call her a walking encyclopedia.
>
> Does not give in easily to physical ailments and incidents that usually cause mental depression.

Very good Bible teacher. Is not afraid to use the vernacular.

Stimulates keen missionary interest among young people and gives largely of herself.

Can work best when independent of other missionaries (which is so necessary anyway in much of our work.)

Has given best years of life; can perhaps give better service in India in the fading years than elsewhere.

She always makes definite accomplishments and leaves a work in better condition than when she takes it on.

Difficulties.

Has never known much about cooperation. It is hard for some others to work with her.

Tries to walk too far and stay out in sun too long.

Expects more of her Indian coworkers than they seem willing and able to give.

Is blunt in her dealings with others, many times not tactful. Often that makes things hard for her and others.[40]

Despite the mixed reviews and the strong evidence of effectiveness on the field, Fales was not allowed to return to India for a fourth term. Instead, she itinerated for the Women's Division and later accepted an appointment as a teacher in Mather Academy, Camden, S. C. She retired September 1, 1948. After her retirement, she made her home with a sister in Saskatchewan. She died in 1953 shortly after celebrating her seventy-third birthday.

CHARLES AND ELIZABETH HASTINGS SCHARER

Certainly, not all the women who left Taylor bound for foreign shores under the auspices of the Methodist Episcopal Church were single. A number of Taylor couples also found their way to various fields. One such couple was Elizabeth Hastings Scharer and Charles Scharer.

Charles Wesley Scharer was born on May 13, 1875 in West Toledo, Ohio. Elizabeth Hastings was born on September 16, 1874 in Spring Mountain, Ohio. They both attended Taylor University, graduating in 1904. They were married in July of that year and in October embarked on their missionary career in educational and evangelistic work in Belgaum and Bidar, South India.

Married women who went to a field such as India faced some of the same problems as their unmarried sisters and some different ones. In the case of the

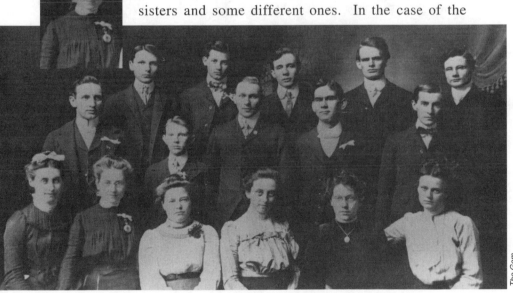

The Gem

Philalethean Literary Society.
Elizabeth Hastings Scharer is second from left in front row.

Scharers, Elizabeth did not have a separate appointment. Even though there was no salary for her, only a spousal allowance, she was still expected to do missionary work. In fact, it was routine for wives to be given full time assignments by the Conference in which their husbands worked. Most often this assignment was either in education or taking charge of the Bible Women who did the evangelistic work among the women and children of the area. Elizabeth Scharer was actively involved in both educational and evangelistic work in cooperation with other missionary wives and the trained Bible Women. The Minutes of the South India Annual Conference for every year beginning with 1906 indicate that "Mrs. Scharer was appointed to do evangelistic work and to work in the schools" on one or more circuits. This continued through the 1918 Minutes with the exception of 1911-12 when they were on furlough— the only one they had in fourteen years. When they returned to India in 1924, Elizabeth Scharer was again appointed to do evangelistic work on one circuit and to supervise a boys school.

In addition to what amounted to a very taxing full time position she also had the responsibility of creating a home. While in India she gave birth to four children, David Oliver, Fletcher Hastings, Earl Wesley and Grace Elizabeth. The Scharers also buried their third son in 1913. It comes as no surprise that by the end of 1919 Elizabeth Scharer was ordered home because she had contracted tuberculosis and needed rest and a good diet. She sailed from India on November 9, 1919 with her three children, leaving her husband behind. Charles wrote the Board informing them of his family's departure.

> I am sorry she had to leave but the doctors said that it was
> absolutely necessary. I had not noticed that her health was so

poorly but other missionaries of the station seemed to be very anxious about her. She will not be able to proceed to her home in Ohio but will remain in Los Angeles. I have commended Mrs. Scharer and the children to the Lord while I remain here and continue Our Father's Business. It was not easy to send away a sick wife but His grace is wonderful. Mrs. Scharer parted looking on the bright side of life. I believe she will recover.[41]

Charles Scharer did not obtain a furlough for the purpose of joining his family for nearly eighteen months. During that time, Elizabeth and the children lived in Los Angeles far from any extended family in rented rooms subsisting on the allowance which was sent from the Board. In addition to her own health problems, she constantly worried about the state of Charles' health, particularly after learning that at the Annual Conference he had been given an even larger work load. She wrote Dr. F. M. North, corresponding Secretary for the Board of Managers, "He was working to the limit before; and I am afraid he will break down unless help is sent soon. I do not want him to break down and me so far away."[42]

Managing on the meager resources which she had must have presented a constant challenge. In May 1920 Charles had requested the Board to send her an extra ten dollars a month and reduce his stipend by that amount because he feared she would not "take the necessary diet of eggs and milk which the Doctor ordered" unless she had more money. However, when Mr. Donohugh of the Board of Managers wrote inquiring as to her financial needs she responded by saying, "We were rather close run sometimes for money... but now Mr. Scharer is sending me an extra $10 per month and my mother is helping me some. I am not needing money at present... I have no special expense on account of my illness."[43]

When Charles did arrive in the United States in May 1921 the whole family traveled to Ohio where they were near parents and uncles and aunts. Both Charles and Elizabeth were convinced that her health was improving and that she would be allowed to return with him to India at the conclusion of his normal furlough. Such was not to be the case. The doctors did not give her medical clearance, and for several months it appeared that Charles would return to India alone and Elizabeth would again remain with the children in California. However, in June 1922 the Board decided to extend Charles' furlough rather than sending him back to India alone. This presented the Scharers with an additional financial dilemma. Charles did not want to draw salary after his regular furlough was ended, but he had no alternative. Eventually he did secure a supply pastor's charge in the Southern California Conference which brought some financial relief and reduced his sense of restlessness about not being allowed to return to India. It was the end of 1923 before they were finally en route to India once again. They had left their oldest son in Pasadena in order that he might finish school, but the other two children returned with their parents.

This time the Scharers' stint on the field was shortened by Charles' illness. He had suffered excruciating back pain for some time. After ruling out a kidney problem, the doctors decided that he had "slight caries of the fifth lumbar vertebra", placed him in a plaster caste and ordered him home. This occurred in January 1926, and they sailed for America from Bombay on February 13, 1926. By 1928 it was clear that they were not able to return to India due to health problems, and they were given retirement status. Charles Scharer continued as a supply pastor in the Southern California Conference for eighteen years. Both of the Scharers died in 1954.

They were survived by their three children, seven grandchildren and several sisters and brothers.

The Scharers were certainly not the only Taylor missionaries to suffer from poor health. Kathryne Bieri and Gertrude Bridgewater were two women who struggled with various health problems which kept them from participating fully in mission work.

KATHRYNE BIERI

Kathryne Bieri was a graduate of the class of 1925. She applied to the Methodist Board of Managers and was appointed to Mussoorie, India where she was to teach in the school for missionary children at Woodstock. She arrived in India in 1928, but was obliged to return to the United States after only a year due to a severe case of stomach ulcers. After spending the summer resting and attempting to recuperate at the shore, Bieri wrote to Ernest Tuck, Associate Secretary for the Methodist Board, that she was feeling "heaps better," but the stomach condition had not cleared up. "I haven't dared to hope that I might again be fit for service with the Board. Its hard to give up ones' calling. But I am trying desperately hard to keep on believing that 'all things work together for good.' " In 1930 she was notified that the Board had found it necessary to remove her name from the list of Methodist Episcopal missionaries due to her continued ill health. She took a position teaching school in Pennsylvania, and in 1935 she again applied to the Board of Missions requesting that she be sent to Woodstock once more

Kathryne Bieri.
Missionary teacher
in India.
Later she worked
for the Methodist
Board of Missions
in New York.

because she believed her health had sufficiently improved to make it possible for her to live successfully in India. The Board was reluctant to take a chance on her given her previous record of poor health. Dr. J. G. Vaughn recommended that the Board not assume full responsibility for costs of ill health, but since "she proposes to cover the Board's financial risk" he would "approve her acceptance on those terms." He then wrote to Bieri reporting his recommendation and telling her, "I do believe you would be acting more wisely if you did not go into missionary service" because of the personal risks involved in doing so.[44]

Nevertheless, Bieri sailed for India in the company of her father, and took up her teaching responsibilities at Woodstock school. Less than a year passed before she and her father received word that conditions at home required them to return. She wrote her resignation letter to Dr. Donohugh on September 18, 1936:

> It seems that the church folk at home feel definitely that I should return and take over the work in the parsonage. Just before I sailed I had promised the folk that if I should be ill or if anything should happen to Muz [mother] I would return to the states. Little did I think that the latter would happen. I have been feeling just fine and thoroughly enjoying my work here at the school. It's one of the hardest things that I have ever done to send in my resignation before completing one year of service.[45]

After returning to the United States, Bieri went to work in the Personnel Department of the Methodist Board of Missions in New York City where she remained until her marriage in 1953 when she moved to Cedar Rapids, Iowa. She served on the Taylor Board of Trustees in the mid 1960s.

GERTRUDE BRIDGEWATER ROBSON

Gertrude Bridgewater was appointed to Chengtu, China in 1914 by the Des Moines branch of the WFMS. She served four years of this term before returning to the United States on the advice of a physician, even though another physician thought her condition did not justify such return. She married a fellow Taylorite, Horace Robson. While she was pregnant with their first child, they applied as a couple to the Board of Managers requesting that they be considered for service in China since Gertrude already knew much of the language and culture. They had a very difficult time securing medical clearance because of her previous early departure from the field.

Gertrude Bridgewater Robson.
Missionary to China.

The report from Dr. J. G. Vaughn to the Personnel Committee indicated that she had suffered from "heart embarrassment" while in China. However, "careful examination of her by three doctors led to their endorsement of her for work on the field." He went on to state that these doctors had concluded that "her symptoms were chiefly functional and of nervous origin." The doctors had further concluded that she suffered no other symptoms of nervousness which might keep her from being appointed. Vaughn concluded his report by saying that: "There is such a borderline of uncertainty in this case that the Medical Department does not desire to carry the responsibility for her going to the mission field."[46]

The Robsons were appointed in October 1922 but they were ordered to go to West Virginia for three months to allow Gertrude to recover from the delivery of their child and to observe whether she was truly healthy enough to return to China. They did sail at the end of the year. Horace Robson served at Nanking University, and in 1927 the couple sustained considerable losses in the Nanking uprising.

ETHEL MABUCE

Some of the young women who went to the mission field under the WFMS in the early years of this century served one or two terms, then returned to the United States where they married or took up other professions. Three of these women were Ethel Mabuce, Ethel Householder, and Floy Hurlbut.

Ethel Mabuce was born in 1886 in Missouri. After completing high school, she attended Mayfield College for a year and then taught four years in country and graded schools. After receiving a call to missionary work, she entered the Chicago Evangelistic Institute, graduating in 1911. She then went to Taylor where she earned a B.A., graduating with the class of 1916. She had been accepted by the WFMS Des Moines Branch before graduation, but she was not sure where she would be sent. Just after graduation she received word that she had been appointed to Burma, but she did not sail until mid November. The trip was far more difficult than anyone anticipated. They were delayed in Japan because

Ethel Mabuce. Missionary to Burma.

248

of passport difficulties, and when they arrived in Singapore, they discovered they could not book steamer passage directly to Burma, but had to go by way of Madras and Colombo. She did not arrive in Rangoon until mid-February of the following year.

Mabuce's first year in Burma was spent in the Rangoon area where she was appointed to do evangelistic work. She also spent the year learning the Burmese language. The following year she was sent to Pegu where she continued evangelistic work. She remained in this area until her furlough in 1921. During her five years in Burma, Mabuce became proficient enough in the Burmese language that she was able to engage in significant translation work. There was a great need for Christian literature in the vernacular, and she fully expected to return to Burma following her furlough to continue in this work. In order to further prepare herself for the next term, she decided to enroll in graduate school at Northwestern University in Evanston, Illinois. While there she completed all the course work for the M.A. but decided not to do the thesis because it was too stressful. That summer she underwent a serious surgical procedure which caused her return to Burma to be postponed.

However, instead of merely being postponed her second term was canceled when she responded to "another call." The Rev. Chris J. Soelberg of Imogene, Iowa proposed. She accepted, and the couple was married in November of 1923. Soelberg had been a missionary to the Chinese-speaking people of Burma for a number of years before returning to the United States and assuming the duties of a parish pastor in the Methodist Episcopal Church.

The couple served rural churches in Iowa and Kansas during their marriage. As a minister's wife, Ethel Soelberg did a great amount of speaking at conferences and other church activities on behalf of missions. After he retired from the active ministry, Chris Soelberg became involved in the promotion of farmer's cooperatives. He was managing one in Kansas when he was stricken with a series of paralyzing strokes. The Soelbergs moved back to Missouri to be near family where Chris died in 1954.

After her husband's death, Mabuce continued an active life of service working at a children's hospital in St Louis until forced to retire at age 65. She then worked as director of an apartment house for women students at the University of Southeast Missouri.

In 1972 Mabuce's niece, Lucille Griffith, persuaded her to edit and publish the large number of letters which she had written to the various members of her family during the years she spent in Burma. This volume, *I Always Wore My Topi,* demonstrated that Mabuce had a real heart for the Burmese people. Many of the letters presented vivid descriptions of life in Burma including many details about climate, flora and fauna, the Buddhist religion, cultural festivals, and social customs. She also clearly described the demands placed on an evangelistic missionary working in a tropical country where travel between the cities and the small villages had to be negotiated by sampan, bicycle or ox cart. The book ended with the following summation of the life of Ethel Mabuce Soelberg:

> She may have been disheartened by the few obvious successes, but often she saw evidence that the Spirit was working among the people. She had never once doubted that the Lord meant for her to be where she was. She had dedicated her whole life to the work of the Master; five of those years she spent in Burma. They were Good years, too, perhaps even the best.[47]

FLOY HURLBUT

Floy Hurlbut and Ethel Householder were classmates,

graduating from Taylor in 1911. They both served two terms in China before returning to the United States where they pursued careers in education after doing further graduate work. Householder taught in the public schools and Hurlbut became a professor at Ball State University in Muncie, Indiana.

Floy Hurlbut was born in a Methodist parsonage in Kearney, Nebraska April 29, 1888. She graduated from Kearney High School in 1906 and attended John Fletcher College for three years before coming to Taylor University where she studied philosophy, mathematics, Greek and Latin. She taught science and mathematics and was Assistant Principal in a high school for one year before going to China. During her two terms of missionary service which stretched from 1913 to 1926 she taught at Foochow Women's College. She earned an A.M. in Geography and Philosophy at the University of Nebraska in 1928, and followed this with a Ph.D. from the same institution in 1930. Hurlbut came to Ball State in 1931 as Professor of Geography. Three years later she established the present Ball State Weather Bureau and provided weather reports for the Muncie Evening Press and WLBC radio station. She was the first woman president of Sigma Zeta, a national science honorary. Her doctoral thesis *The Fukienese: A Study in Human Geography* was

The Gem

Floy Hurlbut. Missionary to China.

subsequently published as a book. She also wrote *The Climate of Fukien Province* which was published by the Natural History Society of Fukien Christian University. Throughout her life she was an active member of High Street United Methodist Church in Muncie. After her retirement from Ball State in 1954 she founded the Muncie Travel Agency in partnership with a former student. In 1965 Ball State named a residence hall in the Studebaker Complex in her honor. She remained in the position of Director of the Muncie Travel Agency until shortly before her death January 2, 1973 at the age of 85.[48]

AMY SPALDING

One Taylor woman whose career in ministry is particularly impressive is Amy Spalding who received her A.B. in 1916. While a student, Spalding was a campus leader and a particularly strong debater for the Soangetahas. In addition, she was a member of the Student Volunteers and the Philalethean Society. It is perhaps not surprising that she would spend her life in ministry. After graduating from Taylor, Spalding taught for two years in God's Bible School in Cincinnati, Ohio while taking graduate work at the University of Cincinnati. In 1920 she took a position with the Indiana Women's Christian Temperance Union. Her job was to work with the foreign born women who were coming into the state. She was sent to Columbia University to attend a summer course in social science and to learn to teach English to the foreign born. She did her practical work in the WCTU Neighbor House on the Lower East Side of New York City. After completing this experience, she was employed as a Field Secretary

Amy Spalding.

with the WCTU. For the next three and a half years she traveled throughout the United States speaking on behalf of temperance in churches and community organizations of every conceivable type. In 1923 she was appointed American Executive Secretary to China. She was assigned to work with Dr. Mary Stone and the Chinese WCTU where over five thousand college students had pledged to bring prohibition to that country.

After her retirement from the WCTU, she continued to lead an active life of service. She moved to Chicago where she became an apartment house manager and still found time to be involved in many Christian organizations. She was President of Business Women's Missionary Fellowship of Moody Church, President of the Women's Auxiliary of the Gospel League and teacher of the Business Women's Bible Class.

CONCLUSION

It is abundantly clear from these representative stories of Taylor women missionaries that each experience was unique in its challenges and opportunities. Many factors, both controllable and uncontrollable, affected the success or failure of these women who found the courage and strength to travel to all the corners of the world where they gave their lives in dedicated service to the end that the Kingdom of God might come upon the earth.

The Ilium

Simon Mungai from Kenya, class of 1989.

Chapter Six

FROM THE CORNERS OF THE EARTH: THE INTERNATIONAL ALUMNI

ince the 1890s Taylor University has attracted a number of international students who have made significant contributions worldwide. However, the presence of internationals at Taylor has not been a steady stream. There have been peak times notably in the first three decades of the twentieth century, and during the last fifteen years. There were also some international students in the late 1940s and early 1950s and in the 1960s. In addition to the story of Samuel Morris from Liberia which is familiar to the Taylor community, there are other international students who have made a significant impact on the world. A number of students came from Africa following the Morris tradition. Even more numerous have been students from the Caribbean region with African heritage. Other significant nations represented among the Taylor student body have been Japan and Canada. Students from other parts of East Asia, the Middle East, Latin America, and Europe have also been drawn to Taylor through the decades. Nearly all the international student alumni attending Taylor University before 1960 entered full-time Christian service either as missionaries or pastors, and most were men.

Until World War II, there was a considerable amount of international attention on campus, particularly with respect to Christian foreign mission opportunities. The international interest waned somewhat during the late 1940s and 1950s, though there existed a small International Club. This interest has become a major factor in campus life during the late 1980s and early 1990s.

EARLY INTERNATIONAL STUDENTS: Hagop Dalkiranian, Sarkis P. Jamcotchian

The first known international student to study at Taylor, then known as Fort Wayne College, was Henry Alson Gladding from Ontario, Canada, who was in the freshman class in 1870-1, and whose course of study was identified as classical in the Collegiate Department. In the late 1870s, Roy F. Davies from Kingston, Ontario was an enrolled student, and was followed in the early 1880s by C.H.W.F. Siemon whom the 1881-2 catalogue identified as from Prussia. The 1889-90 catalogue noted that Gertrude H. Frommholz from Switzerland was one of that year's graduates. Leonard Rubinson from Minsk, Russia was listed in the 1892-3 catalogue. Samuel Morris from Liberia was a student at Taylor University from 1891 until his untimely death in 1893. The catalogue of 1892-3 noted that Morris was in the Biblical course. Also listed in the 1892-3 catalogue were two students - Hagop Dalkiranian and Mikran K. Serailian-from Caesarea, Turkey (now Israel). Both students presumably of Armenian extraction were enrolled in the Biblical course. Unfortunately Dalkiranian died on October 24, 1893 at the age of 26 shortly after the school moved to Upland. The cause of death is not known. A monument was placed in the Jefferson Cemetery, Upland, which still exists today. The inscription, now barely legible, reads: "Hagop Dalkiranian died October 24, 1893 aged 26 years Born of Armenian parents in Caesarea, Turkey Entered Taylor University to qualify himself as a missionary to his people."

This may be the oldest monument in the Jefferson Cemetery. Taylor University purchased a plot at the time, and at least three other people, and perhaps a fourth are buried there.[1]

Nothing is known about what happened to Mikran K. Serailian because he is not listed in any other catalogue. But the 1894-5 enrollment list finds Sarkis P. Jamcotchian, (there are various spellings), also from Caesarea. William Ringenberg in *Taylor University The First 125 Years* noted (page 75) that in 1896 the faculty voted to give $72.00 in financial aid to Jamkotchian and $120.37 to Samuel Culpepper, a student from British Guiana (now Guyana). These were Taylor's first international student scholarships. *The Gem* of 1898 stated that Jamgotchian was Vice President of the Philalethean Literary Society and an associate editor of the student newspaper.

S.P. Jamcotchian, from Caesarera, Turkey (now Israel)

In the 1895-6 catalogue there was also identified in the enrollment list Alfred Dachnowski from Berlin, Germany, and Hebe Wea from Cavalla, Africa (probably Liberia). In the 1897-8 catalogue Dachnowski continued to be listed as well as Samuel G. Noble from Ox Bow, Canada; Marvin Norwood from Caracas, Venezuela; and B.V. Wilson from Liberia, the last names quite possibly being two of the earliest children of overseas missionaries (MKs or TCKs) to attend Taylor.

AFRICA: Samuel Morris

The most famous African student to study at Taylor University was undoubtedly Samuel Morris (1873-1893) from Liberia whose "'spirit-filled' life epitomized what [President Thaddeus] Reade was seeking to accomplish in the lives of all his students."[2] In 1896, three years after Morris' death, President Reade having been deeply moved by the story of this young Liberian, wrote an account of his life.[3] Ringenberg has noted that it was this young man's story as related by Reade more than Morris' personal influence that has made such a significant impact on the history of the institution. Reade wrote his account of this young man of deep faith at a time when the school was struggling for its own survival, having just moved from Fort Wayne to Upland. Reade

Taylor University Archives

Samuel Morris, Liberian Student

was devastated by Morris' death. As Lindley Baldwin's account of Morris noted, Reade had counted on Morris as a major attraction in the cornerstone ceremonies in Upland on June 22 , 1893. Morris was to have spoken and sung.[4]

Baldwin's account of Morris' life was published in 1942. The author at the time was 79 years of age; he had been urged for years by Reade to write this biography. It contains additional information not included in Reade's study. In his Foreword, Baldwin acknowledged his debt to Harriet Stemen MacBeth, teacher of Morris "who knew him better than anyone else." Baldwin was from Fort Wayne, a friend of Dr. Reade, and also had "a fatherly contact with Sammy."[5] Reade wrote his study in 1896 and Baldwin in 1942, but between these two works there was another study of Morris' life. Jorge O. Masa, a Taylor student from the Philippines, wrote *The Angel in Ebony or The Life and Message of Sammy Morris* in 1928 (published by Taylor University Press). Masa noted in his preface that he acknowledged the help among others of Stemen MacBeth, Baldwin, and Miss Grace Husted of Greenfield, Indiana who also knew Morris.

The Taylor community is very familiar with the Samuel Morris story. However, there are some missing details and some contradictions in various parts of the account. There is very little documented material; only one photograph in fact exists of Morris. He was probably born in what is today the West African nation of Guinea somewhere between the Kong Mountains and the Niger River, according to Dr. Charles (Tim) Kirkpatrick who has done considerable research.[6] He was snatched from his parents as a child by slave traders. His earliest childhood memories are living in a Kru village, the adopted son of a chief. Hence he was known as Prince Kaboo (Kuba or Kubah). He recalled constant fighting between the Kru and the Grebo people. According to Kirkpatrick, Kaboo's boyhood home was in the village of Po River near the town of Garraway in southeastern Liberia. Interestingly Bishop Taylor and a party of missionaries came ashore at Garraway in 1888.

Morris recalled he had a "Damascus" experience when he heard an audible voice and saw a light in the sky urging him to flee his captors. After many days he arrived at a coffee plantation presumably near the present city of Monrovia. Methodist missionaries connected with Bishop Taylor visited the plantation every Sunday, noted Kirkpatrick. One of these missionaries was identified as Miss Knolls who according to Lindley Baldwin had been educated at Fort Wayne College and had recently arrived in Liberia. Masa's book was the first publication noting her name. However, the authors of *God's Ordinary People: No Ordinary Heritage* have not found her name on any student lists. It might be noted Reade in his account only mentioned a lady missionary "gave him some instructions in reading and writing and taught him the sweet, simple lessons of the gospel."[7]

Baldwin then recounted that Kaboo was taken into the Methodist Church and baptized as Samuel Morris, a name presumably chosen by Miss Knolls in honor of her benefactor, Samuel Morris. Masa was the first writer to state this fact. However, he did not identify his source.[8] Baldwin noted that Morris was a Fort Wayne banker but Wesley Robinson (class of 1950) in his "Pages from History" in the *Taylor University Magazine* described Samuel L. Morris Sr. as a partner in the law firm of Barrett, Morris and Hoffman.[9] He died in 1922 and is buried in the Lindenwood Cemetery, the same one where Kaboo (Samuel Morris) is buried. Robinson also noted in that article that this Fort Wayne attorney financially supported "Miss Anna Knoll."[10]

After being converted, Morris was determined to share his new found faith with his own people and to learn more of the power of the Holy Spirit. The accounts state that Miss Knolls and Rev. C. E. Smirl, another missionary, advised him to go to America. Jorge Masa in *The Angel in Ebony* noted that Morris became acquainted with another missionary, Elizabeth (Lizzie) MacNeil (see Chapter Two) who knew Rev. Stephen Merritt.[11] Merritt was the secretary of Taylor's mission, the dynamic preacher of the Jane Street Methodist Church in New York City, and considered to be a man of deep faith who emphasized in his preaching the power of the Holy Spirit. Miss MacNeil took a strong interest in Morris. Morris eventually was able to convince the captain of the bark "Liberia" to hire him on as crew member; according to Kirkpatrick the ship left Cape Mount (today Robertsport) in late July 1891. It was a difficult crossing for Morris because of stormy weather and racist attitudes on the part of the crew. The "Liberia" arrived in Kingston Jamaica August 28, and then sailed on to New York City. It arrived in the East River on September 27, and docked at the Pike Street pier not far from today's South Street Seaport restoration. The mission office was at 210 Eighth Street where Morris met Merritt. Merritt and Ross Taylor, one of Bishop Taylor's four sons, were able to get Morris admitted into Fort Wayne College where Morris arrived in late October 1891. He was listed as an "irregular student" the first year, and the following year, as a "Biblical student." He attended the Berry Street Methodist Church in Fort Wayne. Unfortunately Morris acquired a severe cold in January 1893, never regained his health, and died May 12, 1893 in St. Joseph's Hospital, Fort Wayne.

Reade noted the following concerning Morris' death and subsequent funeral:

> So ended this marvelous life. A thousand hearts were full of grief, for we all loved him, and many of us stood in dumb amazement at the Providence which had so quickly terminated what promised to be such a useful life. His plans and ours were all shattered in a moment. But God's ways are higher and better than ours. Sammy's funeral took place from the Berry Street church, to which he belonged, and was one of the largest and by far the most tender and sympathetic one I

ever witnessed in the City of Fort Wayne. The church was packed from the pulpit to the street, hundreds waiting through the whole service outside the door. And strong men bowed themselves that day, and many wept who were not accustomed to weeping.[12]

Morris was buried in the black section of Lindenwood Cemetery, Fort Wayne, and Harriet Stemen MacBeth arranged for a modest stone.

But the memory of Morris and his story continued to fascinate and motivate Taylor's students and faculty. The senior class of 1928 elected one of their own, Filipino Jorge O. Masa, to write a study of Morris which was published under the title *The Angel in Ebony or The Life and Message of Sammy Morris.* The senior class also convinced cemetery officials to reinter Morris' body in a more prominent part of the cemetery. Noted Frances (Thomas '28) Allen whose late husband, Earl '28, chaired the senior class gift committee, "We heard that about 500 people every year would go to visit his grave, even though it was in an inconspicuous place in the cemetery."[13] The simple marker was replaced by a more prominent one with the following inscription:

Samuel Morris
1873-1893
Prince Kaboo
Native of West Africa
Famous Christian Mystic
Apostle of Simple Faith
Exponent of the Spirit-filled Life
Student at Taylor University 1892-3
Fort Wayne, now located at
Upland, Ind. The story of his life
a vital contribution to the
development of Taylor University
The erection of the memorial was

> sponsored by the 1928 class Taylor
> University, and funds were contributed
> by Fort Wayne citizens.

An official of the Lindenwood Cemetery has noted this grave continues to attract more visitors to the cemetery than any other monument.

The impact of the Morris story can be demonstrated in other ways in Taylor's history. The Taylor campus has had a residence hall named for Morris. The original one was built in 1894. The first floor at the outset served as the campus dining hall and kitchen while the second floor was a dormitory for male students. The present Morris Hall was completed in 1958. Throughout the 1920s, 1930s, and 1940s, *The Echo* continued to run articles on Morris' life. In two articles entitled "Spirit of Sammy Morris Influencing Africa" appearing in the May 15 and 31, 1930 issues of *The Echo*, the rapidly growing William Wade Harris independent church movement in west Africa was seen by the author, Robert D. Annand, as a continuation of the Morris spirit. The senior class of 1940 visited the Morris grave in Fort Wayne, as noted in the May 25, 1940 *Echo* issue. Numerous yearbooks have through the years run stories on Morris. In 1954, John C. Wengatz, famed Taylor missionary alumnus, wrote *Sammy Morris Spirit-Filled Life* at the urging of Taylor's Board of Directors. Wengatz noted that he first read the life of Morris in 1906 while a student at Taylor "but have read it many times since, and my tears never cease to flow as I read that unrepeatable story. Each time I find myself again treading on sacred ground."[14] In the Foreword to this book, Evan H. Bergwall, President of Taylor (1951-1959), stated:

> Institutions are the 'lengthened shadows' of individuals. Taylor
> University owes much to the influence of Sammy Morris.

God's Ordinary People:

> Never has greater childlike faith in God been exemplified in a life. Nor has such an unpretentious life had such a far reaching influence on people and institutions. In a day when we are pleased to notice some up-swing in spiritual fervor in evangelical circles across the country and world, we are happy to have the opportunity of telling the story of Sammy Morris once again.

In 1956 the film "Angel in Ebony" was produced which has been viewed by numerous groups.

In more recent times the Morris story continues to attract considerable interest. In December 1988 Professor Kirkpatrick and videographer J. David Ryan (class of 1983) visited Liberia and from that experience produced a thirty minute video documentary entitled "Sammy Morris-100 Years Later Kuba's Amazing Journey."

As part of the October 1995 Homecoming which began Taylor's sesquicentennial celebrations, a Samuel Morris sculpture was dedicated on the Taylor University-Upland campus. A similar sculpture was unveiled in October 1996 on the Fort Wayne campus. The Upland sculpture features three life-size bronze figures creating a narrative symbol of the African's Spirit-filled life. Three figurative components, The Moment of Truth, Heeding the Call, and Sharing the Word are united by circular motifs representing passages, eternity, and the Trinity. The artist-sculptor is Kenneth G. Ryden of Anderson University. The sculpture and surrounding park area were given in memory of Richard H. Schmitz, Ohio businessman and active church member, by the Schmitz family. The Fort Wayne work honors Rachel Lynne Schmitz, wife of Taylor graduate Jamey Schmitz. Another remembrance of Morris is the Samuel Morris Endowed Scholarship Fund for international students attending Taylor University which was first awarded in 1993.

OTHER EARLY AFRICAN STUDENTS: Henry O'Neil, Charles Blooah, Bvuo Nkomo

In *The Angel in Ebony,* Masa mentioned a young African named Henry O'Neil whom Morris had befriended before leaving Liberia for the United States. Masa noted that one day in Fort Wayne, Morris surprised Dr. Reade when he announced his intention of quitting school so that he might to go work. Reade asked for an explanation to which Morris replied he wanted to work in order to get money to bring O'Neil to America. Morris explained that he was his brother in Christ, whom Morris had converted, and that he wanted O'Neil to come to America for an education. Reade's response was that if he were to come, the Lord would open the way and that Morris should pray about it. Morris followed Reade's advice and felt convinced O'Neil would come. Through the efforts of Reade, Stephen Merritt and several missionaries, O'Neil came to this country and attended a school in St. Louis. Apparently the two Africans corresponded with each other. O'Neil then returned to Africa.[15]

Wesley Robinson in his article "Pages from History" in the *Taylor University Magazine* (spring 1988) noted that eleven years after Morris died, O'Neil returned to the United States, this time to study at Taylor which was then located in Upland. O'Neil arrived in Upland by train on August 23, 1904, and was brought to the home of Dr. Burt Ayres. According to Robinson, O'Neil remained at Taylor for three years, and then returned to his home in Freetown, Sierra Leone. In his article, Robinson identified a photograph appearing in *Le Fleuron* (the name of the Taylor yearbook in 1905) of the students of the Elocution Department. Appearing in the photo is an African student whom Robinson identified as O'Neil.

God's Ordinary People:

The 1905-6 *Taylor University Catalog* listed Henry Bezear O'Neil of Freetown, Sierra Leone as an unclassified student in the class of 1905.

There have been at least five other Liberian students who have studied at Taylor. Charles Blooah appeared in *The Gem* of 1909, 1913 and 1915. He was identified as from Garraway, Liberia, apparently the same area where Samuel Morris had grown up. He was a Philalethean, a debater and soloist. *The Taylorite* of January 23, 1913 ran an article written by Blooah entitled "What Africa?"[16]

It was a call for Christian missionaries to Africa. Blooah advised Christians that it might take years of struggle for the Church to be victorious in Africa, but eventually it would happen. Blooah saw parallels between the Church in Africa and John Brown in his efforts to free the slaves:

Le Fleuron - 1905

Henry O'Neil from a photograph of the Elocution Department.

John Brown failed to carry out his plan, but out of his failure sprang the... victory.

We are looking forward to the coming of the day when the Christian Church shall set herself high upon the tower of glory and shall spell out the wood V-I-C-T-O-R-Y over the grave of indifference toward Africa.[17]

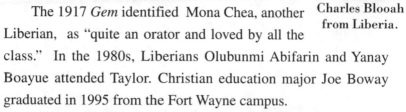

Charles Blooah
from Liberia.

Blooah went on for additional education to DePauw University.

The 1917 *Gem* identified Mona Chea, another Liberian, as "quite an orator and loved by all the class." In the 1980s, Liberians Olubunmi Abifarin and Yanay Boayue attended Taylor. Christian education major Joe Boway graduated in 1995 from the Fort Wayne campus.

In the early days of Taylor's history, the writers of this book have discovered a number of students died while attending Taylor. Hagop Dalkiranian and Samuel Morris, previously noted, were regrettably not the only cases. The life and experiences of Bvuo Nkomo in many ways parallels the story of Morris. Nkomo was born in 1895 in a region called Gazaland in what is today Mozambique. He attended a mission school conducted by the Congregational Board of Foreign Missions. At some point he left his home and walked a three days' journey to Melsetor (Melsetter) in today's eastern Zimbabwe. Again he moved, this time to Old Umtali, a three days' walk from Melsetor, where he found work in a cobbler's shop and where he spent his spare hours teaching. Nkomo then journeyed to Salisbury (Harare) where he was employed as a driver for a Boer farmer. Amazingly he earned enough money to come to America. It was noted that at the mission school at Old Umtali one of the teachers was Miss Pearl Mullikin who gave him a letter of introduction to Professor Newton Wray in Taylor University's Religion Department.[18] Nkomo traveled to the United States via Cape Town and Southampton, England, the journey taking five weeks. In August 1913, at the age of 18, he arrived in Upland and found his way to Professor Wray's home. Nkomo was a student in the Academy. A photograph of several male students in front of the old Samuel Morris Dormitory is believed to include Nkomo.

Tragically Nkomo became ill and for many weeks was nursed in the Morris Dormitory. But his condition worsened, and he was taken to Marion Hospital where he died on May 12, 1918. The death records at the Grant County Health Department noted that

Student residents (1917?) of the original Samuel Morris Dormitory including several international students. Bvuo Nkomo is probably sixth from right.

Taylor University Archives

"Stoic Nkomo" had died of typhoid fever and that he had been studying for the ministry. The death records stated that his date of birth and names of parents were unknown.

The May 23, 1918 issue of *The Echo* included a story of this young African student. At the funeral service, Professor Wray gave the eulogy. The article observed that during his sickness in the hospital "his gentle nature won for him the sympathies of those attending; but in spite of the best of devoted care, he died, a martyr for his native land." *The Echo* obituary noted that he came to Taylor:

> that he might prepare himself to preach and teach his tribesmen... In the passing of Bvuo Nkomo, a unique character has been taken from our midst. His memory will ever be a call to every Christian heart to more zealous missionary efforts. May the mission for which he died never remain unfinished.[19]

The obituary concluded that he was laid to rest in the Jefferson Cemetery, Upland.[20] The authors of this book, however, have not been able to find any records at the cemetery regarding his internment. There are no markers. It is believed by the writers that this needs further investigation. Perhaps Nkomo is buried in the Taylor University plot where three others, including Dalkiranian, are interred. Why there is no record of his burial or any markers is not resolved. There are a couple of possible explanations. There was no money at the time to erect a suitable monument. Or perhaps Nkomo may be the only person of African ancestry buried in the cemetery. In 1918 there was considerable racial animosity in Grant County and possibly no one was willing to erect a monument for fear of vandalism. The writers believe it may be appropriate for the Taylor University community to do additional research on this devout Christian student. This indeed may be a class project similar to the one undertaken by the class of 1928 when it erected a monument to Samuel Morris in the Lindenwood Cemetery, Fort Wayne. Available material on this young African student is admittedly very sketchy, but it makes Nkomo's heroic story even more fascinating. Almost precisely two years after the death of Nkomo, another Taylor international student, Fujihiko Oi also died (May 23, 1920) in the Marion Hospital from typhoid fever.

AFRICAN STUDENTS SINCE WORLD WAR II: William James Humbane, K. Paul and Silas Kasambira, John Kawadza

In the late 1940s and early 1950s, several African students came to Taylor. The 1948 and 1949 *Gem* noted that three Ethiopians-Yohannes (John) Makonnen, Abraham Demere, and Gebbede Gebregiorges - were studying in Upland. Other Ethiopians came to Taylor in the 1980s — Bete Demeke, Kidan and Hanna Alemishet, and Mahedere Mulugeta. Mrs. Marta Gabre-Tsadick of Fort Wayne has been a Taylor trustee during the late 1980s and 1990s. The inspiring story of her Christian faith and her journey to the United States has been published in her book entitled *Sheltered by the King*.[21] Mrs. Gabre-Tsadick and her husband, Demeke Tekle-Wold, have spearheaded Project Mercy, a humanitarian organization to help needy people in Ethiopia and other economically hard-hit areas of Africa. During the 1995 January interterm, a number of Taylor students worked in one of the Ethiopian villages targeted by Project Mercy.

In the early 1950s, Africans Isaac Mensah Apprey from Ghana (then the Gold Coast), Elisha Mutasa from Southern Rhodesia, and A. Ikio Dufegha were students at Taylor. Apprey studied criminal law, and Dufegha was in chemistry with an interest in Christian missions as his life work. The early 1960s brought three students

from Zaire, namely Boniface Chiwengo, Elie Kaputo, and Theodore
Mbualungu. Following graduation in 1965, Mbualungu directed
and taught in a secondary school at the Mukedi station in Zaire.
Bob Wantwadi from Kinshasa, Zaire was a social studies major in
the early 1970s.

From Zimbabwe (Southern Rhodesia) in the mid-1960s came
Josiah Njagu. He was the first of several students with a Zimbabwe
connection. Njagu was a biology major. After graduating from
Taylor, he went on to Ball State University where he earned a

master's degree in biology. Njagu
returned to Zimbabwe where he became
a school principal. He died tragically a
few years ago in an accident. William
James Humbane was a student at Taylor
in the late 1960s and early 1970s.
Humbane, born in Mozambique, had
been Bishop Ralph Dodge's (class of
'31) secretary and chauffeur in
Zimbabwe. In January 1966 he and his
family arrived in Upland. Humbane
majored in French and prepared for
teaching in secondary education. After

William James Humbane
from Zimbabwe.

graduating from Taylor, he enrolled in the Graduate School of
Education at Ball State University, eventually earning his Ph.D.
The family returned to Zimbabwe. Dr. Humbane lives in Harare
and is Executive Secretary of the Methodist Church's Africa Church
Growth and Development Project. This is a partnership of United
Methodist churches in Africa, Europe, and the United States sharing
resources for projects in leadership development, evangelism and

community development, and church construction. Dr. Humbane regularly visits "the 13 annual Conferences of The United Methodist Church in Africa to inspect church projects as well as to perceive their needs and or achievements and subsequently visits the European and American churches to report on how their financial support is being utilized."[22]

Paul and Silas Kasambira, twins from Zimbabwe, born in 1942, were students at Taylor in the early 1970s. They were two of eleven children born to a Methodist preacher and his wife in Umtali (Mutare). Dr. K. Paul Kasambira, related that it was the custom among the Shona people to kill one of the twins at birth. But being Christians the Kasambira family went against this custom. Both Paul and Silas attended Hartzell Secondary School in Old Umtali. Paul Kasambira then went on to Gweru Teacher's College. Because of his superior grades, he was asked to join the teaching staff in his second year. Next he received an invitation to teach at Nyadiri College where he was an instructor for two years, and a deputy headmaster for another two

Dr. K. Paul Kasambira from Zimbabwe.

years. He received a scholarship to study at Taylor University. Interestingly his older brother, Daniel, had sung at Taylor in 1958 with a singing group known as the Ambassadors Quartet. Paul Kasambira arrived in Upland in 1972 with his family.[23] He majored in English, working closely with Dr. Frances Ewbank and Professor Herbert Lee. Following his graduation from Taylor in 1975, Kasambira went on to Ball State University where he earned his Ph.D. in the School of Education. His special interest is educational psychology. Dr. Kasambira is Professor of Teacher Education at Bradley University and a well-established author. His *Lesson Planning and Class Management* was published in 1993 by Longman Press. Silas Kasambira initially began his American education at Ball State University, then transferred to Taylor. He was a biology major. He returned to Zimbabwe and is now a business consultant in Harare. As Paul Kasambira noted, "nine of the Kasambira children went into the field of education - only Silas and another did not. Silas is a white sheep of the family!"[24]

John Kawadza, son of Jonah Kawadza who had been Bishop Ralph Dodge's administrative assistant, graduated from Taylor in 1977. He married Wanda Smith ('76) from the United States. The fall 1988 *Taylor University Magazine* noted that the Kawadzas were living in Harare where John Kawadza was traveling secretary for Fellowship of Christian Union with responsibility for counseling, visiting and coordinating programs for spiritual development among students in higher education. He then went on to teach in a high school in Harare. Wanda Kawadza is an administrator at the University of Zimbabwe. She was Administrative Assistant to the Vice Chancellor of the University of Zimbabwe with responsibility for office administration and involvement with government ministries.[25] Elizabeth Karonga was a Zimbabwean student at Taylor in the early 1980s.

During the late 1960s and 1970s, a couple of Kenyan students were at Taylor. Ruth Kiteka was a biology major. Phil Muinde (class of '73) impressed many people by his deep Christian faith. Rev. Muinde and his family live in Scotland where he is in the Department of Religious Studies at the University of Aberdeen. Stephen (Kip) Koech was a track star, and Martha Okumu, who studied at Taylor for one year, is the daughter of Washington Okumu, a high ranking United Nations diplomat who helped to negotiate a settlement between the African National Congress and the Zulu Inkatha Movement during South Africa's recent presidential elections. Daniel Shani was a business major who graduated in 1981. The fall/winter 1982 issue of the *Taylor University Magazine* featured an article on Shani who was chosen as one of the 1981. Outstanding Young Men of America. He was from a village near Mt. Kilimanjaro, a warrior of the Maasai tribe. Following graduation Shani was with World Vision. In the late 1980s and 1990s at least ten Kenyan students studied at Taylor as well as three others who had been raised in Kenya but who were British subjects.

From South Africa in the 1980s came Betty Ann Botha and Donald and Kenneth Smith. In the late 1970s Charles Masalakulangwa from Tanzania was a student at Taylor. Following graduation in 1978, Masalakulangwa assumed leadership of Inland Press, Mwanza, Tanzania, which prints gospel literature for Africa. In the mid-1980s several West Africans were at Taylor including Robert Taylor from Ghana, Rahila and Yusufu Dankaro from Nigeria, and H. Sona Walla from Cote d'Ivoire. More recently students from Burundi and Zambia have attended Taylor, and one man from Burkina Faso briefly taught French on a part-time basis In addition there are numerous "MKs" who have come to Taylor to study.

It should also be noted that several faculty have either worked in Africa or have traveled there. Charles (Tim) Kirkpatrick and Pat Kirkpatrick were missionaries in Burundi for a number of years. Dr. Milo Rediger, former President of Taylor, made two trips to Africa, a purpose being to locate landmarks significant in the lives of Bishop Taylor and John and Susan Wengatz. Other faculty who have been involved with study trips to Africa or engaged in scholarly research have included Beulah Baker, Faye Chechowich, David Dickey, David Hess, Jessica L. Rousselow, and Alan H. Winquist. Charles Gifford and Steve Beers have led Lighthouse groups to Zimbabwe and Ethiopia respectively. Recently several students have studied at Daystar University, Nairobi.

The special Taylor connection with Africa indeed has been long standing and of great significance.

THE CARIBBEAN
GUYANA (formerly British Guiana): Samuel Culpepper

Samuel Culpepper was born in British Guiana in 1880. As a child his family moved to Trinidad and at the age of six his education began in a Roman Catholic school on the island. From there he went to Caracas, Venezuela, and then on to Taylor University to prepare for the ministry. In June 1898 he completed the academic course, and two years later received his AB degree with high grades. While a student, Culpepper was President of the Philalethean Literary Society in 1900. He was also listed as Professor of Spanish at Taylor during the 1900-1 academic year.

Culpepper was a member of the North Indiana Conference of the Methodist Episcopal Church. In 1901 he was appointed Professor of Latin and Greek at Washington Institute, San Juan, Puerto Rico. This institute was a Methodist school founded in September 1900 to train "young people of Porto Rican and American families not willing to send their children to the public schools and not able to send them to the United States."[26] The same report noted that Culpepper came about April 1, 1901 from Taylor, and rendered "very efficient service in all departments of the Mission."[27]

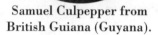

Samuel Culpepper from British Guiana (Guyana).

In 1902 Culpepper was ordained a deacon, and in 1905 an elder. He served churches in several locations in Puerto Rico including San Juan and Arecibo. He married a Puerto Rican woman in 1907 and fathered four children, one of whom later was enrolled as a student at DePauw University. Culpepper was known as an effective evangelist. He died in 1928 after a period of declining health. The obituary observed that:

> The altars were never empty when he gave the sweet invitation to the sinners; so then, on his last night on earth, 23 persons came to the altar, and he, full of enthusiasm, said: 'One more, one more; I do not want to retire tonight without giving you an opportunity; I want to have a clear conscience,' and the warrior... felt happy. Then he retired, happy, without the least thought that it was his last night on earth.[28]

In the early 1950s Taylor had another student from British Guiana named Patrick A. Bacchus. *The Gem* of 1952 noted that he came from Georgetown. Following graduation Bacchus enrolled at Garrett Biblical Institute, Evanston, Illinois, and accepted a call as assistant minister at the First Methodist Church in Pekin, Illinois. He was voted membership in the Illinois Methodist Conference, the first black minister in that conference.

BARBADOS: Joseph P. Blades

One of the most outstanding students at Taylor during the second decade of the twentieth century was Joseph Blades. In 1951 Dean Burt W. Ayres, then Vice President Emeritus of the University, wrote *Honor to Whom Honor Is Due The Life Story of Joseph Preston Blades.* In the preface, Ayres noted that:

> The two lives [Samuel Morris, Joseph Blades] brought together in Taylor's history-though not face to face-are complementary to each other and present together a wonderful beauty, richness, and balance of the mystical, rational, and ethical in Christian experience, life, and character as manifested in the black race.[29]

Ayres hoped this small volume would in some way make a significant contribution to race tolerance because while a student Blades experienced racial discrimination. One such incident was when he fell on the ice and broke his cheek bone during an Upland winter. A local doctor refused to treat him. It was Robert E. Brown, professor of chemistry and future missionary doctor in China, who then came to his aid. Ayres also recounted incidents in which Blades was refused service in Marion and Muncie restaurants.

Ayres quoted from Blades how he first learned of Taylor University. While walking down a road in Barbados one day, he saw a piece of paper. The headline of the paper read "Taylor University."

> I began to read the story which told of the life of Samuel Morris. I read and reread the story of his life. Finally I said I would like to go to that University where this young man had gone. This seemed fantastic, for I did not know where Taylor University was, only that it was in America. Neither had I any money to get there.[30]

Blades then decided to join his brother on the island of St. Lucia to find work opportunities. He remained there for six years engaged in a variety of jobs. After a brief return to Barbados, Blades set out for the Panama Canal Zone to stay with a Christian friend whom he had met in St. Lucia. Eventually he found employment in Panama which allowed him to save enough money in three years to get himself to the United States. He was headed for a Bible school in Cincinnati, Ohio upon the advice of a missionary in Barbados. He remained for two years at that school, and then transferred to Taylor in 1909. He took courses both from the Academy and College, and finally obtained his A.B. degree in 1918.

Joseph P. Blades from Barbados. Photo taken in 1950.

Honor to Whom Honor is Due

Ayres recollected that Joe, as Blades was known on campus, was:

so humble, courteous and kind,

278

that I believe every one in the student body and faculty loved him and had great respect for him as a Christian gentleman in the true sense of that term; and recognized in him more than an ordinary depth of spirituality. He was a positive spiritual force in the school. When he led in public prayer, his distinct articulation, his clear tenor voice mellowed with tenderness, his easy flow of simple but beautiful language, the flexibility of modulation and emphasis, as if face to face with the Divine, made it a real leading in prayer, because it had an attraction and kindling power in others that lifted their aspirations, and they really emotionally blended their prayers with his. He was not loud and boisterous, but earnest, articulate, and meaningful...[31]

Blades had the highest praise and appreciation for Dr. Monroe Vayhinger, Taylor's President at the time he was a student. Vayhinger helped to get Blades through Taylor financially. In Blades' own words:

One cannot think of Taylor without thinking of the lives and spirit of those who have made Taylor great. I think now of Bishop Taylor, who, it is said, when he was dying asked to be put on his knees in order that he might spend his last moments on earth praying for Taylor University. So now the spirit of that great man of God hovers over Taylor. Also the spirit of Dr. Reade [Thaddeus Reade]... still prevails.[32]

The Gem (1919) noted that Blades along with Lee Tan Piew from Singapore, both Eulogonians, defeated the Eurekans in a debate in 1914. He was also a Philalethean "and best of all a winner of souls among the students."[33]

After graduating from Taylor, Blades went on to Drew Seminary in Madison, New Jersey. A number of students in the 1910s were drawn to Drew. A major reason no doubt was the influence of George Shaw and Newton Wray, two Bible professors at Taylor who were Drew graduates.[34] The latter seemed to have had a particular fondness and understanding for international students. Wray was Professor of Bible history, theology and New Testament Greek. He had received his A.B. from DePauw University in 1875 and a B.D. from Drew Theological Seminary in 1887.

Blades received his B.D. from Drew in 1921. Just prior to graduation he married Lucile Frazier. She was from Columbus, Ohio and had graduated from Ohio State University in 1914 with the degree of Bachelor of Science in Education. After graduation, Blades became supply pastor in Marietta and Mt. Pleasant, Ohio from 1921 to 1924. In 1924 he was secretary of the Colored YMCA in Columbus, Ohio. He was unsuccessful in gaining entrance to the Methodist Episcopal Church Annual Conference which was a great disappointment to him. In 1925, he was given the opportunity to become pastor of the Monroe Avenue Christian Church of Columbus, Ohio. Blades then became a Presbyterian pastor in Kentucky, and was the first black minister to be elected from the Logan Presbytery in the Kentucky Synod. In 1954 he retired to Columbus, Ohio and was active with the Taylor alumni group of that city well into the 1960s.

JAMAICA: Percy Smith

Several Jamaicans have studied at Taylor, the first being Percy Smith. Rev. Burt Opper in his book *Fifty Years Among the Telugus* recounted his friendship with Smith:

> My first acquaintance with him was on the first night I arrived [the year was 1908] at Taylor University.. I inquired of one of the students, a young man from Jamaica, if the college provided sheets for our beds... The Jamaican man, Percy Smith, informed me that the college did not provide sheets. I went out for a walk after getting settled in... and when I came

back to my room I found my bed made up neatly with clean linens-and Percy conspicuously absent. This was the beginning of a lifelong friendship.[35]

After completing his education at Taylor in 1912, Smith went to India as a missionary. He served under a small mission but then stepped out on his own. He lived in central India and was very effective in leading numerous people to the Christian faith.[36] Rev. Smith or "Uncle Percy" as Opper's family referred to him had been in India for 41 years when some friends collected money for him to return to Jamaica and the United States for his first furlough. Opper noted that:

Percy A. Smith from Jamaica.

Fifty Years among the Telugus

> Whenever I have a problem or need, there is always one person I know I can depend upon for help in prayer. Uncle Percy will take any of my burdens as his own and pray through until the problem is solved. Thank God for praying friends like Percy...[37]

Rev. Smith spent a total of fifty-seven years on the mission field with one furlough. He died in India in 1969 at the age of 96. As one missionary educator noted, "He was a saint in the real spiritual sense of the word. He was a man full of the Holy Spirit."[38]

J.W. Brown, from Kingston, Jamaica, graduated from Taylor in 1922. He had been a student at Leland University before coming to Taylor. He was a member of the Volunteer Band and was a debater. In 1950 Ivan Samuels, also from Kingston, graduated from Taylor. He became an Associate Professor of Education at

Purdue University-Calumet campus. The spring 1969 issue of the *Taylor University Magazine* noted that he passed away earlier that year.

CUBA: Armando O. Bustamante

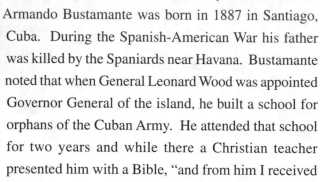

The Gem

Armando Bustamante from Cuba.

Armando O. Bustamante, his sister, Belen Portela, and Joseph P. Arbona, all from Cuba, attended Taylor in the 1910s. Armando Bustamante was born in 1887 in Santiago, Cuba. During the Spanish-American War his father was killed by the Spaniards near Havana. Bustamante noted that when General Leonard Wood was appointed Governor General of the island, he built a school for orphans of the Cuban Army. He attended that school for two years and while there a Christian teacher presented him with a Bible, "and from him I received the first glimpses of what the real teachings of Christ were."[39] After being converted, young Bustamante joined the Methodist Church, and was then asked by a missionary if he would like to help in the missionary work.

Bustamante completed his education at the Taylor University Academy in 1914. He had been a member of the Philaletheans. His sister, Belen Portela, was also in the Academy as of 1917. From 1914 to 1917 Armando Bustamante attended Ohio Wesleyan University where he received his B.A. degree. He volunteered in the American Army, and completed his naturalization papers for American citizenship in 1918. In that year he married an American woman, and then began studies at the Boston University School of Theology where he received his S.T.B. degree in 1920.

At this time Bustamante and his wife were accepted as

missionaries. He was assigned to Panama, but became the center of an unfortunate controversy. J. Tremayne Copplestone in his *History of Methodist Missions* explained in detail the situation which developed.[40] As Bustamante was about to depart for Panama the summer of 1920, a cable arrived at the Methodist Board of Mission's office in New York from the Superintendent of the Panama Mission with the following message: "Spanish workers have strong prejudice against Bustamante. It will be advisable to delay departure for the present. Mission station begs Board to reserve decision until further correspondence..."[41] The controversy was that some Spanish-speaking workers had jumped to the conclusion that Bustamante had been hand-picked over their heads. The suggestion was made that Spanish people would dislike a black missionary. It was apparent that racism was at the center of the controversy. Fortunately the American leadership prevailed, and Bustamante was sent to Panama with the result that there were few difficulties. But a deep racial cleavage in Methodist missions in Panama had been exposed. Bustamante served in the town of Chitre as well as in Panama City. His preaching was described by Copplestone as "eloquent and easily heard."[42]

Bustamante and his wife were transferred to Cuba but this move did not satisfy Bustamante whose love was the work in Panama. In 1928 they withdrew from missionary service, and Bustamante then served the Florida Conference, Central Jurisdiction, as a preacher. He died in 1946 leaving his wife and three grown children.

PUERTO RICO

Several students in the first two decades of the twentieth century came from Puerto Rico. *The Gem* of 1907 noted three Puerto Ricans were studying in the Business College —Juan Deliz, Jose M. Hernandez, and Jose S. Soler. Susan Talbott who would marry John Wengatz spent a considerable amount of her free time tutoring them in the English language. Hernandez taught Spanish at Taylor during the 1907-8 academic year. He graduated in 1911 with the intention of becoming a medical missionary. But *The Gem* of 1925 in an article entitled "Where Are Taylor Alumni?" noted that Hernandez after his graduation from Taylor had become an instructor in Spanish at the University of Michigan, then a Professor of

Jose M. Hernandez from Puerto Rico.

Spanish at the University of Oklahoma, and in 1925 was working toward his doctorate at Harvard University. Carlos Daniels and William B. O'Neill in the late 1910s were also students from Puerto Rico. Daniels taught Spanish at Taylor and *The Gem* of 1917 noted that "on account of his frank disposition and manliness, he is held in high esteem by all his classmates." The 1930 *Echo* listed Miguel Palacio from Mayaguez. Palacio was a poet, and an *Echo* article of April 17, 1929 noted that he published his poems under the title "First Poems in the English Language." These poems focused on his life at Taylor, in the United States, and his Christian faith.

BAHAMAS AND OTHER WESTERN HEMISPHERE NATIONS (excluding Canada)

During the past fifteen years, Taylor University has experienced a noticeable increase in international students. Though few in relation to the entire student body, the annual average has been around forty to forty-five students. The largest group of international students has been from the Bahamas. The first Bahamian student graduated in 1980. Since that time nearly fifty Bahamians have studied at Taylor. They have developed a strong Taylor Alumni Club in the Bahamas, and have become successful in a variety of professions including teaching, business, and government work. During that same time period there have been students from the Cayman Islands, British Virgin Islands, Haiti, Honduras, Mexico, and Venezuela. In the early 1960s, three students from Panama and one from Trinidad studied at Taylor.

In the 1920s, there were three students from Callao, Peru. They were Senefelder Vallejo, a Philalethean; Edilberto Chaves who was in the Commercial Department; and Leonardo J. Diaz in the class of 1927. After graduation, Diaz returned to Peru where he was a teacher and also served a number of churches as pastor and district superintendent. He retired in 1959. Diaz was a biology major, and a member of the Thalonians and Cosmopolitan Club. Anbel Castro from Guatemala was noted in the 1927 yearbook.

ASIAN STUDENTS
JAPAN: K.S. Hiraide, Taeko Obara, Kan Ori

There has been a steady stream of Japanese students attending Taylor from the beginning of this century to the present. Perhaps the most well-known of the earlier students was K.S. Hiraide whom an *Echo* article of February 1, 1916 called the Japanese "Billy Sunday."[43] Hiraide was born in Nagano, Japan in 1882. He graduated from Tokyo Bible Institute in 1906, and then preached for four years in his native land. He came to the United States in 1910, spent one year at Adelphia College (Seattle, Washington), and then entered Taylor in 1911. He was "an interesting speaker and often addressed large audiences regarding the condition and needs of the Japan of today."[44] He was a Thalonian and Eulogonian. He received his B.A. degree in 1914 and the B.D. in 1915. *The Gem* of 1915 stated Hiraide intended to establish a Bible school and college when he returned to Japan.

From Taylor, Hiraide enrolled at Drew Theological Seminary where he received his Bachelor of Divinity degree in 1916. He also attended Boston University. Hiraide returned to Japan in 1917 and married a Japanese woman. He frequently wrote back to Taylor, and several articles appeared in *The Echo* and the *Taylor University Bulletin* through the years about Hiraide. He was very appreciative of the Taylor community. Shortly after returning to Japan, he wrote *The Echo*:

> Yes, you have assisted me while I was going through Taylor University, Drew Theological Seminary and Boston University. You have prayed much for my camp meeting work and evangelistic campaign while I was with you. I trust you will continue to do so while I am absent from you in flesh and preaching the unsearchable riches of Christ and spreading the Scriptural Holiness in the Far Eastern Sunrise Kingdom - my native land. I thank you very much for the kind hospitality and assistance you have so generously rendered me during my stay among you. I pray the Father's richest blessings to rest upon you continually.[45]

In 1932 he wrote a letter from Hiroshima to Taylor's President

Taylor University Archives

K. S. Hiraide from Japan.

R.L. Stuart which appeared in the July 1932 *Taylor University Bulletin.* He spoke warmly of his alma mater:

> ....I have never forgotten my dear Alma Mater though seventeen years have rolled away since I left her. My appreciation and my heart's affection are never changed. And I am determined today to pray for her more and more. I am very glad to hear of the great revival that God has given to

Taylor. Glad also, to know of the renewed determination of
T.U. to remain true to God...

I want to report to you that the students of our school-Japan
Alliance Theological Seminary-are praying for T.U. every day
from six to six thirty o'clock A.M.

I entered T.U. by a miraculous leading of the Lord in
September of 1911. Received B.A. in 1914; and B.D. in 1915.
Then went to [Drew] in the fall of 1915, then to [Boston
University], two outstanding institutions of America. I
returned to Japan in 1917. But I want to testify that the key to
open the Holy Scripture; the vision of the Living Christ; the
passion for the world-wide evangelism, I got from Taylor
University...

Well, I see in the Bulletin that T.U. is struggling for the
financial difficulty. The financial difficulty is everywhere.
Indeed it is very keenly felt in Japan too. But I feel I must
help T.U. So, I hereby pledge one hundred yen, $100.00... I
have no [more?] money to send now; but I pledge by faith,
praying the Lord to enable me to send an expression of my
love for my dear Alma Mater.[46]

Hiraide encouraged Japanese students to come and study at
Taylor. Fujihiko Oi was one such student, but his experiences in
the United States were not happy ones. Twenty year old Oi arrived
in Upland in February 1920, and tragically was a student at Taylor
for only three months. He died May 23, 1920 in the Marion General
Hospital from typhoid fever. *The Echo* obituary of June 9, 1920
noted that his father was a prominent citizen of the town of
Yokosuka, Japan.[47] When Oi arrived in Upland on February 12, it
was cold and he was alone, having given no previous notice of his
arrival. By chance two men, one of whom was President Monroe
Vayhinger, picked him up in their car. Apparently Oi contracted a
disease on the long trip from Japan; he never regained his health at

Taylor. *The Echo* article noted that:

> his seemingly premature death reminded us of that of Samuel
> Morris, who likewise had purposed to prepare his life for work
> in his own land, but at his funeral three students volunteered
> to take his place in Africa. This was also true with respect to
> Mr. Oi's death. The same divine hand who had called him
> away so early in life has been placed upon the hearts and
> lives of worthy young students to take his place in Japan.

The main eulogy at the funeral service was given by Professor
Wray. In attendance was a Japanese YMCA secretary who read an
obituary, and then took the body to Chicago for cremation. The
remains were then sent to Japan.

Hiraide became an evangelist in Japan, was the head of a school,
an editor of a Christian publication, and a writer of Biblical
commentaries. The September 1931 *Taylor University Bulletin*
noted that Hiraide returned to the United States for a series of
evangelistic meetings. The *Bulletin* stated:

> The Beulah Beach Bible Conference was the scene of a recent
> dramatic moment. During the course of one of the services
> the work of Keitsu Hiraide, the great Bible school worker of
> Japan, had been described and given the great praise which it
> deserves. Immediately afterward, Dr. R.L. Stuart, Taylor's
> new president, was introduced. A most pleasing and cordial
> reception was given him. However, imagine the interest and
> enthusiasm of the audience when the next speaker arose and
> made the following statement, 'And Hiraide came from Taylor
> University.'[48]

Hiraide continued to come back to the United States, and
returned to his alma mater on several occasions. The March 1950
issue of *The Taylorite* noted that:

> K.S. Hiraide spoke in a chapel service at Taylor in February.
> Since arriving in Seattle last fall, he has spent several months
> traveling in Canada. He is now touring the United States.

> While at Taylor, he also spoke in prayer meeting and at a
> service in the Methodist church in Upland.[49]

The *Taylor University Bulletin* of December 1953 reported on
another visit of this celebrated preacher:

> K.S. Hiraide, who is president of the Japanese Association of
> Evangelicals visited the campus during December while he
> was in the United States on a speaking tour. He is also founder
> and president of Japan Evangelical Seminary and a member
> of the General Committee of the World Evangelical
> Fellowship. Two books on the Bible have been written by
> Rev. Hiraide...[50]

Hiraide became pastor of Seijo Church, Tokyo, in 1947. On January
17, 1975 he died at the age of 92; the funeral was held in that
church he had pastored for 28 years.

Between 1900 and 1960 there were at least twenty other
Japanese or possibly in some cases, Japanese-American students
who came to Taylor. Though many of them are merely mentioned
in past yearbooks, for some there is some biographical information
available. Perhaps the earliest Japanese student to attend Taylor
was R. Takemaye who was a friend of Joseph Blades.[51] *The
University Journal* of February 10, 1906 printed an article by
Takemaye entitled "Some Prophecies Fulfilled" in which he called
for a converted Japan to arise. "Arise Japan! Illuminate a degenerate
world with the truth of God. Drive out Asiatic religion by the love
of Christ."

James T. Ishii, an Academy senior in 1915, was a class officer
who had an interest in becoming an evangelist and social reformer.
He wrote a well-written and thoughtful essay for the 1915 *Gem*
entitled "The Doom of War." Talayoshi Fujihara was a member of
the graduating class of 1921. Prior to coming to Taylor, he had

been a student at a college in Shanghai, China. His major at Taylor was mathematics. After his graduation, Fujihara was in charge of a Japanese art store in Indianapolis and attended Butler College.[52] Shigeru Kobayashi was in the graduating class of 1924. She may have been the first woman international student to attend Taylor. Kobayashi had attended Women's Christian College, Tokyo, before coming to Taylor. Kobayashi was a member of the Volunteer Band. Her major was voice, and there were references to her fine singing abilities. *The Gem* of 1924 noted that Kobayashi intended to go back to Japan with the Women's Foreign Missionary Society of the Methodist Episcopal Church, and become involved with social and religious work in Tokyo. Another 1924 senior was Shigetomi Ogawa who had attended the Agricultural College, Tokyo before being admitted to Taylor. He was a history and social science major with the goal of working in the field of public finance. A 1925 senior education major was Otoshige Takechi; the following year Shigeki Doi from Tokyo, a religion major, graduated.

At the outbreak of World War II in 1939, Taeko Obara received her B.A. degree from Taylor, majoring in English. She had been a member of the Volunteer Band and the Holiness League at Taylor. In 1940 Taeko Obara was a graduate student at Taylor, working on her Master of Arts degree in theology. Her goal was to return to Japan and work in her home church. Her father, Rev. Tsoja Obara, was a minister in Tokyo. World War II prevented her return until its conclusion. *The Taylorite* of March 1948 noted that she, five sisters, and her father were trying to rebuild the church which was destroyed in a 1945 American air raid.[53] During the war, her father had been arrested by the Japanese authorities[54]

God's Ordinary People:

> Ever since the end of the war, we have been fully engaged in the reestablishing of our church, which was ordered dissolved one year after the arrest. The Lord has been with us in such a definite way that we have finally accomplished the buying of the lot and building of the church and the building of the parsonage. Now [1949] we are ready for the third project, which is the building of the permanent auditorium that will hold from fifteen hundred to two thousand people...[55]

In 1952 Obara visited the Taylor campus on her return to Saitama, Japan where she was pastor of the Shiki Church, an independent congregation. Earlier that year she had been a Japanese delegate at the meeting in West Germany of the International Missionary Council. She also attended the Commission on Work of Women in the Church held in Oxford, England. The winter 1967 issue of the *Taylor Magazine* noted that Obara, identified as Mrs. Okomoto, was living in southern California employed by the Social Science Department of the Rand Corporation.

The Gem

Taeko Obara from Japan.

Kan Ori from Osaka was a student at Taylor in the early 1950s. Before coming to Taylor he was in Hawaii as a student at a community college and as reporter with the *Honolulu Star Bulletin*. At Taylor he was a psychology major and received his A.B. degree in 1956. A student leader, he was managing editor of *The Echo*, and editor-in-chief of the 1956 *Gem*. Ori then went on to graduate studies in political science at

Indiana University where he earned his doctoral degree, focusing on the American government. Ori returned to Taylor in the early 1960s as Assistant Professor of Political Science. According to Professor Philip Loy, Ori established Taylor's political science department, and was a mentor to him. During the 1970-1 academic year, Ori taught at the Indiana University extension in Gary. Then he became Professor of Political Science at Sophia University, Tokyo. Ori also had a post-doctoral fellowship at Oxford University. He wrote a number of published works in his field including *Japanese Public Opinion of Sino-Japanese Relations, 1969-1972* (Tokyo: Sophia University, 1972); *A New Perspective on the Japanese Higher Civil Service: An Empirical Study of its Prestige* (Tokyo: Sophia University, 1974); and *Political Parties and Elections in PostwarJapan* (Tokyo: Japan Foundation, Office for the Japanese Studies Center, 1982). Along with Roger Benjamin,

The Gem

he co-authored *Traditions and Change in Postindustrial Japan The Role of the Political Parties* (New York: Praeger Publishers, 1981). He was married with three children. Ori died in March 1995.

During the last thirty-five years there have been at least seven or eight Japanese students at Taylor as well as several from neighboring Korea. There were two students from Korea in the 1910s, Tuk Sung Kim and Young Han Choo. The former came to the Hawaiian Islands in 1906 and

Kan Ori from Japan.

293

was a student there until 1910. He entered Taylor in 1911, and graduated in 1915 from the English Theological course. He returned to Korea as a missionary. Young Han Choo joined the staff of a Methodist school in Seoul after graduation. Song W. So, class of 1963, was working for the Pacific Chemical Industrial Company in Seoul in 1977.

SINGAPORE, CHINA, HONG KONG: Lee Tan Piew

In the past fifteen years, the second (only after the Bahamas) largest group of international students at Taylor have been Singaporeans. Nearly 30 Singaporeans have studied at Taylor, many coming as a result of the Taylor in Singapore Program begun in the late 1980s in conjunction with Singapore Youth for Christ. They have become successful upon their return to Singapore. Also from Southeast Asia have come students from Vietnam and Malaysia. Kashwinder Kaur, from Malaysia, is currently working as an Admissions Office counselor and is serving as the international student's coordinator. In the 1910s, Lee Tan Piew was a student from Singapore. He had spent some time at the Anglo-Chinese School before arriving at Taylor in 1910. Lee was a very talented and energetic student with strong leadership abilities. *The Gem* of 1913 and 1915 noted he was President of the Academy class of 1913, *The Gem* art editor during the same year, a member of the Thalonian Literary Society, and a debater. *The Gem* of 1915 featured a summary article of the Thalonians written by Lee. After graduating in 1915, Lee received a scholarship to study medicine at the University of Michigan. He also attended Ohio Wesleyan University.[56] As a student at Taylor, his aim was to enter medical missionary work. He became a medical doctor in Hong Kong.

Many years later B.R. Opper, missionary to India and Taylor alumnus, recounted in *Fifty Years Among the Telugus* his accidental meeting with Lee in Hong Kong. They spent time together reminiscing about their student days at Taylor.[57]

Another student of Chinese extraction from Southeast Asia was Dorothy Dzao. She was from Indonesia, and studied at Taylor in the early 1950s. She was the recipient of a scholarship from World Vision. Her father, Dr. Timothy Dzao, was founder and president of Ling Liang World-Wide Evangelistic Mission, established in Shanghai, China in 1942, but headquartered in Hong Kong after the communist victory in China in 1949.

The Gem

Lee Tan Piew from Singapore

Dr. Dzao was awarded an honorary Doctor of Divinity degree by Taylor at the matriculation day exercises in September 1955.

Several students from China have attended Taylor. The first was probably Frank H. Lee (Lee Tuam Hong) from Canton (Guangzhou). *The Gem* of 1919 noted he was a Thalonian and the quote next to his photograph stated, "A merry heart maketh a cheerful countenance." Three years later *The Gem* (1922) indicated

295

Lee had returned to China and was attending Canton University. Chung Ying Chu, also from Canton, was another Chinese student in the 1920s; he had previously attended Defiance College and Johns Hopkins University and his goal following his 1925 graduation was Christian work. *The Echo* in 1930 featured an article entitled "China to Taylor via Chicago" and was about how Tsing Wong from Canton found his way to Taylor. He moved from place to place across the United States, first to California to attend a teacher's training school, followed by a period of time at Columbia University in New York City, and then Chicago. "It was in a Y.M.C.A. in Chicago that a friend told me of Taylor University. I was greatly interested and decided to come here."[58]

Probably the individual who has done the most in establishing contacts for Taylor in China is Don J. Odle, former Athletic Director. This was achieved through the Venture for Victory basketball program, an idea originally conceived by Youth for Christ. That organization encouraged Odle to gather a group of Christian basketball players

The Ilium

Yue Xuan Gu (Pamela Gu) from China

296

and bring them to Taiwan during the summer of 1952. The program found support with Madame Chiang Kai-shek. Many thousands of Taiwanese became Christians through this program. In following years, Odle made fifteen trips to Asia with American basketball teams. Odle attracted Billy Hwang, a basketball Olympic star from Hong Kong, to enter Taylor as a freshman in the fall of 1961. In the early 1980s, Odle visited Mainland China, and through that experience made contact with Yue Xuan Gu (Pamela Gu), a young woman from Shanghai. Gu's education had been interrupted by the Cultural Revolution, and for five years she worked in a factory. But her goal was to obtain further education. Don and Bonnie Odle agreed to sponsor her studies at Taylor where she majored in Communication.[59]

In recent years additional students from Hong Kong and Taiwan have attended Taylor.

THE PHILIPPINES: Alfredo Gonzales, Jorge O. Masa

The Methodist Episcopal Church had a considerable mission work in the Philippines, and it was, therefore, natural for some Filipinos to find their way to Taylor in the early years. Alfredo Gonzales came to Taylor undoubtedly through the encouragement of Mr. and Mrs. Joshua Frank Cottingham, missionaries to the Philippines. Gonzales graduated in 1920 and returned to the Philippines where he became Professor of Philosophy and Education, and then Dean of Central Philippine College, Iloilo. He was one of the contributing editors of the *Philippine Observer*, a leading journal of religion, and a regular writer for the *Philippine Journal of Education.*

In a letter to Dr. Burt Ayres which was published in *The Echo*

(November 28, 1922), Gonzales noted that he was encouraging a number of young Filipinos to get further education at Taylor. Esteban Cunbam and Manuel E. Alojado were students in the 1920s. The former was a member of the Holiness League and the Prayer Band; the latter, from Antique, was a member of the orchestra and

was on *The Echo* staff. Alojado's majors were English and education.

An outstanding young man who came to Taylor in the mid-1920s was Jorge O. Masa from Sibalom, Antique, on the island of Panay, some 300 miles south of Manila. Prior to his education at Taylor, he had done some studies at the University of the Philippines. He came to Taylor in his mid-

Jorge Masa from Philippines

twenties with his wife, Consuelo, and during the time he was a student a daughter, Eugenia, was born in 1926. Masa was a very energetic student, being President of the Cosmopolitan League (an organization for international students), a member of the Volunteer Band and Gospel Team, and a Thalonian. His majors were philosophy, psychology, history, and social science. The most memorable legacy Masa left at Taylor was the writing in 1928 during his senior year, at his classmates' encouragement, *The Angel in Ebony or The Life and Message of Sammy Morris*. John Paul, President of Taylor from 1922 to 1931, in the introduction to this book made the following comments about Masa:

> His [Masa] desire to come to America was fostered by a graduate of Taylor University who was operating in the Philippine field, and he was encouraged to come to Taylor for his higher education 'for one great reason, that it is a clean school, from the moral standpoint, and is free from race prejudice of any kind.'

With his aims directed toward the medical profession, Mr. Masa came to America and to his alma mater with 'a bitter antagonism,' using his own expression, 'to anything that had a religious element in it.' Naturally he was shy of the spiritual influences at Taylor and not entirely satisfied with first impressions. But to his mind there was power in friendship. The friendly atmosphere that dominates the student life at Taylor led him to investigate the spiritual force which lay back of it. His mind was philosophical enough to see that there was a reason. He found what he conceived to be the reasons, in the prominence that was given to Jesus Christ, and the simple faith that was reflected in the testimony of his associates.

It was not long until Mr. Masa acquired a new and better view of religion.

Following graduation from Taylor, Masa and his family went to New York City where he pastored a church and was a leader in a Filipino student movement. He received degrees from Columbia University and Yale Divinity School. The Masas returned to the Philippines and worked on the island of Panay. He was a member of the Executive Committee of the National Christian Council of the Philippines, and was a leader of the United Evangelical Church which he helped organize in 1941. He also organized a high school in Pikit on Panay.

Masa was recognized a World War II hero during the difficult days when the Philippines was under Japanese occupation. The *Taylor University Bulletin* of November 1949 featured an article which appeared in *Christian Century* (October 3, 1945) recounting Masa's heroism:

When the Japanese army captured Pikit, Jorge gained from the commandant of the Gasisang prison camp permission to serve as chaplain for the 6,000 Filipino and 2,000 American soldiers and civilians interned there. But the permission was withdrawn after six weeks. Then he and his family returned to Pikit to begin their Filipino Christian 'counter-attack.' Through church members they organized a campaign of 'no friendship' for the Japanese invaders. Groups of Filipinos in the streets, men engaged in the inevitable chess games and others simply stopped talking and walked away when Japanese soldiers seeking companionship approached. Jorge never carried firearms. He continued his ministry all during the occupation, making one trip of 230 miles afoot to visit congregations in the conference. But he refused to be a puppet. He turned down several requests to speak when the 'new' republic was inaugurated in 1943. When Pikit was attacked by the guerrillas, the Masa family was warned ahead of time to evacuate. But they had not gone when the attack came. Jorge shepherded thousands of his townsmen to the river, where he had them protect themselves beneath the banks while shells whistled overhead. He stood all night in water to his shoulders to demonstrate what his people must do, holding his five-year old daughter in his arms. For five months Jorge was in bed as the result of pneumonia contracted that night. When planes of the invading American army began to bomb Pikit, Jorge took charge of the evacuation of 20,000 civilians. With a loss of only two lives, he got them into an evacuation center where they lived for two months. He also saved scores of collaborators by arranging for them to surrender to him upon the assurance from guerrilla chiefs that their lives would be spared. Later, he turned them over to the guerrilla forces, and finally to the American army.[60]

In the same *Taylor University Bulletin,* Masa wrote an article in which he expressed his enthusiasm for the Ayres Library project. He added:

> ...When we can save a little sum we hope to be able to send something if only to remind ourselves of the contribution that the venerable man [Burt W.Ayres] made to our preparation at Taylor, and as expression of gratitude to what Taylor has done for us and has meant to us. If only the last war had not interrupted our life in the Philippines, we could have immediately responded to the appeals... But we were left

with nothing except our lives and hopes when the liberation forces came. All our houses, farm implements, et al were completely lost during the occupation of this country by the invaders. In a year more we hope to be able to rehabilitate ourselves.[61]

Masa returned to Taylor for his class' 25th reunion in 1953 and was given a special award from his alma mater. He was teaching at Silliman University in the Philippines until his retirement in 1968. The spring 1977 *Taylor University Magazine* noted that this eminent Filipino had died at his home in Sibalom, Antique on November 22, 1976.

At least five additional Filipinos have studied at Taylor since the 1950s. Currently three students from Palau are attending Taylor.

INTERNATIONAL STUDENTS FROM INDIA, MIDDLE EAST, EUROPE, CANADA

Taylor has not had many students from the Indian subcontinent. In the early 1930s, however, Cleophas Stanley Speake from the state of Uttar Pradesh, India was a student. *The Gem* of 1933 noted that he was a sociology major, that he had attended Lucknow Christian College and Lucknow University, and that his life work would be teaching. In the 1990s several young people of Indian and Sri Lankan citizenship have been part of the Taylor community.

At least six students from Iran have studied at Taylor. The earliest was Maryum Margaret Yonan. *The Gem* (1915) noted that she came to Taylor after studying in the Chicago public schools, that she was an officer of the Thalonian Society, and that she expected to devote her life to missionary work. She graduated from Taylor in 1913. She married Rev. Paul Newey who founded the Assyrian Congregational Church in Chicago. The church was organized to serve immigrants who fled from Iran, Iraq, and Turkey during World War I as a result of religious persecution. The June 1953 *Taylor University Bulletin* observed that the Neweys celebrated the 40th anniversary of Rev. Newey's ordination at that church. The article noted they had aided more than 1,000 Assyrian-Iranians to become U.S. citizens.

At least one Arab student from the Middle East has studied at Taylor, and he was Waleed Alibraheem from Kuwait who transferred from Tri-State University in Angola, Indiana, and graduated in 1984. Essa G. Sackllah, an Arab-American of the class of 1977 has been actively involved in a number of Arab organizations in this country. He has been on the national board of directors of the Palestine Human Rights Campaign, and a national board member of the Save Lebanon Movement. He is a resident of Houston, Texas, and is president of a large Houston delicatessen and catering business.

Like other areas of the world, the early Europeans who studied at Taylor generally were interested in Christian missions or the Methodist ministry as their life work. This was true of John B. Vickery from Cork, Ireland (class of 1913), Alfred V. Patton from Liverpool, England (1914), D. Shaw Duncan from Scotland (1904), Kathryn Hettelsater born in Norway (1903), Ernest A. Mathews from Devonshire, England

International Students - 1949.

The Gem

302

(1907), Niels August Christensen from Denmark (1915), Archie Ericksson from New Zealand (1899-1900), and others. Since 1950 students have come from Australia, Belgium, Bosnia, Germany, Ireland, Italy, Macedonia, the Netherlands, Norway, Switzerland, and the United Kingdom.

In looking at the entire history of Taylor, one can say the largest group of international students who have studied at this institution have come from Canada. Before 1950 fully three dozen Canadian students attended Taylor, and after 1950 that figure grew to at least one hundred. They have come from several provinces, the majority being from Ontario. An early graduate was Ernest W. Bysshe from Ottawa who was listed in the 1899-1900 catalogue and who became a Methodist missionary to France in 1909. He attended Drew Theological Seminary. J.C. Eason from Ontario from the class of 1913 also attended Drew, and then went into the Methodist ministry J.S. Bain from Ontario was in the class of 1907 and also went into the ministry of the Methodist Episcopal Church. In more recent years Ralph Bell (class of 1959) from St. Catherine, Ontario, has been an evangelist with the Billy Graham Association.

CONCLUSION

There is no question that a college which can attract international students will also become a much more cross culturally aware campus. The increased number of "overseas" students including sons and daughters of missionaries at Taylor during the past ten years has contributed to a greater interest and emphasis on internationalizing the curriculum. These include foreign travel/ study and Christian service opportunities sponsored by the University or in conjunction with larger consortium programs such as the Coalition of Christian Colleges.

An International Studies major has been developed; this program exists under the history department. There is a required cross cultural component in the general education program. Taylor is a member of the Cincinnati Council on World Affairs and the Indiana Consortium for International Programs. A large number of the faculty have been afforded the opportunity to study, teach, or travel overseas during the past decade. Another clear indication of the increased interest in international affairs is the number of featured articles appearing in *The Ilium* and the *Taylor University Magazine* during the past ten years.

An important program at Taylor is a support group for international students. Societies have existed for these students from time to time during Taylor's history. For example, in the late 1920s the Cosmopolitan Club (or League) was active. The 1964 and 1971 yearbooks featured photographs of the International Club which also included "MKs." For the past twenty years a separate group has existed for international students known as the International Student Society.[62] A well-organized orientation program for new international students has been developed as well as a series of activities through the academic year including a major campus-wide spring event known as the World Food Festival. Currently there are forty-three international students studying at Taylor from eighteen nations in Asia, Africa, Europe, Latin America, and the Pacific Islands. It should also be noted Taylor continues to attract a sizeable number of "MKs" from around the world (currently 140 from thirty-five nations), and there is an active society for these students known as Mu Kappa.

Current international student alumni are found in a variety of professions and occupations. But the emphasis on Christian service and ministry continues to play an important role. This emphasis inspired by Bishop William Taylor one hundred years ago will continue to play a major role in the life of Taylor University and its alumni into the next century.

Cosmopolitan Club

God's Ordinary People:

OTHER TAYLOR ALUMNI WHO HAVE SERVED AS METHODIST MISSIONARIES (Selected List)

AFRICA:

Ila May Scovill (class of 1924) - began work in Southern Rhodesia in 1925. She was from Pioneer, Ohio, attended Ohio Wesleyan University before coming to Taylor. She was an active member of the Holiness League, Philaletheans, and President of the Student Volunteer Band. Her major was Biblical literature.

Marguerite Deyo (class of 1931) - from St. Paul, Minnesota with majors in sociology, economics, religious education, and Biblical literature. She was President of the Soangetahas, Vice President of the Volunteer Band, and a debater. Deyo became a Methodist missionary to Southern Rhodesia and worked in Old Umtali.

Charles Melvin Blake and Doris Brown Blake (class of 1940)- Charles Melvin Blake and Doris Brown Blake were missionaries to Angola. In 1943, Charles Blake received his B.D. degree from Drew Theological Seminary. They arrived in Luanda in 1948; the following year Charles Blake was appointed director of the Luanda Mission. In Angola he was an evangelist. Bishop Dodge noted that he and Blake "saw eye to eye on most issues." In 1957 he succeeded Dodge as Executive Secretary for Africa of the Board of Missions of The Methodist Church, Division of World Missions. In 1960 Taylor University conferred upon him the honorary Doctor of Divinity degree. Blake has been a keen observer and interpreter of Angolan events which have unfolded during the past thirty-five years. In the *Taylor University Bulletin The Alumnus* (February 1962) he wrote an article entitled "Anguish in Angola." (pp. 8-10) (Mr. and Mrs. C. Melvin Blake folder 1047-1-3:21-22 — 1946-49, General Commission on History and Archives, The United Methodist Church, Madison, New Jersey).

Kenneth D. Enright (class of 1945) - a Biblical literature major, member of the Thalonians, Holiness League, and President of the Student Volunteers. Wtih his wife, Enright has been a Methodist missionary to the Congo (Zaire) for some 48 years. Three of their children have attended Taylor. In the *Taylor University Fiftieth Reunion* booklet, Enright noted that Robert Stuart, President of Taylor University from 1931 to 1945, had a great influence on his life. He was appreciative of Stuart's "common sense stand on faith" and "his practical manner."

Marie Heinemann (class of 1938) - she was a Free Methodist missionary in Burundi, and later changed to the National Holiness Missionary Society. Heinemann was born in Huron, South Dakota into a German Methodist home, and eventually became a Methodist minister. In 1945 she embarked on her first missionary assignment by boarding a troop ship heading for Asia to pick up soldiers after the end of World War II. After two weeks on the troop ship with sixteen other missionaries, Heinemann arrived in Egypt and spent almost three more weeks traveling by nearly every imaginable mode of transportation to reach Burundi where she began teaching school. Heinemann was instrumental in founding the Olson School in Keyero, Burundi which was named for Grace Olson's parents. The school was dedicated on February 12, 1950. The Olson family were major contributors to the school. Heinemann spent a total of thirty-six years as a missionary in Burundi. She has written two books, *Of Eagles and Angels,* and *On Eagles' Wings,* which are accounts of a Hutu pastor, Toma Mbindigiri, and his fight for freedom. (Information from Dr. Hazel Butz Carruth).

ASIA:

J. Theron Illick (class of 1910) - He was born in Cherry Valley, Pennsylvania in 1888, the son of a Methodist minister. He entered Taylor in the fall of 1906, and received the A.B. degree four years later. *The Gem* of 1909 showed him as a member of The Taylor University Quartette (another member of that group was Burt Opper - see below). After graduating from Taylor, Illick studied zoology at Syracuse University, and earned a Ph.D. at Princeton University. In 1916, he and his wife whom he had met at Syracuse University sailed for China. Illick taught biology at Nanchang Academy, using Chinese in his classes. In 1920 he was appointed to the University of Nanking where he organized the Department of Biology, described as the finest in East Asia. During 1936-7, while the Illicks were on furlough in the United States, word came that the Japanese invasion would prevent their return to China. Dr. Illick joined the Zoology Department at Syracuse University where he remained professor until his retirement seventeen years later. In 1955, Illick was appointed Dean of the College of Science at Christian Tunghai University in Taiwan. In two years he was able to complete a science building at that institution. He then accepted an invitation to become Dean of the faculty at Chung Chi College, Hong Kong. In 1959 he retired to Modesto, California where he died in 1967. (Illick, J.T. and Bernice R. folder 1467-1-2:44, General Commission on History and Archives, The United Methodist Church, Madison, New Jersey).

Mark R. Shaw - attended Taylor during the first decade of this century. He then went on to Ohio Wesleyan University, graduating in 1914, and Boston University Theological School (1920). Shaw was active in the temperance movement of the Methodist Episcopal Church. In 1922 he made an extensive survey of the results of prohibition in Chicago. He spent six years (1922-28) in Japan under the Methodist Episcopal Church promoting temperance. The *Taylor University Bulletin* of March 1953 noted that at that time Rev. Shaw was living in Melrose, Massachusetts, and was an unsuccessful candidate for election to the U.S. Senate on the Prohibition ticket. He served for years as vice chairman of that party, and had twice been the party's candidate for governor of Massachusetts. In 1953 Shaw was engaged in peace education as New England secretary of the National Council for Prevention of War. (M. Shaw folder 1047-6-3:21, General Commission on History and Archives, The United Methodist Church, Madison, NJ)

L. Chester Lewis (class of 1912) **and Emma Tanner Lewis** (class of 1912) - L. Chester Lewis was born in Ohio in 1891, and entered Taylor in the fall of 1908 where he was active in the temperance movement. He was also an officer of both the Young

Men's Holiness League and the Philalethean Literary Society. Emma Tanner was from Rensselaer, Indiana, and entered Taylor in 1909. *The Gem* of 1911 noted that "we have learned to love her for her amiable disposition, high ideals, and sweet Christian character." She was President of the Prayer Band. Following graduation, L. Chester Lewis became a pastor in Ohio, then went on to Princeton Theological Seminary, and Garrett Seminary. In 1919 Chester and Emma Lewis sailed for India and worked in Cawnpore. However, things did not work out well for them in India. Mr. Lewis found it difficult working with the Indians, and Mrs. Lewis was in poor health. They returned to the United States in 1926 and withdrew from the Mission Board. Mrs. Lewis died in Ohio in 1929. The following year Lewis became pastor of an Ohio Methodist church.(Lewis, Mr. and Mrs. L. Chester Lewis folders 1111-5-1:4 and 1467-2-3:09, General Commission on History and Archives, The United Methodist Church, Madison, NJ)

Dr. Arthur Howard (class of 1934) and **Esta Herrman Howard** (class of 1936) - After graduating from Taylor, Art Howard received an M.A. degree from the University of Michigan. He was named Athletic Director at Taylor in 1936. From 1938 to 1944, he was Athletic Director at Huntington College. On November 19, 1944, Mr. and Mrs. Howard had their service of commission at First Methodist Church, Huntington, Indiana, to be missionaries to India. As a teacher of physical education and coach, Art Howard was appointed to head the Physical Education Department of Lucknow Christian College, Methodism's leading educational institution in India. The school had a reputation of being a leader in the promotion of sports in India and had been represented at the

Olympic Games on several occasions. In 1959 he was awarded an honorary LL.D. degree from Taylor University. Esta Howard was born in India, the daughter of Methodist missionaries who had served in the Philippines and India. After her studies at Taylor, she became a registered nurse. (Howard, Mr. and Mrs. Arthur folder 1111-4-3:40-42 - 1944-49, General Commission on History and Archives, The United Methodist Church, Madison, NJ)

*L*ATIN AMERICA

Walter Oliver (1896-1979) and Anna Skow Oliver (1895-1963) (class of 1918) - *The Gem* of 1917 noted that Walter Oliver was a member of the Volunteer Band. As students at Taylor, they first met in a German language class. Following graduation, they were married and began teaching in a two-room school in New Jersey. In 1923 the Olivers first went to Panama where Mr. Oliver became the Director of Instituto Pan-Americano, a school under the auspices of the Methodist Episcopal Church. The Olivers were responsible for overseeing the growth of this school from less than one hundred to nearly eight hundred students. In 1943 Mr. Oliver began teaching in the Canal Zone school system. They were involved in educational leadership in Panama and the Canal Zone from 1923 to 1959. In 1955 government officials decided that Spanish would be used as the primary language of instruction in all schools, including those where English-speaking West Indian workers children were attending. Mr. Oliver was appointed to develop a Spanish-language curriculum and to train all the English-speaking West Indian teachers' to become bilingual. The program was a success. In recognition of their pioneer work in education, the Olivers received

Panama's highest honor in 1956, membership in the Order of Vasco Nunez de Balboa. This was the first time both a husband and wife received the honor. The Olivers maintained close contact with Taylor. They had a special fondness for their alma mater. In 1959 Mr. Oliver was awarded an LL.D. from Taylor. From 1959 to 1963, he was instructor of Spanish at Taylor. During that time, Dale and Barbara Murphy were students and were very much influenced by the Olivers. In 1992 they

Walter Oliver missionary, educator in Panama.

presented to Taylor University the Walter and Anna Skow Oliver Memorial Endowed Scholarship. The scholarship is to be awarded annually to a Taylor student who plans to be engaged in fulltime Christian service in Latin America or to an international student from Latin America or to an "MK." (Oliver, Mr. and Mrs. Walter folders 1185-2-3:22-28 — 1923-40, General Commission on History and Archives, The United Methodist Church, Madison, NJ; information from Charles Stevens).

Charles Raymond Illick and Lois Allen Illick (class of 1915) C.R. Illick was born in Tannersville, Pennsylvania in 1886. He joined the Methodist Episcopal Church in 1902. Following education at a trade school in Pennsylvania, Illick entered Taylor in 1910. He was President of the Thalonian Literary Society, and the Eulogonian Debating Club. Following graduation, Illick spent some time at the Detroit School of Medicine and Surgery, but always felt led to go into missions work. In 1919 Dr. and Mrs. Illick left for Mexico. Their first assignment was in Guanajuato where Dr. Illick worked with a veteran medical missionary. Mrs. Illick had special training and experience in evangelistic singing. She taught children in the mission's church school. The following year the Illicks were transferred to Mexico City. Later Dr. Illick was a surgeon at a hospital in Puebla. From correspondence, one concludes that the Illicks had a difficult experience in Mexico. He was outspoken about the shortcomings of his fellow missionaries. He was concerned that the medical people were not keeping up with current medical practice or engaged in proper medical procedures. He found other missionaries were displaying "selfishness and greed and utter inconsiderateness which are ... almost appalling to behold... I firmly believe in my work, I want to be a good missionary and I want to encourage others to go to fill the great needs. However my heart is greatly saddened by the unnatural and unappropriate (sic) spirit shwon (sic) by some missionaries as I have observed them." (Letter to Dr. Farmer, New York, August 26, 1921 - file folder 1415-5-3:05 - General Commission on History and Archives, The United Methodist Church, Madison, NJ). The Illicks left the mission in 1928, and C.R. Illick took up medical practice in California. The Illicks were very appreciative of their Taylor education. Lois Illick wrote to *The Echo* (November 24, 1931):

> I'll never get over being thankful for Taylor, and all the consecrated professors who sacrificed in order to give poor young people a chance. (also in *Alumni News*, November 1931, p. 16).

FORMER NON-METHODIST MISSIONARIES TO ASIA:
TAYLOR ALUMNI (Selected List)

Burton Raymond Opper and Hazel Newlon Opper - B.R. Opper began attending Taylor in 1909. He was born in Ohio, and had been a public school teacher before attending Taylor. He was president of the Philalethean Literary Society, the Eulogonian Debating Club, and the Prohibition League. He was also a member of the Taylor University Quartette and editor-in-chief of *The Echo*. He was also instructor of penmanship between 1912 and 1914. In 1916 after hearing Rev. Benjamin Davidson, founder and director of the Ceylon and India General Mission, speak in chapel, Opper received "from God a definite call to serve Him in India." (*Fifty Years Among the Telugus,* p. 33). Opper attended Moody Bible Institute following his graduation from Taylor, and then sailed for India in 1916. He became engaged to Hazel Newlon, a former Taylor student, and they were married in 1919 in the Methodist Church in Bangalore, India. The Oppers were still living in India in 1968 when Mr. Opper wrote *Fifty Years Among the Telugu* (published in Secunderabad, India by Deccan Literature Printers, 1968). Articles appeared in various Taylor magazines and *The Echo* about their ministry in India. Betty, one of their daughters, married Paul Pixler who taught theology at Taylor for several years in the mid-1950s.

Paul Clasper and Helen Aleshouse Clasper (class of 1942) - In 1952 they went as missionaries to Burma (Myanmar) under the American Baptist Missionary Society. Paul Clasper taught at the Baptist Burma Divinity School in Insein, Burma, and trained

God's Ordinary People:

Christian pastors for engagement in Christian-Buddhist dialog. He became Vice President of the school. During the 1963-4 academic year, while on furlough, he taught at Andover Newton Theological School in Boston, Massachusetts. When political conditions made it impossible to return to Burma, Clasper taught ecumenical theology and Asian religions in a number of seminaries in the United States including Drew University and the Graduate Theological Union, Berkeley, California. He returned to Asia in 1975 as an Anglican priest, serving in that capacity at Christ Church, Kowloon, Hong Kong. He was also a senior lecturer in the Chinese University of Hong Kong. In 1980, Clasper's stimulating and thought-provoking *Eastern Paths and the Christian Way* was published by Orbis Books (Maryknoll, New York). The publisher noted that this book "is an introduction for thoughtful people concerned with the quality of Christian faith as it encounters the great traditions of the Asian Paths. Paul Clasper's conviction is that for many in our time a sensitive appreciation of the Asian Paths may be a step toward a deeper and renewed understanding of the Christian Way."

NOTES

CHAPTER ONE NOTES

[1] An Address: Delivered at the anniversary celebration of the Methodist Episcopal Sabbath School in the City of Fort Wayne, Jan 27, 1845, by Joseph K. Edgerton. *Fort Wayne Times*, Mar 8, 1845.

[2] *Fort Wayne Sentinel,* Dec 12, 1846.

[3] *Fort Wayne Sentinel,* Nov 9, 1844.

[4] *Fort Wayne Times and Press,* Oct 3, 1845.

[5] *Fort Wayne Sentinel*, June 26, 1847.

[6] *Catalogue and Register of the Fort Wayne Female College and Fort Wayne Collegiate Institute, 1853-54.* Indianapolis: Indiana State Journal Steam Press print. 1854, p. 17.

[7] *Fort Wayne Times,* Aug 22, 1850.

[8] *Proceedings of the Fort Wayne Female College Board of Trustees,* May 14, 1853.

[9] *Catalogue and Register of the Fort Wayne College for the Year Ending April 2, 1858.* Fort Wayne: J. W. Dawson, printer, p.19.

[10] George B. Manhart. *DePauw Through the Years. Vol I.* Greencastle, Indiana: DePauw University, 1962, p.81.

[11] *Catalogue of the Alumni of Oberlin Institute, 1845-46,* pp.27-31.

[12] *Oberlin Institute Catalogue, 1846-47,* pp. 34-36.

[13] Robert Samuel Fletcher.   *A History of Oberlin College From Its Foundation Through the Civil War.* Vol II. Oberlin, Ohio: Oberlin College, 1943, p.716.

[14] *Twenty-fourth Annual Catalogue of Fort Wayne College.* Fort Wayne, Ind: Daily Gazette Steam print, 1871, p. 21; *Fort Wayne City Directory*, 1864-65.

[15] *Catalogue and Register of the Fort Wayne Collegiate Institute.* Indianapolis: Indiana State Journal Steam Press Print, 1854. p.20.

[16] *Catalogue of the Fort Wayne College for the year ending June 20, 1889.* pp.10-13.

[17] George B. Manhart, *DePauw Through The Years,* Vol I. Greencastle, Indiana: DePauw University 1962, p.78.

[18] Proceedings of the Board of Trustees of the Fort Wayne Female College, January 1, 1848.

[19] *The Fort Wayne Times,* Aug 22, 1850.

[20] *Indianapolis Sunday Star,* May 6, 1928.

[21] *Proceeding of the Board of Trustees of the Fort Wayne Female College,* April 21, 1852.

[22] *Catalogue of Fort Wayne College For The Year 1877-8-9.* Fort Wayne: Gazette Co., Printers, 1880, p. 30.

[23] *The Fort Wayne Gazette,* Dec 13, 1873.

[24] *The Fort Wayne College Index,* Vol I, No 5. Aug, 1885, pp.2-4.

[25] *The Fort Wayne College Index,* Vol I, No 7. Oct, 1885, pp.1-3.

[26] *Catalogue and Register of the Fort Wayne College, for the Year Ending April 2, 1858.* Fort Wayne: J. W. Dawson, printer, 1858, pp. 12-14.

[27] *The Fort Wayne College Catalogue, 1884-85.* Fort Wayne: Gazette Co, Book and Job Printers, 1885.

[28] *Catalogue of the Taylor University for the Year Ending June, 26, 1890.* Fort Wayne: Archer House and Co., 1890, p. 8.

[29] Much of the impetus for the nineteenth century Holiness Movement came from the ministry of Phoebe Palmer. She was born in New York City in 1807 and married W. C. Palmer, M.D. when she was twenty years old. She was one of the earliest female Methodist class leaders in the city. She also was an active tract distributor and was Manager and Secretary in Methodist female benevolent societies. She started prayer and study meetings on Tuesday afternoons for the promotion of holiness. These prayer meetings were one of her most important contributions to the interest in holiness which eventually burgeoned into a full scale inter-denominational movement with its roots in Methodism. They were attended by large numbers of ministers and lay persons from various

denominations. She was an evangelist, hymn writer and author. Her books included: *The Way of Holiness*; *Faith and Its Effects; Incidental Illustrations; Four Years In The Old World;* and *Tongues of Fire*. During the last fifteen years of her life she traveled with her husband conducting revival meetings throughout the U.S., Canada and Great Britain. Richard Wheatley. *The Life and Letters of Mrs. Phoebe Palmer.* New York: Garland Publishing, Inc. 1984.

[30] *Catalogue and Register of the Fort Wayne Female College and Fort Wayne Collegiate Institute, 1853-54.* Indianapolis: Indiana State Journal Steam Press Print, 1854.

[31] *Twenty-fourth Annual Catalogue of Fort Wayne College, 1870-71,* Fort Wayne: Daily Gazette Steam Print, 1871, p.17.

[32] *Catalogue of Fort Wayne College For the Years 1877-78-79.* Fort Wayne: Gazette Co. Printers, 1880, p.30.

[33] *The Fort Wayne College Catalogue, 1884-85.* Fort Wayne: Gazette Co., 1885, p.35.

[34] *Catalogue of the Fort Wayne College for the Year Ending June 20, 1889,* p.25.

[35] *Catalogue of Taylor University Fort Wayne, Indiana, 1891-92,* p.7.

[36] *Catalogue of Taylor University of Upland, Indiana, 1893-94,* p.4.

[37] *Catalogue of Taylor University, Upland, Indiana, 1895-96,* p.4.

[38] *Catalogue of Taylor University of Upland, Indiana, 1893-94,* p.17.

[39] *Catalogue of Taylor University of Upland, Indiana, 1897-98.* Fort Wayne: The Archer Printing Co., 1898, p.6.

[40] *Catalogue of Taylor University of Upland, Indiana, 1897-98,* pp.12-15.

[41] *Catalogue of Taylor University of Upland, Indiana, 1897-98.* Fort Wayne: Archer Printing, 1898, pp.6-7.

[42] *Catalogue of Taylor University of Upland, Indiana, 1897-98.* Fort Wayne: Archer Printing, 1898, pp.11-12.

[43] *Catalogue and Register of the Fort Wayne College for the Year Ending April 3, 1858.* Fort Wayne: J. W. Dawson, Printer, 1858, p.12.

[44] *Twenty-fourth Annual Catalogue of Fort Wayne College, 1870-71.* Fort Wayne: Daily Gazette Steam Print, 1871, p. 3.

[45] *Catalogue Fort Wayne College, 1875-76,* Fort Wayne: Daily News Printing House, 1876, p.2.

[46] *Catalogue Fort Wayne College, 1875-76,* Fort Wayne: Daily News Printing House, 1876, p.2.

[47] *Fort Wayne College Catalogue,1881.*Fort Wayne: *Gazette* Book and Job Print, 1881, p.3.

[48] *Catalogue of the Fort Wayne College for the year ending June 23, 1882. Fort Wayne*: Daily News Book Print, 1882, p.3

[49] *The Fort Wayne College Catalogue, 1884-85.* Fort Wayne: Gazette Co, Book and Job Printers, 1885, pp.3-4.

[50] *Catalogue of the Fort Wayne College for the Year Ending June 20, 1889,* p 4.

[51] *Catalogue of the Fort Wayne College for year ending June 23, 1881.* Fort Wayne: Gazette Book and Job Print, 1881, pp.41-42.

[52] *Catalogue of the Fort Wayne College for Year Ending June 23, 1882.* Fort Wayne: Daily News Book print, 1882, pp.33-34.

[53] *Catalogue of the Fort Wayne College for Year Ending June 23, 1882.* Fort Wayne: Daily News Book Print, 1882. p.32.

[54] *Catalogue of the Fort Wayne College for Year Ending June 23, 1882.* Fort Wayne: Daily News Book Print, 1882 p.32.

[55] *Catalogue of Taylor University for the Year Ending June 23, 1892.* Fort Wayne: Archer Housh and Co., 1892, p.3.

[56] *Catalogue of Taylor University of Upland, Indiana, 1893-94.* Fort Wayne: Archer Housh and Co. 1894 p.3.

[57] *Catalogue of Taylor University of Upland, Indiana, 1895-96.* Marion, Indiana: E. L. Goldthwait & Co, 1896, p.3.

CHAPTER TWO NOTES

[1]   Interview with Jay Kesler, Upland, Indiana, May 1996.

[2]   Interview with Jay Kesler, May 1996. A useful reference book on Holiness sources is: William Kostlevy, *Holiness Manuscripts. A Guide to Sources Documenting the Wesleyan Holiness Movement in the United States and Canada.* (ATLABibliography Series #34). Metuchen, N.J., London: The American Theological Library Association and The Scarecrow Press, Inc., 1994.

[3]   William Taylor, *Story of My Life.* New York: Eaton & Mains, 1896, p.26.

[4]   John Paul, *The Soul Digger or Life and Times of William Taylor.* Upland, Indiana: Taylor University Press, 1928, p. 21.

[5]   W. Taylor, *Story of My Life*, p. 26.

[6]   W. Taylor, *Story of My Life*, p. 26.

[7]   W. Taylor, *Story of My Life*, p. 17

[8]   Anne Taylor died in 1905.

[9]   Quoted in David Bundy, "Bishop William Taylor and Methodist Mission: A Study in The Nineteenth Century Social History - Pt. 1 - From Camp Meeting Convert to International Evangelist", *Methodist History*, July 1989, 27:4, p. 201.

[10]   D. Bundy, *Methodist History*, July 1989, p. 201.

[11]   J. Paul, *The Soul Digger,* pp. 315, 316; interview with Stanley Koskinen, Salinas, California, May 1995. The author was privileged to make contact with Edmund Chambers and Diana Johnson, Edward and Barbara Jean Koskinen, and Stanley and Ellen Koskinen on a visit to California in May-June 1995. They were extended invitations to attend the Taylor University sesquicentennial homecoming in October 1996.

[12]   William Taylor, *Seven Years Street Preaching in San Francisco, California; Embracing Incidents, Triumphant Death Scenes, etc.* ed. W.P. Strickland. New York: Carlton and Porter, 1856, (reprinted in 1974 and 1875), p. 282.

[13]   Information from author's visit to San Francisco and Oakland, May-June 1990.

[14] The complete list of Taylor's books with the original date of publication (all were reprinted several times) are:

Address to Young America, and a World to the Old Folks (1857)

Africa Illustrated: Scenes From Daily Life on the Dark Continent with Photographs Secured in Africa by Bishop William Taylor, Dr. Emil Holub and the Missionary Superintendents (1895)

California Life Illustrated (1858)

Cause and Probable Results of the Civil War in America. Facts for the People of Great Britain (1862)

Christian Adventures in South Africa (1867)

The Election of Grace (1868)

The Flaming Torch in Darkest Africa (1898)

Four Years Campaign in India (1875)

Infancy and Manhood of Christian Life (1867)

Letters to a Quaker Friend on Baptism (1880)

The Model Preacher: Comprised in a Series of Letters Illustrating the Best Mod Of Preaching the Gospel (1859)

My Kaffir Sermon, or, The Gospel Savingly Preached to the Heathen in a Single Sermon (no date)

Our South American Cousins (1878)

Paul's Methods of Missionary Work (1879)

Reconciliation, or, How to be Saved (1867)

Seven Years Street Preaching in San Francisco, California; Embracing Incidents, Triumphant Death Scenes, etc. (1856)

Story of My Life; an account of what I have thought and said and done in my ministry of more than fifty-three years in Christian lands and among the heathen, written by myself (1895)

Ten years of Self-Supporting Missions in India (1882)

[15] William Taylor, *The Model Preacher: Comprised in a Series of Letters Illustrating the Best Mode of Preaching the Gospel.* Cincinnati: Swormstedt and Poe, 1859 (reprinted in 1859, 1860, 1861), p.169.

[16] D. Bundy, "Bishop William Taylor and Methodist Mission: A Study in Nineteenth Century Social History. Pt. II: Social Structures in Collision", *Methodist History*, October 1989, 28:1, p.10.

[17] D. Bundy, *Methodist History*, October 1989, p.10.

[18] D. Bundy, *Methodist History*, October 1989, p.12.

[19] A selected list of source materials on Bishop William Taylor's life includes: E. Davies, *The Bishop of Africa; or the Life of William Taylor, D.D. with an Account of the Congo Country, and Mission.* Reading MA: Holiness Book Concern, 1885; John W. Landon, *From These Men* (chapter 18- "In Seven-League Boots The Story of Bishop "William Taylor") Des Moines, Iowa: Inspiration Press, 1966; Ivan Henry Nothdurft, *The Significance of William Taylor's Work in Self-Supporting Missions* (MA thesis) Evanston, Illinois: Northwestern University, 1945. Some of Bishop Taylor's correspondence may be found in the General Commission on History and Archives, The United Methodist Church, Madison, New Jersey; and Commission on Archives and History, The United Methodist Church California-Nevada Conference, Berkeley, California.

[20] J. Paul, *The Soul Digger*, p.115.

[21] Sources for Taylor's South African preaching ministry in William Taylor, *Christian Adventures in South Africa* New York: Phillips & Hunt, 1880; Daryl M. Balia, "Bridge over Troubled Waters: Charles Pamla and the Taylor Revival in South Africa," *Methodist History,* January 1992, 30:2, pp.78-90.

[22] Quoted in D. Balia, *Methodist History,* January 1992, p.80.

[23] D. Balia, *Methodist History*, January 1992, p.78.

[24] D. Balia, *Methodist History*, January 1992, p.78.

[25] W. Taylor, *Christian Adventures in South Africa*, p.123.

[26] W. Taylor, *Christian Adventures in South Africa,* p.451.

[27] Information from D. Balia, *Methodist History,* January 1992, p.88.

[28] D. Balia, *Methodist History*, January 1992, p. 90.

[29] Wade Crawford Barclay, *History of Methodist Missions, pt. 2 - The Methodist Episcopal Church 1845-1939* New York: The Board of Missions of The Methodist Church, 1957, p. 869.

[30] W. Taylor, *Story of My Life,* p.691. The General Commission on History and Archives, The United Methodist Church, Madison, N.J. has material on Mary Sharpe - Folder 1467-4-3:77. For a description of the problems of the Methodist Episcopal Church in Liberia prior to 1885, see W.C. Barclay, *History of Methodist Missions, pt.2 - The Methodist Episcopal Church 1845-1939.*

[31] W. Taylor, *Story of My Life*, p. 692.

[32] Amanda Smith came to Liberia in 1883. See *An Autobiography The Story of The Lord's Dealings with Mrs. Amanda Smith the Colored Evangelist* Oxford: Oxford University Press, 1988 reprint (first published in 1883).

[33] Agnes McAllister, *The Lone Woman in Africa Six Years on the Kroo Coast* New York: Eaton & Mains, 1896. The General Commission on History and Archives, The United Methodist Church, Madison, N.J. has material on McAllister - Folder 1467-3-1:01

[34] W.C. Barclay, *History of Methodist Missions*, Part 2, p. 902.

[35] Elizabeth McNeil's name was also spelled McNeill or McNeal in other sources. Elizabeth McNeil folder 1465-5-2:28, The General Commission on History and Archives, The United Methodist Church, Madison, N.J.

[36] William Taylor, *The Flaming Torch in Darkest Africa* New York: Eaton & Mains, 1898, p.457.

[37] Interview with Dr. Clarice Lowe, Houston, Texas, November 1995.

[38] Unpublished personal reflections of Diana McNeil Pierson, in possession of Dr. Clarice Lowe, Houston, Texas; information from "A Romance of Providence," *The Pacific Christian Advocate*, September 19, 1920, p. 13.

[39] Unpublished personal reflections of Diana McNeil Pierson.

[40] Interview with Dr. Clarice Lowe, November 1995.

[41] "First Black Grad of USC An African-Born Missionary," *Houston Chronicle*, July 24, 1970.

[42] Interview with Dr. Clarice Lowe, November 1995. Dr. Lowe and her son, Edwin, were invited to attend the Taylor University sesquicentennial homecoming, October 1996.

[43] W.C. Barclay, *History of Methodist Mission*, Pt. 2, p. 904.

[44] Quoted in W. C. Barclay, *History of Methodist Mission*, Pt. 2, p. 904. There may have been 43 in the first party.

[45] Recollections of Herbert Withey. Diaries and Papers of Rev. Herbert Cookman Withey in General Commission on History and Archives, The United Methodist Church, Madison, N.J., folders 1467-6-3:21-23.

[46] W. Taylor, *Flaming Torch in Darkest Africa*, p.467.

[47] W. Taylor, *Story of My Life*, p.714.

[48] Three daughters of Mr. and Mrs. Amos Withey died; only their son, Herbert, born 1873 in Lynn, Massachusetts, survived - he became a noted linguist, translated the New Testament into Kimbundu. Information on the Angola mission found in *Minutes of the Liberian Annual Conference* (1880s, 1890s); *Minutes of the West Central Africa Mission Conference* (turn of the century); *Official Journal of the Angola Mission Conference* (early part of the twentieth century).

[49] A.E. Withey, *Minutes of the Liberian Annual Conference*, 1896, p. 26 - quoted in W.C. Barclay, *History of Methodist Missions*, Pt. 2. p.913. General Commission on Archives and History, The United Methodist Church, Madison, N.J. has papers of Rev. Amos E. Withey folder 1467-6-3:20.

[50] W.C. Barclay, *History of Methodist Missions*, Pt. 2, pp. 922-931.

[51] W.C. Barclay, *History of Methodist Missions*, Pt.2, p. 924.

[52] W.C. Barclay, *History of Methodist Missions*, Pt. 2, pp. 924, 925.

[53] W.C. Barclay, *History of Methodist Missions*, Pt. 2, p. 925.

[54] Herbert C. Withey, "The Methodist Mission in Angola" unpublished document in General Commission on History and Archives, The United Methodist Church, Madison, N.J., folder 1467-6-3:23. Withey died in the mid-1930s.

[55] Susan Collins folder 1465-6-1:35; Martha Drummer folder 1465-6-3:17 in General Commission on History and Archives, The United Methodist Church, Madison, N.J.

[56] Article by Salla Webba in M. Drummer folder 1465-6-3:17, General Commission on History and Archives, The United Methodist Church, Madison, N.J.

[57] J. Tremayne Copplestone, *Twentieth-Century Perspectives (The Methodist Episcopal Church, 1896-1939)* in W.C. Barclay, *History of Methodist Missions* Vol. IV, New York: The Board of Global Ministries, The United Methodist Church, 1973, p.520.

[58] J.T. Copplestone, *Twentieth-Century Perspectives*, p.522.

[59] Quoted in J.T. Copplestone, *Twentieth-Century Perspectives*, p.523.

[60] J.T. Copplestone, *Twentieth-Century Perspectives*, p.574.

[61] J.T. Copplestone, *Twentieth-Century Perspectives*, p.934.

[62] Quoted in J.T. Copplestone, *Twentieth-Century Perspectives*, p.935.

[63] Quoted in J.T. Copplestone, *Twentieth-Century Perspectives*, p.935.

[64] J.T. Copplestone, *Twentieth-Century Perspectives*, p. 936.

[65] Quoted in J.T. Copplestone, *Twentieth-Century Perspectives*, p. 937.

[66] Information from "Angola Reunion Newsletter" - a monthly newsletter - Article by Burl Kreps, November 1995, no. 3.

[67] Information from Tom Logsdon, Area Executive Secretary for Southern Africa, General Board of Global Ministries, The United Methodist Church, New York, August 1996. B. Kreps commented that on his visit Quessua "had the appearance of a ghost town."

[68] B. Kreps, "Angola Reunion Newsletter", November 1995.

[69] Letter from Herbert Withey to Rev. W.L. Matthew, dated June 11, 1929- letter in Commission on Archives and History, The United Methodist Church California-Nevada Conference, Berkeley, California.

[70] *The New York Times*, April 10, 1885, p. 4.

[71] D. Bundy, *Methodist History*, October 1989, pp. 14-20.

[72] W.C. Barclay, *History of Methodist Missions*, Pt. 2, pp. 927, 929, 930.

[73] Quoted in W.C. Barclay, *History of Methodist Missions*, Pt. 2, p.930.

[74] *The Echo*, April 1917, p.13.

[75] *Taylor University Bulletin*, May 1926, 17:8.

[76] *The William Taylor Foundation Annual Report*, 1989?

[77] J. Paul, *The Soul Digger*, pp.317, 318.

[78] *Taylor University Bulletin*, May 1956, 49:1.

[79] The project was spearheaded by Alan H. Winquist; Jerry Hodson, Department of Art, did the matting and framing.

[80] The walking stick was obtained by Alan H. Winquist, May 1995.

[81] W. Taylor, *The Model Preacher*, p.169.

[82] William Ringenberg, *Taylor University The First 125 Years*. Grand Rapids, Michigan: William B. Eerdmans Publishing Co., 1973, p.70.

[83] J.M. Buckley in *Christian Advocate*, June 12, 1902; quoted in *Dictionary of American Biography*, edited by Dumas Malone, New York: Charles Scribner's Sons, 1943, p.345.

CHAPTER THREE NOTES

[1]   *The Echo,* June 15, 1914.

[2]   *The Echo,* June 15, 1916.

[3]   *The Echo,* June 22, 1920.

[4]   *The Echo,* Oct. 1, 1914.

[5]   *The Echo,* Nov. 16, 1914.

[6]   *The Echo,* Jan. 13, 1920.

[7]   *The Echo,* Jan. 13, 1920; *The Echo,* Nov. 2, 1920; *The Echo,* Nov. 21, 1928; *The Echo,* Jan. 9, 1929.

[8]   *The Echo,* Feb. 15, 1916; *The Echo,* Jan., 1917.

[9]   *The Echo,* Dec. 1, 1914; *The Echo,* March, 1917; *The Echo,* May, 1917; *The Echo,* Nov. 25, 1919; *The Echo,* Nov. 16, 1927; *The Echo,* Jan. 16, 1929.

[10] *The Gem,*1921.

[11] *The Echo,* Sept. 14, 1927.

[12] *The Echo,* Dec. 3, 1926; *The Echo,* Feb. 22, 1928; *The Echo,* April 13, 1934.

[13] *The Echo,* Feb. 22, 1928.

[14] *The Echo,* Mar. 7, 1928.

[15] *The Gem,* 1925, pp. 86-87.

[16] *The Echo,* Jan. 18, 1927; *The Echo,* Feb. 25, 1927; *The Echo,* Mar. 1, 1927.

[17] *The Echo,* April 4, 1928; *The Echo,* April 11, 1928; *The Echo,* April 17, 1929; *The Echo,* Mar. 23, 1934.

[18] *The Echo,* May 26, 1920.

[19] *The Gem,* 1907.

[20] *The Gem,* 1909.

[21] *The Echo,* Jan. 15, 1916.

[22] *The Echo,* Nov. 9, 1927.

[23] *The Echo,* Feb. 25, 1919; *The Echo,* Oct. 28, 1919; *The Echo,* Oct. 16, 1929; *The Echo,* Oct. 12, 1918; *The Echo,* Oct. 12, 1927; *The Echo,* Jan. 9, 1929.

[24] *The Echo,* Oct. 25, 1917; *The Echo,* Oct. 28, 1919; *The Echo,* Nov. 9, 1927.

[25] *The Echo,* Mar. 12, 1926; *The Echo,* May 14, 1926.

[26] *The Echo,* Mar. 12, 1926.

[27] *The Echo,* Mar. 12, 1926; *The Echo,* Nov. 5, 1926; *The Echo,* Nov. 19, 1926.

[28] *The Echo,* Nov. 12, 1926; *The Echo,* Nov. 16, 1927; *The Echo,* Nov. 2, 1927.

[29] *The Echo,* Nov. 9, 1927; *The Echo,* Oct. 29, 1926.

[30] *The Echo,* Nov. 19, 1926.

[31] Telephone interview with John Monroe Vayhinger, July, 1996.

[32] The Flying Squadron of America was a speaking campaign launched by the WCTU in its efforts to enact prohibition. The campaign was nationwide visiting two hundred cities in the forty-eight states. They held three-day meetings in each city, focusing particularly on educational institutions. There were twenty-one speakers who were a part of the Squadron. Culla Vayhinger was one of these speakers.

[33] *The Echo,* Nov. 1, 1913.

[34] *The Echo,* Nov. 1, 1913.

[35] *The Echo,* April 15, 1914.

[36] *The Echo,* Mar. 5, 1926; *The Echo,* Mar. 12, 1926.

[37] *The Echo,* April 12, 1927.

[38] *The Echo,* Feb. 22, 1928; *The Echo,* Feb. 29, 1928.

[39] *The Echo,* Nov. 30, 1940.

[40] *The Echo,* Nov. 30, 1940.

[41] *Taylor University Bulletin,* May, 1914, pp. 48-49.

[42] *The Gem,* 1907.

[43] *The Gem,* 1913 p. 12.

[44] *The Echo,* Feb., 1917.

[45] *Taylor University Bulletin,* May, 1925, p. 15.

[46] *The Echo,* June 7, 1927.

[47] Interview with Don and Bonnie Odle, Upland, Ind., July, 1996.

[48] Interview with Hazel Butz Carruth, Marion, Ind., July, 1996.

[49] *Catalogue of Fort Wayne College For the Years 1877-8-9.* Fort Wayne: Gazette Co. Printers, 1880, pp. 24-25.

[50] *Catalogue of the Fort Wayne College.* Fort Wayne, 1888, p. 28.

[51] *Catalogue of the Fort Wayne College.* Fort Wayne, 1888. P. 29.

[52] *Catalogue of Taylor University of Upland, Indiana, 1894-95.* Marion, Indiana: E.L. Goldthwaite and Co., 1894.

[53] *The Gem,* 1911.

[54] Faculty Committee membership lists appear in the *Taylor Bulletins* 1931-1961.

[55] *The Echo,* Oct. 26, 1935.

[56] *The Taylor University Gem,* 1948, p. 7.

[57] Interview with Alice Holcombe, Decatur, Ind., July, 1996.

[58] Interview with Don and Bonnie Odle, Upland, Ind., July, 1996.

[59] *Taylor University Bulletin,* May, 1954.

[60] *Taylor University Alumni Magazine,* April, 1958.

[61] *The Taylor University Gem,* 1934, p. 30.

[62] *Taylor University Catalogue,* 1914, p. 29.

[63] *The Echo,* Dec. 3, 1938.

[64] Interview with Iris Abbey, Warren, Ind., September, 1995.

[65] *Catalogue and Register of the Fort Wayne Female College and Fort Wayne Collegiate Institute, Fort Wayne, Indiana, 1853-54.* Indianapolis: Indiana State Journal Steam Press Print, 1854, p. 20.

[66] *Catalogue of Fort Wayne College, 1870-71.* Fort Wayne: Daily Gazette Steam Print, 1871, p. 16.

[67] *Catalogue of Fort Wayne College for the Years 1877-8-9.* Fort Wayne: Gazette Co., Printers, 1880, pp. 28-29.

[68] *Catalogue of Fort Wayne College for the Year Ending June 23, 1882.* Fort Wayne: Daily New Print, 1882, p. 36.

[69] *Catalogue of the Fort Wayne College for the Year Ending June 14, 1888.*

Fort Wayne: W.D. Page, Printer and Publisher, p. 32.

[70]   *Catalogue of Taylor University of Upland, Indiana, 1893-94.*   Fort Wayne: Archer Housh and Co., Printers, p. 20.

[71]   *Catalogue of Taylor University of Upland, Indiana.*   Fort Wayne: The Archer Printing Co., 1896, p. 4.

[72]   *Catalogue of Taylor University.*   Upland, Ind., 1900-01, p. 6.

[73]   *The Gem,* 1923, p. 16.

[74]   Interview with Alice Holcombe, Decatur, Ind., July, 1996.

[75]   *Taylor University Bulletin.* Vol XVII, No. 1, May 1925, p. 17.

[76]   *The Gem,* 1935.

[77]   Interview with Don and Bonnie Odle, Upland, Ind., July, 1996.

[78]   *The Gem,* 1934, p. 29.

[79]   *Taylor University Bulletin,* Vol XLIII, No. 11, Feb, 1951.

[80]   *Taylor University Bulletin,* Vol XLIII, No. 11, Feb., 1951.

[81]   Interview with David Dickey, Upland, Ind., July, 1996.

[82]   Interview with David Dickey, Upland, Ind., July, 1996.

[83]   Interview with Elmer Nussbaum, Upland, Ind., July, 1996.

[84]   Interview with Hazel Carruth, Marion, Ind., July, 1996; Interview with Alice Holcombe, Decatur, Ind., July, 1996; Grace Olson file, Taylor University Archives.

[85]   *Taylor Magazine,* Dec., 1992.

[86]   Interview with Don and Bonnie Odle, Upland, Ind., July, 1996.

[87]   Interview with Elmer Nussbaum, Upland, Ind., July, 1996.

[88]   *The Taylor University Gem,* 1942, p. 7.

[89]   *The Taylor University Bulletin,* Vol XXXVII, No. 1, Mar., 1994, p. 6.

[90]   *The Gem,* 1913, p. 77.

[91]   Interview with David Dickey, Upland, Ind., July, 1996.

[92]   Interview with Elmer Nussbaum, Upland, Ind., July, 1996.

[93]   *Taylor University Bulletin,* May, 1955.

[94]   *The Echo,* Feb. 26, 1926.

[95]   Letter from Miss Grace Olson to Dr. Herbert Lyons. Mar. 5, 1945. The

Grace Olson Collection. Taylor University Archives, 22:6:3 BX 2.

[96] Interview with Alice Holcombe, Decatur, Ind., July, 1996.

[97] Interview with Hazel Butz Carruth, Marion, Ind., July, 1996.

[98] The Grace Olson Collection. Taylor University Archives, File 22:6:3 BX 2.

[99] The Grace Olson Collection. Taylor University Archives, File 22:6:3 BX 2.

[100] Interview with Hazel Butz Carruth, Marion, Ind., July, 1996.

[101] The Grace Olson Collection. Taylor University Archives, File 22:6:3 BX 2.

[102] Interview with Ruth Brose Rogers, Francis Johnson Willert, and Alice Rocke Cleveland, Upland, Ind., July, 1996.

[103] Interview with Don and Bonnie Odle, Upland, Ind., July, 1996.

[104] Telephone interview with Phil Loy, Upland, Ind., August, 1996.

[105] The Grace Olson Collection. Taylor University Archives, File 22:6:3 BX 2.

[106] *Taylor University Bulletin,* May, 1915, p. 75.

[107] *Taylor University Gem,* 1915, p. 83.

[108] *The Echo,* Feb. 15, 1927.

[109] Interview with Jennie Andrews Lee, Upland, Ind., Dec., 1995.

CHAPTER FOUR NOTES

[1] *The Gem*, 1907, no page number given.

[2] This was a large percentage of the student population - the total student body in 1911 was 105.

[3] W. Ringenberg, *Taylor University The First 125 Years*, p. 115.

[4] W. Ringenberg, *Taylor University The First 125 Years*, p. 115. The Annual Reports of the Board of Foreign Missions of the Methodist Episcopal Church include directories of missionaries from the early 1900s to the 1930s.

[5] Hale J. Moody, *Life Story of Oliver Mark Moody by His Father,* no publisher, date, or place noted; additional information from Moody, Oliver Mark folders 1259-5-1:46 and 1467-3-2:48 in the General Commission on History and Archives, The United Methodist Church, Madison, N. J.

[6] H.J. Moody, *Life Story of Oliver Mark Moody,* p.13.

[7] H.J. Moody, *Life Story of Oliver Mark Moody,* p.13.

[8] H.J. Moody, *Life Story of Oliver Mark Moody,* p.23 - quoting a letter Oliver Moody had written to his parents dated January 15, 1905, from Angola.

[9] H.J. Moody, *Life Story of Oliver Mark Moody,* pp.23, 24.

[10] H.J. Moody, *Life Story of Oliver Mark Moody,* p.25.

[11] H.J. Moody, *Life Story of Oliver Mark Moody,* p.52.

[12] H.J. Moody, *Life Story of Oliver Mark Moody,* p.29.

[13] H.J. Moody, *Life Story of Oliver Mark Moody,* p.61.

[14] H.E. Withey observation, in Wengatz, Rev. and Mrs. John folder 1467-6-2:18, General Commission on History and Archives, The United Methodist Church, Madison, N.J.

[15] Sadie Louise Miller, compiler. *In Jesus' Name Memoirs of the victorious life and triumphant death of Susan Talbott Wengatz*, no publisher or place indicated, 1932, p.8.

[16] Interview with Dr. K. Paul Kasambira, July 1996, Upland, Ind.

[17] John Wengatz, *Miracles in Black   Missionary Experiences in the Wilds of Africa* New York: Fleming H. Revell Co., 1938, p.9.

[18] J. Wengatz, *Miracles in Black*, pp.100, 101.

[19] J. Wengatz, *Miracles in Black,* p.10.

[20] J. Wengatz, *Miracles in Black,* p.56.

[21] Wengatz, Rev. and Mrs. John folder 1467-6-2:18, General Commission on History and Archives, The United Methodist Church, Madison, N.J. The Taylor University Archives has an extensive collection of papers, photographs, and memorabilia of Rev. and Mrs. John Wengatz.

[22] Wengatz folder 1467-6-2:18, General Commission on History and Archives, The United Methodist Church, Madison, N.J.

[23] Wengatz folder 1467-6-2:18, General Commission on History and Archives, The United Methodist Church, Madison, N.J.

[24]   J. Wengatz folder 1467-6-2:18, General Commission on History and Archives, The United Methodist Church, Madison, N.J.

[25] S. Miller, *In Jesus' Name,* pp.55, 56.

[26] J. Wengatz folder 1467-6-2:18, General Commission on History and Archives, The United Methodist Church, Madison, N. J.; see also William Taylor Memorial School folder 1467-6-2:18, General Commission on History and Archives, The United Methodist Church, Madison, N.J.

[27] *The Christian Advocate,* November 22, 1934, p.935.

[28] Report from Rev. Geraldo Manuel Xavier, Bishop Moises Domingo Fernandes, February 10, 1994, Malange, Angola.

[29] Herbert C. Withey, "Ascended in a Chariot of Fire", in J. Wengatz folder 1467-6-2:18. General Commission on History and Archives, The United Methodist Church, Madison, N. J.

[30] Interview with Alice Holcombe, Upland, Ind., October 1995.

[31] Interview with Bishop Ralph Dodge, Dowling Park, Florida, November 1995.

[32] *The Unpopular Missionary* Westwood, N.J.: Fleming H. Revell, 1964; *The Pagan Church The Protestant Failure in America* Philadelphia: JB Lippincott Co., 1968; *The Revolutionary Bishop Who Saw God at Work in Africa An Autobiography* Pasadena, California: William Carey Library, 1986.

[33] Abel T. Muzorewa, *Rise Up and Walk The Autobiography of Bishop Abel Tendekai Muzorewa*, edited by Norman E. Thomas, Nashville, Tennessee: Abingdon, 1978, pp.44, 47, 48.

[34] A.T. Muzorewa, *Rise Up and Walk*, p.60.

[35] Dickson A. Mungazi, *The Honoured Crusade Ralph Dodge's Theology of Liberation and Initiative for Social Change in Zimbabwe.* Gweru, Zimbabwe: Mambo Press, 1991, p. ix.

[36] Interview with Bishop Ralph Dodge, Dowling Park, Florida, November 1995.

[37] *Taylor University Magazine,* summer 1981, p.6.

[38] *Taylor University Magazine,* summer 1981, p.7.

[39] Murphree, Mr. and Mrs. Marshall folder 1467-3-2:87, General Commission on History and Archives, The United Methodist Church, Madison, N. J.; also information from the Journals of the Rhodesia Mission Conference of the Methodist Episcopal Church.

[40] Interview with Dr. K. Paul Kasambira, Upland, Ind., July 1996.

[41] *Africa Christian Advocate,* April-June 1967, p.2.

[42] Interview with Dr. K. Paul Kasambira, Upland, Ind., July 1996.

[43] A. T. Muzorewa, *Rise Up and Walk,* p. 4.

[44] A.T. Muzorewa, *Rise Up and Walk,* , pp. 5, 6.

[45] A.T. Muzorewa, *Rise Up and Walk,* p. 41.

[46] A.T. Muzorewa, *Rise Up and Walk,* p. 33.

[47] Brown, Dr. and Mrs. Robert folders 1041-2-2:12,14; and 1465-5-2:15, General Commission on History and Archives, The United Methodist Church, Madison, N. J.

[48] Burt Ayres, *Honor to Whom Honor is Due The Life Story of Joseph Preston Blades,* Upland, Indiana: published by the author, 1951, p. 24.

[49] B.R. Opper, *Fifty Years Among the Telugus* Secunderabad, India: Deccan Literature Printers, 1968, p. 31.

[50] Article found in the Brown, Rev. and Mrs. Robert folder 1041-2-2:12, General Commission on History and Archives, The United Methodist Church,

Madison, N.J.

[51]   *The Echo*, April 2, 1930.

[52]   Fulkerson, Epperson Robert folder 1465-7-1:75, , General Commission on History and Archives, The United Methodist Church, Madison, N. J.

[53]   Chinzei Gakuin folder 1461-2-3:49, General Commission on History and Archives, The United Methodist Church, Madison, N. J.

[54]   Cottingham, Dr. and Mrs. Joshua Frank folder 1465-6-1:61, General Commission on History and Archives, The United Methodist Church, Madison, N. J.

[55]   Abbey, Mr. and Mrs. Vere folders 1465-4-2:01 and 1109-4-3:37, 38, General Commission on History and Archives, The United Methodist Church, Madison, N. J.

[56]   *The Echo,* November 27, 1929.

[57]   *The Echo,* February 28, 1925, letter dated December 1, 1924, Rangoon, Burma.

CHAPTER FIVE NOTES

[1]   *Constitution of the Women's Foreign Missionary Society. Article II.*

[2]   *Year Book Women's Foreign Missionary Society of the Methodist Episcopal Church.* 1883. P. 20.

[3]   *Year Book Women's Foreign Missionary Society of the Methodist Episcopal Church.* 1885, p. 25.

[4]   *Year Book Women's Foreign Missionary Society of the Methodist Episcopal Church.* 1887, p. 25-26.

[5]   *Year Book Women's Foreign Missionary Society of the Methodist Episcopal Church.* 1886, p. 24.

[6]   *Year Book Women's Foreign Missionary Society of the Methodist Episcopal Church.* 1888.

[7]   Information for the General Office, New York. Wellesley Girls' High School, Naini Tal, *U.P., 1918.* General Commission on Archives and History. The United Methodist Church, Madison, N.J.

[8]   *The Indian Witness,* May 28, 1924, p. 341.

[9]   Mrs. J.T. Gracey. *Boarding School Series.* Calcutta, India, 1898, p. 8. General Commission on Archives and History. The United Methodist Church, Madison, N.J.

[10]   *The Indian Witness,* May 28, 1924, p. 341.

[11]   *Year Book Women's Foreign Missionary Society of the Methodist Episcopal Church,*1898, pp. 33-34.

[12]   *Year Book Women's Foreign Missionary Society of the Methodist Episcopal Church,* 1900, p.141.

[13]   *Reports and Minutes of the Eighteenth Session of the Women's Missionary Society of the Methodist Episcopal Church in Bengal, 1904.* Calcutta: The Methodist Publishing House, 1905, p.36.

[14]   *Reports and Minutes of the Nineteenth Session of the Bengal Women's Conference of the Methodist Episcopal Church in Bengal, 1906.* Calcutta: The Methodist Publishing House, 1906, pp.28-29.

[15]   *The Indian Witness,* May 28, 1924, pp.5-6.

[16]   *Year Book. The Annual Report of the Women's Foreign Missionary* Society, 1898, p.64.

[17]   *Minutes of the South Japan Mission Conference of the Methodist Episcopal Church.* 1899, The Methodist Publishing House, p.24.

[18]   *Third Annual Report to the South Japan Mission Conference of the Methodist Episcopal Church,* 1900, p.28-30.

[19]   *Minutes and Reports of the Fifth Session of the Women's Mission Conference of the Methodist Episcopal Church in South Japan,* 1903, pp.21-24.

[20]   *Ninth Annual Report. South Japan Women's Conference,* 1907, pp.23-27.

[21]   *Eleventh Annual Report. South Japan Women's Conference,* 1909, pp.15-19.

[22]   *Twelfth Annual Report. South Japan Women's Conference,* 1910, pp.45-48.

[23]   *Twelfth Annual Report. South Japan Women's Conference,* 1910, pp. 27.

[24]   *Eighth Annual Report to the South Japan Women's Conference,* 1906, pp.20-21.

[25]   *Eighth Annual Report to the South Japan Women's Conference,* 1906, p.23.

[26]   *Year Book. The Forty-Second Annual Report of the Women's Foreign Missionary Society.* 1911, p.192.

[27]   *Year Book. The Forty-Third Annual Report of the Women's Foreign Missionary Society,* 1912, pp. 177-78.

[28]   *Women's Missionary Friend,* Feb, 1925, p.68.

[29]   Letter from Leota Ratcliffe to A. B. Leonard. Nov 29, 1907. General Commission on Archives and History, The United Methodist Church. Madison, N.J.

[30]   Information in this paragraph is taken from Ratcliffe's application to the Board of Missions; a letter from Ratcliffe to A. B. Leonard dated Nov 29, 1907; and a letter from A. R. Archibald to A. B. Leonard, Dec 10, 1907. General Commission on Archives and History, The United Methodist Church. Madison, N.J.

[31] Letter from I.B. Scott to Leota Ratcliffe, Oct 18, 1907. General Commission on Archives and History, The United Methodist Church. Madison, N.J.

[32] Letter from A. B. Leonard to Leota Ratcliffe, Nov 25, 1907. General Commission on Archives and History, The United Methodist Church. Madison, N.J.

[33] Letters from A. B. Leonard to Leota Ratcliffe dated Dec 6, 1907; April 21, 1908; and April 22, 1908. General Commission on Archives and History. The United Methodist Church. Madison, N.J.

[34] Life Sketch of Rev. John Hamilton Reed, D.D. Clipping File. General Commission on Archives and History, The United Methodist Church. Madison, N.J.

[35] Letter from Leota Ratcliffe to A. B. Leonard, July 27, 1908. General Commission on Archives and History, The United Methodist Church. Madison, N.J.

[36] Letter from I.B. Scott, Bishop of Africa to Leota Ratcliffe, Sept 1, 1908. General Commission on Archives and History, The United Methodist Church. Madison, N.J.

[37] Letter from A. B. Leonard to Leota Ratcliffe, Sep 17, 1908. General Commission on Archives and History, The United Methodist Church. Madison, N.J.

[38] Letter from Mary Sharp to A. B. Leonard, Sept 16, 1908. General Commission on Archives and History, The United Methodist Church. Madison, N.J.

[39] Letter from Leota Ratcliffe to A. B. Leonard, Dec 16, 1908. General Commission on Archives and History, The United Methodist Church. Madison, N.J.

[40] Field Reference Committee's Report on Missionary Service. Women's Foreign Missionary Society of the Methodist Episcopal Church. Esther Shoemaker, Aug 30, 1941. File 1465-7-1:04 General Commission on Archives and History, The United Methodist Church, Madison, N.J.

[41] Letter from C. W. Scharer to Dr. F. M. North, Corresponding Secretary of the Board Of Managers. Nov 11, 1919. General Commission on History and Archives, The United Methodist Church, Madison, N.J.

[42] Letter from Elizabeth Scharer to Dr. F. M. North, Feb 17, 1920. General Commission On Archives and History, The United Methodist Church, Madison, N.J.

[43] Letter from Elizabeth Scharer to Thomas S. Donohugh, Board of Managers, Nov 15, 1920. General Commission on History and Archives, The United Methodist Church, Madison, N.J.

[44] Kathryne Bieri File 1109-3-1:07, General Commission on History and Archives, The United Methodist Church. Madison, N.J.

[45] Letter from Kathryne Bieri to Dr. Donohugh, Board of Managers, Sept 18, 1936. File 1109-3-1:07, General Commission on History and Archives, The United Methodist Church. Madison N.J.

[46] Memo from J. G. Vaughn to Dr. Ward, Personnel Committee, Oct 5, 1922. File 1109-3-1:07 General Commission on History and Archives, The United Methodist Church. Madison, N. J.

[47] *I Always Wore My Topi: The Burma Letters of Ethel Mabuce, 1916-1921.* Edited and with preface and introductions by Lucille Griffith. The University of Alabama Press, 1974. p. 322.

[48] Personnel File for Floy Hurlbut. Ball State University Archives, Muncie, Indiana.

CHAPTER SIX NOTES

[1] Donald Leon Roye - 1960; Ellen Haakonsen - 1961; Lily Haakonsen - 1981; perhaps Bvuo Nkomo - 1918.

[2] W. Ringenberg, *Taylor University The First 125 Years,* p.71

[3] Thaddeus Reade was President of Taylor University from 1891 to 1902. His 12 page account of Samuel Morris was entitled *Samuel Morris (Prince Kaboo),* published by Taylor University in 1896 (reprinted in 1921, 1924).

[4] Lindley Baldwin, *Samuel Morris* Minneapolis: Bethany House Publishers, 1942, p.73.

[5] Jorge O. Masa, *The Angel in Ebony Or The Life and Message of Sammy Morris* Upland, Ind.: Taylor University Press, 1928, preface.

[6] Interview with Charles (Tim) Kirkpatrick, Upland, Ind., June 1996; L. Baldwin, *Samuel Morris,* p.10.

[8] Baldwin stated that Kaboo "was the first fruit of her [Miss Knolls] missionary labor, and she named him 'Samuel Morris' in gratitude" - L. Baldwin, *Samuel Morris,* p.21.

[9] *Taylor University Magazine,* fall 1988, p.22. W. Robinson wrote, "Specializing in corporate law, he [Samuel Morris] became one of the most prominent attorneys of the time in Indiana."

[10] Further research is necessary to clarify Mr. Morris of Fort Wayne and Miss Knolls or Knoll.

[11] J. O. Masa, *The Angel in Ebony,* pp.41, 42. Other sources spelled her name McNeal or McNeill.

[12] T. Reade, *Samuel Morris (Prince Kaboo),* p.27.

[13] Quoted in *The Taylor Magazine,* summer 1993, p.13.

[14] J.C. Wengatz, *Sammy Morris Spirit-Filled Life,* preface.

[15] J.O. Masa, *The Angel in Ebony,* pp. 71-73.

[16] *The Taylorite,* January 23, 1913, 1:4.

[17] *The Taylorite,* January 23, 1913, p. 1.

[18] Her name was spelled Mulligan in Nkomo's obituary in *The Echo,*

May 23, 1918, 5:16. Pearl Mullikin was listed in the *Methodist Directory of Missionaries.* Her home was identified as Wilmore, Kentucky. She had gone to Rhodesia in 1909 and was working in Old Umtali; in 1928 she was in Mrewa.

[19] *The Echo,* May 23, 1918, 5:16.

[20] The official Grant County death records also certified the burial location was Jefferson Cemetery.

[21] Marta Gabre-Tsadick, *Sheltered by the King.* Lincoln, Virginia: Chosen Books, 1983.

[22] Letter from William Humbane to Bishop Ralph Dodge, December 11, 1995; also information from Tom Logsdon, Area Executive Secretary for Southern Africa, General Board of Global Ministries, The United Methodist Church, New York.

[23] *Taylor Magazine,* spring 1973, pp. 11-13 featured an article about Mrs. Paul (Irene) Kasambira.

[24] Interview with Paul Kasambira, Upland, Ind., July 1996.

[25] *Taylor Magazine,* fall 1988.

[26] *Official Minutes of the First Annual Meeting of the Porto Rico Missions of the Methodist Episcopal Church,* 1902, p. 20.

[27] *Official Minutes... Porto Rico Missions of the Methodist Episcopal Church,* 1902, p.20.

[28] *Puerto Rico Mission Conference, The Methodist Episcopal Church,* 1928, p. 57 - obituary written by Jose T. Nieves.

[29] Burt W. Ayres, *Honor to Whom Honor Is Due The Life Story of Joseph Preston Blades,* preface (iii).

[30] Quoted in B. Ayres, *Honor to Whom Honor Is Due*, p.14.

[31] B. Ayres, *Honor to Whom Honor is Due,* p.19.

[32] Quoted in B. Ayres, *Honor to Whom Honor Is Due,* p.27.

[33] *The Gem,* 1919, p.157.

[34] In 1915 there were five Taylor University graduates studying at Drew University, ranking Taylor sixth among colleges represented in the Drew student body.

[35] Burt R. Opper, *Fifty Years Among the Telugus,* p.106.

[36] Information from Wesley Robinson's column, *Taylor Magazine,* summer 1990, p.36.

[37] B.R. Opper, *Fifty Years Among the Telugus,* p.110.

[38] Wesley Robinson's column in *Taylor University Magazine*, summer 1990, p.36.

[39] Unpublished paper by A. Bustamante entitled "A brief sketch of my conversion and call to ministry," in A. Bustamante folders 1185-2-3:12, 1465-5-2:50, General Commission on History and Archives, The United Methodist Church, Madison, N. J.

[40] J. Tremayne Copplestone, *History of Methodist Missions,* vol. IV, pp.1084-1091.

[41] Quoted in J.T. Copplestone, *History of Methodist Missions,* vol. IV, p.1084.

[42] J.T. Copplestone, *History of Methodist Missions,* vol. IV, p. 1090.

[43] Also noted in *The Echo*, December 1916, p. 25; *The Gem,* 1920.

[44] *The Gem,* 1913.

[45] *The Echo,* December 20, 1917.

[46] *Taylor University Bulletin,* July 1932, 14:2.

[47] There was also an obituary in the *Marion Leader-Tribune*, May 25, 1920, p.10.

[48] *Taylor University Bulletin,* September 1931, 23:4, p.4.

[49] *The Taylorite,* March 1950, 3:1.

[50] *Taylor University Bulletin,* December 1953, 46:9, p.8.

[51] B. Ayres, *Honor to Whom Honor Is Due,* p.30.

[52] *The Gem,* 1922, p. 120.

[53] *Taylor University Bulletin*, 1945, 1:2, p.6.

[54] Taeko Obara's father had visited his daughter upon her graduation from Taylor in 1940. Earlier he had written a heart-warming letter to his daughter in response to her description of the positive experience she was having at Taylor. The letter was published in the *Taylor University Bulletin*, December 1937, 29:8, p.3.

[55] *Taylor University Bulletin,* November 1949, 43:9.

[56] *The Gem*, 1920.

[57] B. Opper, *Fifty Years Among the Telugus,* pp.89, 90.

[58] *The Echo,* April 9, 1930.

[59] *Taylor Magazine*, fall/winter 1982, pp. 16-17.

[60] "More About Masa" by E.K. Higdon.

[61] Masa noted that his daughter Esther was planning to come to Taylor in 1950 to study music.

[62] Advisers to the International Student Society have included Tara Davis, Alan H.Winquist, Cassandra Smith, and currently Kashwinder Kaur.

No Ordinary Heritage